T0153056

THE
MIDEAST PEACE
PROCESS

THE
MIDEAST PEACE
PROCESS
AN AUTOPSY

NEW AND EXPANDED EDITION:
FROM OSLO TO DISENGAGEMENT

EDITED BY NEAL KOZODOY

ENCOUNTER BOOKS
NEW YORK, NEW YORK

Copyright © 2006 by Neal Kozodoy

Revised Edition

All rights reserved. No part of this publication may be reproduced, stored in a retrieval system, or transmitted, in any form or by any means, electronic, mechanical, photocopying, recording, or otherwise, without the prior written permission of Encounter Books, 900 Broadway Suite 400, New York, New York, 10003.

First edition published in 2002 by Encounter Books, an activity of Encounter for Culture and Education, Inc., a nonprofit, tax exempt corporation.

Encounter Books website address: www.encounterbooks.com

Manufactured in the United States and printed on acid-free paper.

The paper used in this publication meets the minimum requirements of ANSI/NISO Z39.48-1992 (R 1997)(*Permanence of Paper*).

Library of Congress Cataloging-in-Publication Data

Kozodoy, Neal
    The Mideast peace process / Neal Kozodoy
    p.   cm.
    ISBN 1-59403-191-6
    1. Arab-Israeli conflict—1993—Peace   2. Israel—Politics and govern-
ment—1993.   3. Palestinian Arabs—Politics and government—
1993.   I. Kozodoy, Neal.
    DS119.76.M468   2006
    956.04—dc22

                                                            2006025761

10 9 8 7 6 5 4 3 2

Table of Contents

Preface to First Edition

Only the principals knew for sure, on that September day in 1993, how the world-historical agreement being signed in brilliant sunlight on the lawn of the White House, and sealed with a handshake before an assemblage of transfixed dignitaries and guests, was even then in the process of being subverted—had already been subverted.

At the signing ceremony, one party, Israel—through its prime minister, Yitzhak Rabin, and its foreign minister, Shimon Peres—was formally recognizing the Palestine Liberation Organization (PLO) as the representative of the Palestinian people and committing itself to the peaceful resolution of their differences. The other party, the PLO, having (in the days leading up to this moment) silently withdrawn its previous undertakings to Israeli negotiators, was still not agreeing to declare an end to armed struggle, or even to set a date for renouncing its official aim of destroying the Jewish state. To the contrary, on the day of the signing itself, Yasir Arafat, the chairman of the PLO, would broadcast to the Palestinian people in Arabic that the peace accord to which he had affixed his name was nothing more than a first step in a longstanding plan for the "phased" elimination of Israel.

So, in deception and self-deception, began the Middle East "peace process," a chain of events that would emerge as the first if not the costliest folly of the post-cold-war age. Among the questions likely to engage future historians contemplating this folly, a good number will surely concern what may or may not have been in the minds of Israeli negotiators and politicians who had to be aware of the nature of the partner with whom they were dealing and the activity in which they were engaged, and yet, averting their faces and the world's from what they knew, plunged ahead anyway. Questions such as these:

When it entered into secret negotiations at Oslo and then into its "partnership" with the PLO, a radical terrorist group just then at the nadir of its own political fortunes, was Israel being unwillingly dragged by developments, either in its region or internationally, which it felt it had no choice but to accommodate? Conversely, did it perceive itself, in the aftermath of the collapse of the Soviet Union and the defeat of Iraq in the Gulf war, to be in a unique and possibly ephemeral position of regional strength, a position enabling it, at a stroke, to preempt and sub-due one threat to its security while at the same time creating a buffer between itself and other, still larger ones? To what degree may it have been motivated by feelings of historic guilt vis-à-vis the Palestinian Arabs in the territories it had controlled since the Six-Day war of June 1967? What role was played, after more than four decades of armed conflict, by simple weariness; or by "post-Zionist" aspirations toward a society rid of the burdens, physical and moral, of an occupying power; or by sheer utopianism?

Most troublesome of all, how could any, or even all, of these con-siderations have sufficed to induce Israel to throw to the winds its decades-old strategy of deterrent strength and embrace as its "peace partner" the most implacable and ambitious of its enemies? How could it then have proceeded to bring this enemy home from exile, to rehabil-itate its sunken international credit, invest it with political authority, help to equip it with arms and money, acquiesce in its indoctrination of young Palestinians in the hatred and killing of Jews, suffer its every resort to violence, whitewash its every lie?

We need not, as it happens, wait very long for such questions to be asked. In the fiery months after the implosion of the Oslo peace process in September 2000, no one would pose them more plaintively, or bitterly, than hundreds of thousands of crushed Israelis, including some who had been Oslo's most ardent champions within the country's political and cultural establishments. Indeed, a new question would quickly be added to the list: why, even after the deceptions and self-deceptions of Oslo had at last been unmasked and reality could no longer be denied, were voices still to be heard insisting with grotesque inconsequence that, in the words of the then-departing American ambassador to Israel, "just because the Middle East peace process failed does not mean it should be abandoned"?

To answer these questions adequately will no doubt require whole dissertations in politics and psychology. But in any survey of relevant factors, what should not be overlooked is the volume of sustaining *applause* that was generated worldwide by the news of the Oslo accords, amplified a hundredfold at the September 1993 ceremony on the White House lawn and then supplemented with equal parts of international and, especially, American cajolery and blandishment as year to year the process wended its tortuous way, from declarations of brotherly intent to violation after violation by the PLO to concession after concession by

Israel to renewed acts of Palestinian violence and so forth in dismal progression.

Yet through all this, and no matter how brutal the serial effects, not least on those Palestinians who had been relegated to life under Yasir Arafat's regime, the peace process never lost its aura of sanctified approval among the West's enlightened classes. In the print media and on the air, in churches and synagogues, in universities and diplomatic circles, in foundations and international forums, the rightness of the enterprise lay stubbornly beyond question. This consensus became, in itself, a chief weapon in the hands of Oslo's backers and apologists, wielded with effectiveness to silence any who might raise a doubt as to its origins, its course, or its likely consequences. For who, after all, could be against "peace"?

· · · · ·

That is where this book comes in. The essays in it have been selected out of a much larger number on the subject that were published in *Commentary* magazine over the course of the Oslo years. By presenting them chronologically, in the order in which they appeared, we hope to give some sense of the way in which the peace process itself developed, and of its shifting nuances and priorities. But since the very first such article there could certainly be no mistaking the magazine's general perspective. In stark contrast to almost every editorialist and columnist and political observer who thought and wrote about the Oslo peace process, the magazine's authors not only failed to applaud or endorse it, but took a deeply skeptical view: skeptical of Oslo's origins, its course, and its likely consequences.

They were not afraid that Oslo might succeed in bringing peace. They saw that it rested on a deep misreading of the true disposition of the Arab side, and that its implementation could not allay but rather only inflame extremist passions among Palestinians, not enhance but worsen Israel's physical security, not mitigate but excite the Arab determination to achieve the eventual destruction of the Jewish state. In short, they were afraid it was calculated to end in disaster, to bring not peace but war. So indeed it gives every indication of having done.

That the dissenting position taken by *Commentary*'s writers should, at the time, have been quite so isolated as it was—and so harshly attacked and condemned—is itself a pertinent fact, redolent of the atmosphere of willed, illusory expectation, coupled with moral bullying, in which the peace process was manufactured and sold. Now that Oslo's moment has passed and the human price of its folly is being paid, and paid again, these essays can perhaps be appreciated at their truer worth: as astute and remarkably prescient exercises in contemporary historical analysis. Case studies of a temptation to which democratic societies of all kinds and places have been peculiarly susceptible, may they also serve, however fleetingly, as a warning in the face of similar temptations to come.

Note to This Edition

The essays included in the first (2002) edition of this book traced the steps of the misnamed Oslo peace process from its universally applauded beginnings in 1993 to its effective demise with the Arab launching of the "second *intifada*" in September–October 2000. The subtitle of the book, "An Autopsy," was thus appropriate—but, as things turned out, significant in another, unexpected sense as well. For, between the completion of the manuscript in the summer of 2001 and the date of publication more than six months later, the world was shaken by the events of September 11, and the United States was, suddenly, at war. Only in an afterword included in the first edition was the novelist Mark Helprin able to undertake an interim assessment of the meaning of the new, post-9/11 strategic environment for the Middle East in general and for the security and survival of Israel in particular.

Long before 9/11, however, there had already been "every indication," as I noted in the preface to the first edition, that the Oslo peace process had itself been leading inexorably not to peace but, through continuing Arab rejectionism and violence, to war. The essays included in the 2002 edition, all of them drawn from the pages of *Commentary* magazine, analyzed the evolving history of this reckless and immensely costly experiment in international wishful thinking. Still, that experiment, despite its larger reverberations, had seemed limited to a single theater: the conflict between Israel and the Palestinian Arabs under the rule of Yasir Arafat. After 9/11, it was no longer so easy to deny the deep resemblances between the long war of annihilation being fought by Arabs and Muslims against the existence of the democratic state of Israel and the larger war declared by al-Qaeda and its millions of sympathizers around the world against the existence of the United States, and indeed of the democratic West.

That larger war provides the implicit (and sometimes the explicit) context for this revised and updated edition of *The Mideast Peace Process: An Autopsy*. In the interests of brevity, a number of items from the 2002 edition have been eliminated; at the same time, six new essays, once more from *Commentary*, have been added, bringing the story up past the Israeli disengagement from Gaza in the summer of 2005. This edition thus strives to preserve the still pertinent lessons to be learned from the Oslo experiment—lessons of an entirely negative kind—while conveying a vivid sense of the no less hazardous but very different choices facing both Palestinians and Israelis in the wake of the American response to 9/11, the invasion of Iraq and the toppling of Saddam Hussein, the ongoing contest of the West with radical Islam, and perhaps above all the enunciation and implementation of the Bush Doctrine, with its basic commitment to the spread of political, economic, and religious freedom in a region long mired in dictatorship and violent extremism.

The years since 2001 have witnessed terrible assaults, both physical and ideological, on Israel and on the Jews; they have also witnessed a resilient and versatile response to those assaults and, on the part of Israel, a post-Oslo determination to set, insofar as possible, its own destiny as a Jewish and democratic state. Five years after 9/11, six years after the onset of the second *intifada*, a year after the disengagement from Gaza, this chapter of history has really only begun. To some Israelis and outside observers, including a number of contributors to the first edition of *The Mideast Peace Process*, the vicious actions of jihadists, terrorists, and annihilationists of every stripe have made this a chapter steeped only in blood and in the missteps of their own side—the preeminent such misstep having been the disengagement itself. For the most part, though, the writers included here already see something else: hardly an immediate end to armed struggle or bitter conflict, something never in itself promised by disengagement, but rather, if the forces of mayhem, brutality, and despotism can be crushed, the glimmerings at last of a more hopeful political order—more hopeful not only for the peace-starved people of Israel but also for the Arab and Muslim Middle East, and thus for the world at large.

Whether the chance will be grasped is the question yet to be decided.

—*July 7, 2006*

David Bar-Illan

Israel's New Pollyannas

U ntil recently, it was not difficult to define the main obstacle to a peace agreement between Arabs and Israelis: the very minimum the Syrians and Palestinians could accept exceeded the maximum Israel could give.

In practical terms, this meant that since Hafez al-Assad's Syria could accept no less than what Anwar Sadat's Egypt had received—every inch of land lost to the Israelis in war—and since Israel could not afford to relinquish all this land (which would bring the border to within yards of the Sea of Galilee), an agreement with Syria was impossible.

Similarly, no Palestinian leader could accept anything less than total Israeli withdrawal to the 1949 armistice lines (usually described as the 1967 borders—that is, the borders until the Six-Day war in June of that year) and the establishment of a Palestinian state with the eastern half of Jerusalem as its capital, while no Israeli government could allow this to happen. Ergo, the prospects of a Palestinian-Israeli agreement were nonexistent.

All the procedural arguments—for instance, the Arabs' insistence on an international conference to decide the issue rather than direct talks between the parties—were merely a function of these differences. The Arabs, correctly assuming that Israel—no matter who was in the government—would not deliver their minimal demands, saw in a UN-sponsored conference a venue in which the world tribunal would impose an unpalatable settlement on Israel.

That is why the Madrid conference of 1991 was considered a small miracle. Israel, Jordan, Lebanon, Syria, and the Palestinians actually sat down to negotiate in bilateral, direct talks. This, despite the fact that the then-Israeli government was a hawkish Likud-led coalition, headed by the stubborn Yitzhak Shamir, and that to expect it to bend to Palestinian demands for sovereignty in Judea, Samaria, and Gaza, or to accept Syrian claims to all of the Golan Heights, was ludicrous.

But the meeting took place at least partly because it was conceived in deception. In secret private letters, the Bush administration was able to convince each participant that the U.S. would support its position. Thus, Syria was promised not only that the American (and Soviet) sponsors of the talks would play an important mediating role when it mattered, but that Washington saw "the return of territories according to UN Resolutions 242 and 338"—a formula which to the Arabs translated into total withdrawal—as applicable to the Golan.

Similarly, the U.S. assured the Palestinians that it was still committed to the general outline of the Rogers plan of 1969, which called for virtually complete Israeli withdrawal to the 1949 armistice lines, and that it considered the Israeli annexation of the eastern part of Jerusalem illegal. In the eyes of the U.S., the Palestinians were reminded, east Jerusalem was still "occupied territory." (As it happens, even west Jerusalem has not been recognized by the U.S. as part of Israel.) The message was unmistakable: the U.S. would support the establishment of a Palestinian homeland in the territories with east Jerusalem as its capital. Indeed, for the first time since 1967, an American administration refused Israel's request to say that it actively opposed a Palestinian state.

To assuage Israel's fears of American support for a Palestinian state, however, the Bush administration did specifically agree to exclude the PLO from the negotiating process, and to insist on a joint Jordanian-Palestinian delegation, thus eliminating any semblance of a separate, independent Palestinian entity. Israel also received a commitment that only inhabitants of the territories could become delegates to the talks. That is, neither residents of Jerusalem nor members of the Palestinian "diaspora" would be eligible.

Furthermore, Israel was assured that the U.S. stood by President Gerald Ford's commitment to "give weight" to Israel's security concerns in the Golan Heights, that the Jerusalem question would be raised only at a later stage of the negotiations, and that the negotiations would be based on the formula worked out at Camp David in the 1978 talks leading up to the breakthrough agreement between Israel and Egypt. This last meant an interim period of Palestinian autonomy for five years, with negotiations for a permanent solution beginning after the third year. All options would be left open—including the possibility of an Israeli demand for sovereignty over the territories.

. . . . .

These assurances to the various parties were clearly irreconcilable. Charitably, they were white lies intended to get everyone together in the hope that differences would be ironed out at the negotiating table. A more cynical interpretation would characterize them as a stratagem designed to create an irresistible momentum which would force Israel to yield to the prevailing world demand for total withdrawal. Either way, then-Prime Minister Yitzhak Shamir did not appreciate their import. When asked about the American assurances to the Arabs, he said Israel was not bound by American promises. All that mattered was that the talks were bilateral and direct, and that the U.S. would not interfere.

But conflicting promises have a way of exploding. On the very first day of the Madrid conference, the Palestinian representatives, who were supposed to be included in the Jordanian delegation, were allotted the same space at the table as the other delegations and allowed a separate time slot for their addresses. Armed with American support for them as a distinct delegation, they stalled the negotiations for months until the Israelis yielded. Washington also allowed Faisal Husseini, a resident of Jerusalem and a member of Yasir Arafat's Fatah organization—and therefore doubly ineligible for participation—to head an "advisory team" attached to the delegation. He and the team's spokeswoman, Hanan Ashrawi, promptly became the most sought-after stars of the peace talks. The Jordanian delegation faded into the background.

In addition, the Bush administration circumvented the ban on the PLO by letting senior PLO figures enter the U.S. for post-Madrid negotiations in Washington. Setting up shop in the delegates' hotel, they were ostentatiously consulted by the official Palestinian participants before and after every session. The commitment to exclude "diaspora" Palestinians was also broken, when Mohammad Khalaj, a member of the Palestine National Council who lives in America, was included in the negotiations on refugees at the multilateral talks on regional problems. And the final obliteration of the American commitment to exclude the PLO and Jerusalem residents came when Israel (now led by Yitzhak Rabin) agreed, as part of the deal with the U.S. (now led by Bill Clinton) following the expulsion of 400 Hamas agitators, to the formal recognition of Husseini as head of the Palestinian delegation.*

· · · · ·

But far more disturbing than the American manipulations were those practiced by the Israeli government itself. For some three years, the Syrians had been spreading the word that Assad had had a change of heart. Having lost the sponsorship of the Soviets, he purportedly now realized that he would never achieve strategic parity with Israel—a euphemism for a military capability which would enable him to vanquish Israel on his own. Forced to get closer to the West to survive, and aware that the West wanted peace, he was ready to sign an agreement with Israel.

This line was startlingly similar to the argument made in 1990 by Saddam Hussein and *his* supporters in the West and in Israel. (Among those convinced at the time that Saddam was so eager to curry favor with the West that he would be a natural candidate for a peace treaty with Israel was Ezer Weizman, now Israel's President.) That Saddam himself proved the fallacy of the argument—he not only betrayed his promises but started a war in the Gulf without Soviet backing—seemed to be forgotten.

President Hosni Mubarak of Egypt, who weeks before Iraq's invasion of Kuwait had assured Israel of Saddam's benignity, was credited both with persuading Assad of the advantages of peace and with convincing the U.S. that the Syrian dictator was sincere. As Egypt had discovered in the late 1970s, lost land (in Egypt's case, the Sinai peninsula) could be retrieved from Israel more easily through peace than by war. And Assad, a reputed pragmatist who had repeatedly vowed to destroy Israel if it took 200 years, now saw that sitting with Israel at the negotiating table made sense. True, to mitigate an implied recognition of the Jewish state, the Syrians insisted on calling the negotiations an international conference, but in reality they agreed to participate in strictly bilateral talks.

The Syrians at first found the role of peace partners a little unnatural. But eager to get their country off the State Department list of states

---

*Predictably, this made the Palestinians assume they could bring up the matter of Jerusalem immediately, rather than at the negotiations on the permanent solution. This in turn caused an impasse in the negotiations which prompted the Clinton administration to send a diplomatic team headed by Dennis Ross to Israel to reconcile PLO and Israeli positions.

that sponsored terrorism, they even chimed in with a confidence-building measure, allowing the gradual emigration of Syrian Jews provided they did not go to Israel. And as soon as the Israeli delegation, under the Labor government, announced Israel's readiness to withdraw from the Golan Heights, they switched from displays of cold fury to smiles and handshakes. These prompted the new Israeli Foreign Minister, Shimon Peres, to proclaim that the developments in Damascus were nothing short of sensational.

What the Syrians made clear, however, was that they expected the negotiations to bring nothing less than full Israeli withdrawal not only from the Golan Heights—small in area but strategically vital for the defense of Israel's north—but from all areas occupied by Israel in 1967 and 1982. This meant the complete evacuation of Judea, Samaria, Gaza, east Jerusalem, and Israel's security belt in southern Lebanon.

Nor was Syria willing to sign a full-fledged peace treaty in return. It interpreted UN Resolution 242 to mean that Israel must withdraw from *all* captured territory on *all* fronts (a transparently false reading), and that in return Israel was entitled to nothing more than an end to the state of belligerency that would not include a peace treaty and normalization of relations.

Though aware of the Syrian position, Rabin—who a day before the Israeli election had said that anyone abandoning the Golan Heights would be guilty of forsaking Israel's security—predicted that "within months" Israel and Syria would sign on the dotted line. Members of the cabinet, including Police Minister Moshe Shahal who was known for his closeness to Rabin, openly advocated relinquishing the entire Golan.

To be sure, Rabin himself kept stressing that he would consider withdrawing only *on* the Golan Heights, not *from* them. But he kept all options open by allowing that the extent of withdrawal depended on the quality of peace Syria was prepared to offer. This was generally understood to mean that for a full-fledged peace treaty, which would include an exchange of ambassadors and a free flow of people and goods between the two countries, Rabin would forfeit Israeli sovereignty in the Golan and effect a gradual but complete withdrawal. In that case, leaks from government offices averred, to ensure against Syrian aggression, Rabin would insist that the area be demilitarized and the U.S. station troops between Syrians and Israelis.

Rabin's "you tell me first what kind of peace you want and I'll tell you how much land I'll give" created the impression that the Syrians had not made their position clear. Yet soon after the resumption of negotiations under the Labor government, the Syrian delegation submitted a document summarizing its position. It indicated that Damascus had not budged an inch from its insistence on total Israeli withdrawal to the 1949 armistice lines on all fronts, and that in return it was willing to commit to no more than a state of nonbelligerency.

This document so disappointed the Israeli government that it asked the Syrian delegation not to publish it, a request that may have constituted a historic first: a democratic government asking a dictatorial regime to keep an exchange secret for fear that the information would adversely affect public opinion. To this day, the only open source of the document's contents is the Arab press to which it was leaked by the Syrians. Israel has yet to release it.

· · · · ·

This, however, was a relatively minor episode in a much more elaborate effort by the Israeli government—one in which the press collaborated—to sell Assad not only as a leader who needed and wanted peace but as a man of honor. The evidence for this, said ministers and columnists, was there for all to see: the 1974 separation agreement on the Golan Heights, which had been observed by Syria for twenty years (with the exception of a few forays by terrorists, for which the Syrians were not held responsible). Assad might be a ruthless dictator, but his signature on a contract would be binding.

Forgotten were a few pertinent facts. The reason the Syrians have been careful not to provoke the Israelis on the Golan Heights is that the Israeli army there is within striking distance of Damascus. In Lebanon, where Israeli retaliation can hurt only Hezbollah cadres, Palestinian terrorists, and Shiite villagers, Syria's scruples about agreements have seemed to disappear.

Indeed, Assad's record of broken agreements easily matches that of other Middle Eastern dictators. In 1983, he broke a pledge he had made to the Reagan administration (via the Saudis) that he would accept the Israeli-Lebanese peace treaty and withdraw his troops from Lebanon. He did the opposite: as soon as Israel began to get out, he poured more troops into Lebanon. He completed the effective annexation of the country in 1990, after having joined the anti-Iraq coalition and being rewarded by the Bush administration with carte blanche in Beirut. And recently his Foreign Minister, Farouk al-Sharaa, declared that Lebanon and Syria were "like one country."

Assad is also in violation of the Saudi-sponsored Taif agreement, endorsed by all the Arab states, which stipulates the withdrawal of Syrian troops and the restoration of Lebanese. sovereignty. September 1993 marks precisely a year since Syrian troops were supposed to have left Beirut.

Even more puzzling is the current Israeli government's support of the notion—a favorite of European and American diplomats—that Assad is pursuing peace. Hezbollah, the Iranian-financed organization whose almost daily attacks on Israeli targets finally led to the retaliatory strikes of late July, trains its 3,000–5,000 highly motivated fighters in Syrian camps, under Syrian supervision, in Lebanon's Bekaa valley. It is equipped with Syrian arms, including potent Sager missiles, and Iranian arms brought through Damascus. The organization could not have mounted a single major operation against Israel without Syrian approval. Yet as soon as Labor came to power, Hezbollah became an "Iranian organization" operating independently. Indeed, it was only after the cease-fire ending the fighting in late July that Syria's role in "standing behind" Hezbollah was alluded to by Rabin (which did not prevent him from praising Assad a few days later).

Ignored, too, has been Syrian sponsorship of the Palestinians who openly call for the destruction of the Jewish state by force of arms. Last year, Syria held a conference of the ten "rejectionist" groups—among them Hamas, Islamic Jihad, and the radical PLO factions—in Damascus, where many of these organizations have their headquarters. Syria also directs the operation of Radio Al Quds, beamed to the administered territories, which incites Palestinians against the "traitors" in their midst who negotiate with Israel. Unlike their Israeli apologists, the Syrians are quite frank about supporting the "armed struggle" as long as Israel occupies "Arab land." And they have flatly rejected Israeli demands to disarm Hezbollah and the Palestinians in southern Lebanon. In the peace talks the Syrians have rejected all Israeli suggestions to discuss a truce in Lebanon.

Nor has Assad slowed down the feverish pace of Syrian arming. Having replenished and modernized all branches of its armed forces, Syria surpasses Israel in virtually all major classes of military equipment, let alone in the number of troops. In April, Syria began to manufacture Scud-C missiles in factories near Hama and Aleppo.

Occasionally, Prime Minister Rabin and Foreign Minister Peres mention Syrian missile acquisitions and continued Syrian testing of sophisticated missiles. Israeli field commanders on the northern front also talk gravely of Syria's formidable new power. But mostly government spokesmen suggest that the Assad regime's march to peace is inexorable and must not be interrupted with irritating cavils about arms build-ups or backing Hezbollah.

The press is even worse. Not unlike Soviet apologists in the West during the cold war, Assad's promoters in the Israeli media explain that Syria is just as concerned about an Israeli attack as Israel is about Syrian aggression. Only when ambushes and shelling by Hezbollah cost the lives of Israeli soldiers in July did the press begin to question Syria's role, gingerly. Yet after the mini-Lebanese war caused by these attacks, Syria was given credit for helping to end it.

The army brass, too, has collaborated in pushing the notion that an agreement with Syria is a *sine qua non* of peace. The chief of the General Staff, Ehud Barak, making the kind of political pronouncement men in uniform are usually expected to avoid, has warned that failure to achieve an agreement with Syria would trigger a countdown to war. To which one wag responded, "Does such a countdown mean that Syria would start arming?" Barak also extolled Assad as a "responsible leader" following the cease-fire in Lebanon.

A similar make-believe approach has dominated the government line on the Palestinians. Terrorist attacks on Israelis are routinely attributed either to lone Muslim fanatics suddenly driven to murder Jews, or to the actions of Hamas cells. Yet the truth is that a majority of terrorist acts, against both Jews and Palestinian Arabs accused of "collaboration," are committed by the secular Fatah, Arafat's own group in the PLO. And despite the reputed rivalry between the PLO and Hamas, some of the operations are mounted by them as joint efforts. Arafat himself has repeatedly taken credit for every "execution" in the territories. ("I approve every file," he once said, "if not before the execution, then after it.")

Nevertheless, government spokesmen prefer to pretend that the killers are not operatives of the "moderate" Arafat, supporter of the peace talks, but "enemies of the peace process" such as Hamas, Islamic Jihad, and PLO radicals like the Habash, Hawatmeh, and Jibril groups. The not unreasonable assumption behind this charade is that the public might resent continued talks with proxies of the "mainstream" PLO in Washington while its gunmen are killing Israelis back home.

The separation between negotiators and killers was reinforced by Peres when he was asked why the subject of continued terrorism, both in Israel and the administered territories as well as on the Lebanon border, was not brought up at the peace talks. "Because the people who are doing the talking are not the people who are doing the shooting," he answered.

Yet leaving aside whether it makes sense to negotiate with people who do not control those "who are doing the shooting," the government is perfectly aware of Arafat's connection with terrorist activity. In early July, Minister of Health Haim Ramon, a rising Labor-party star who often represents the government in Knesset debates, was reported to have contacted Arafat with the proposal of a trade: direct Israeli negotiations with the PLO in exchange for the cessation of terrorism. The answer was a flat no.

This points to another government-propagated myth. When asked about the absence of reciprocal gestures by the Palestinians, Peres said, "There is nothing the Palestinians could give us. We just have to decide what we want to give them." In fact, however, a halt to terrorism is only one "confidence-building" gesture the Palestinians might make. Another would be to lift the boycott on Israeli goods in the territories and to appeal to the Arab states to terminate their economic boycott against Israel. But the Palestinians have been doing the exact opposite. When Kuwait announced that it was lifting the "secondary" boycott—the banning of foreign companies that do business with Israel from Arab markets—the Palestinian leadership yelled treason.

What Israel's government seems unwilling to admit, perhaps even to itself, is that terrorist activity and guerrilla warfare are not "a campaign against the peace process." Individual members of groups like Hamas and Hezbollah may indeed believe that the peace process is a satanic Zionist-American plot, but the Arabs participating in the peace negotiations who use the services of these organizations—Syria and the PLO—are simply following a traditional totalitarian strategy of shooting while talking.

The immediate purpose of the shooting is to inflict as many Israeli casualties as possible. ("I want Israel to see a funeral a day on the TV screen," Assad said during the Israeli withdrawal from Lebanon in 1984.) The ultimate goal is to create internal pressure in Israel for a speedier peace settlement that would presumably stop the killing. A grieving mother from the northern Israeli town of Kiryat Shemona was shown on television after a Katyusha bombardment from Lebanon, crying, "Enough, give them what they want, it's time to make peace." Similarly, clashes with the army are aimed at demoralizing Israel's soldiers. If peace is really at hand, getting killed defending a piece of land slated to be relinquished makes little sense.

· · · · ·

It is, of course, possible that branding the terrorists "enemies of the peace process" is the government's way of deflecting criticism from its Left flank for its tough anti-terrorist measures. After all, Rabin sold his super-dovish Meretz coalition partners on the expulsion of 400 Hamas agitators by assuring them that it would strengthen the PLO's position and help the peace process. And following this year's Black March, in which terrorist killings—mostly inside the Green Line—occurred almost daily, the government imposed an open-ended closure on the administered territories with nary a peep from Meretz. (Had a Likud government deprived 120,000 Arab workers of their livelihood for any length of time, the Left would have been in an uproar heard around the world.)

In the first weeks of the closure, terrorist attacks ceased almost completely. That Palestinian laborers were prevented from crossing the Green Line caused hardship and losses not only to them but to Israeli builders, industrialists, and farmers. Yet the public reacted with a sigh of relief. At which point the Labor government began to view the closure as more than a security measure; now it was seen as a brilliant political move. The assumption was that the luxury of life free of terrorism would make a majority of Israelis long for the day when Israel would relinquish the territories.

What seems to have been overlooked in this picture was that only the Israeli army's presence in the territories made the closure effective. Nor was this effectiveness a product of the separation in itself. Greatly assisted by the forced immobility of the population, the army could now make virtually unhindered house-to-house searches, discover terrorist cells, and round up known individual terrorists by the hundreds. The results were nothing short of spectacular. Most of the men wanted for killings of Israelis and "collaborators" were either apprehended or forced to flee the country (mainly to Egypt).

It was this blow to the terrorist organizations, rather than the closure—which was in effect suspended within weeks—that reduced terrorist activities to a minimum. But the government, preferring to attribute the relaxation to "the separation," continued to perpetuate the myth that the closure was still in effect well after 60,000 registered Palestinian workers and 10,000 others had returned to work in Israel.

The government also seems to have overlooked something else. The brief initial separation of the Palestinians in the territories from Jerusalem made *them* realize how dependent they are on their leaders and their offices, institutions, newspapers, and information services, all of which are located in the eastern part of the city. Ultimately, the most dramatic accomplishment of the closure may have been the sharpening of the Palestinian demand for the inclusion of east Jerusalem in the autonomy plan and the future Palestinian state. "The Israelis and the Americans had better realize," said the Palestinian negotiator Haidar Abdel Shafi in mid-July, "that without an Arab Jerusalem there will be no peace."

Shafi's observation is probably correct. His assessment of the ten rounds of talks in the twenty months since Madrid as utterly devoid of results is also far more accurate than Peres's glowing expressions of optimism. (Rabin has been more restrained.) Even the agreement with Jordan—"all we need is a pen to sign it with," said Peres before the beginning of the tenth round—proved a chimera. The delegations had come together on a draft according to which Israel would relinquish areas on the Jordan river bank and south of the Dead Sea, in return for Jordan's willingness to sign an agenda containing the words, "it is anticipated that the process will culminate in a peace treaty." But the draft, subject to approval by the respective governments, came back from Amman with "minor clarifications": the Jerusalem issue must be resolved first; all the administered territories must be referred to as "occupied"; and the reference to a peace treaty at the end of the road must be eliminated. Here, too, the negotiations were back to square one.

· · · · ·

The Labor government's negotiating strategy is not easy to fathom. From the start, Rabin made one concession after another without a hint of reciprocation. Before the tenth post-Madrid round he declared—implicitly acknowledging what he had been doing up to that point—that the time of one-sided concessions was over. But he never said what he expected from the Arab side.

Concomitantly, the government has been portraying developments in rosy terms when in fact no progress has been registered. Even the one concession the Syrians had made to the Likud government of Yitzhak Shamir—allowing Syrian Jews to emigrate—was withdrawn soon after Labor came to power in early 1992. Nor did the hoped-for moderation of Palestinian demands—which was supposed to follow Israel's agreement to include Jerusalemite Faisal Husseini in the Palestinian delegation—ever materialize. On the contrary, the question of Jerusalem, which must be postponed to a later stage if any progress is to be made on the interim arrangements, became the central issue.

Overly optimistic pronouncements are probably unavoidable during negotiations. They are often used to create momentum and place the ball in the adversary's court. But under present circumstances it is difficult to see the purpose of a consistently Pollyanna-ish Israeli campaign. One possible explanation is that the government is deceiving itself about the willingness of the Arabs to make peace on terms that do not entail full Israeli withdrawal from the Golan Heights, as well as all other territories taken in the Six-Day war, and a Palestinian state with east Jerusalem as its capital. Another, less charitable, explanation is that the dovish faction led by Peres hopes to make the expectation of peace so overwhelming that prices that seemed prohibitive to the Israeli people only yesterday will seem worth paying tomorrow.

The Palestinians, like all the Arab regimes, enjoy an advantage democracies do not have. They can be intransigent and hard-nosed without fear of internal pressures for concessions and compromises. On the contrary, they must fear assassination if they *do* make concessions. Whatever some Israeli doves may imagine, it is a given that the Palestinians will not budge from the demand that autonomy—and later sovereignty—include half of Jerusalem. And it can be taken for granted that they will not agree to any substantial compromises on the territorial definition of autonomy: it will have to extend to all of Judea, Samaria, and Gaza. Nor will they give up on officially including the PLO in the talks.

Against these demands stands Yitzhak Rabin, who still insists on a few traditional Labor-party "no's": no discussion of the permanent solution before autonomy is established; no return to the 1949 armistice lines; no relinquishing of the Jordan valley and Gush Etzion settlements; no direct negotiations with the PLO; and no compromise on Jerusalem, which must stay undivided under Israeli sovereignty. But Deputy Foreign Minister Yossi Beilin, who voices Peres's opinions, has indicated a willingness to yield on *all* these points—with the possible exception of Jerusalem.

If Peres, Beilin, and the dovish faction in the government have their way, the gap between the Arabs' minimum and Israel's maximum will become so narrow as to be imperceptible. And what until recently was quite unthinkable—the establishment of a Palestinian state in the administered territories, the relinquishment of the Golan Heights, and perhaps even the division of Jerusalem into two capitals—may become official government policy.

—*September 1993*

Yigal Carmon

The Story Behind the Handshake

he August 1993 agreement reached in Oslo between Israel and the PLO, and then signed (with some modifications) on the White House lawn a month later, was negotiated in the deepest secrecy. So far, the story behind it has been told only selectively and only by participants or supporters who see it as a triumphant historical breakthrough. But a very different picture emerges when that story is told more fully.

Oslo was by no means the first place in which PLO officials had met with Israelis. From the 1970s on, symposia, conferences, and "dialogues," open as well as clandestine, were held in cities throughout the world under various organizational, semiofficial, and even UN auspices, usually with the host countries' participation. As time went on, the Israeli participants became bolder, notwithstanding the Israeli law which prohibited direct unauthorized contact with members of the PLO. (This law was repealed shortly after the Labor party came to power in 1992.)

The Scandinavian countries had always seemed particularly eager to play the role of host in encounters between the PLO, an organization whose cause they had consistently espoused, and Israeli "peace activists" or dovish American Jews. It was in Stockholm that a group of such Americans, including Rita Hauser and Menachem Rosensaft, met with Yasir Arafat in 1988, clearing a path to the dialogue with the PLO that was begun in the last days of the Reagan administration.

That dialogue was suspended when Arafat refused to condemn a May 1990 terrorist attack on a beach near Tel Aviv by one of the mainstream PLO factions. Washington was particularly miffed when it discovered that the group had intended to attack not only Israelis, but also the American embassy. However, Arafat's refusal to dissociate himself from Abu Abbas, the group's leader, did not have the same effect on the Israeli "peace camp" as it did on the U.S. government. Israeli doves continued to meet with the PLO throughout the world, with at least one major colloquy made into an hour-long program that was widely distributed by PBS.

Among the various hosts of these meetings, a think tank called FAFO (the Norwegian acronym for Institute for Applied Social Science) was outstanding in its dedication and zeal. Early in the summer of 1992, its executive director, Terje Rod Larsen, sought out Yossi Beilin, then head of the Israeli research institute ECF (Economic Cooperation Foundation), and a protégé and very close confidant of Shimon Peres, one of the main leaders of the Labor party. Larsen told Beilin that the Palestinians were tired of the *intifada*, the campaign of violence that had been launched against Israel in 1987, and were ready to reach an agreement. If the coming election brought Labor to power, the opportunity should not be missed. Beilin responded by putting Larsen in touch with a friend, Professor Yair Hirschfeld of Haifa University, a fan of the late Austrian Chancellor Bruno Kreisky, who was famous for his Pollyanna-ish notions about the Arab-Israeli conflict.

Following the Labor victory in early 1992, Yitzhak Rabin became Prime Minister, Shimon Peres became Foreign Minister, and Peres appointed Beilin as his deputy. Larsen—whose wife was administrative assistant to the Norwegian Foreign Minister, Johan Jorgen Holst, while Holst's own wife was the FAFO chairman—now offered the services of the Norwegian government to Beilin. Holst himself was known to be "possessed" by the idea of making peace between Israel and the PLO. There could be no cozier arrangement.

Beilin could not officially participate in direct contacts with PLO representatives—they were still illegal—but he assured Larsen that Hirschfeld and a former student of his, Ron Pundik, an academic with a Scandinavian background, could do the job. At the time, says Beilin, he considered the encounter no more than an intellectual exercise.

Nor did the PLO take the Hirschfeld-Pundik pair too seriously—not until Hanan Ashrawi, the PLO spokeswoman whose home they used to visit, realized how close they were to Shimon Peres's new deputy and closest confidant. At that point, Ashrawi arranged for them to see the PLO's "Finance Minister" Abu Ala in London, and it was there that the idea of drafting a proposal for an Israel-PLO agreement was formed.

Hirschfeld suggested that meetings continue in Oslo, and the PLO people concurred.

Pundik and Hirschfeld kept stressing to their PLO counterparts that the Israeli government might disavow them at any moment. But this only served to convince the Palestinians that their Israeli interlocutors were indeed representing the government. In fact, however, virtually no one in Israel knew of the talks. Hirschfeld and Pundik's only contact at the time was with Beilin, and it is not quite clear at what stage Beilin reported their dealings to Peres.

What *is* certain is that Prime Minister Yitzhak Rabin was entirely unaware of these developments, at least until December 1992, when the Oslo negotiators came up with a document which was, according to Beilin, essentially identical to the Declaration of Principles of August 1993. It called for an almost complete Israeli withdrawal from the Gaza Strip and Jericho, to be followed shortly thereafter by the extension of Palestinian self-rule to the entire West Bank.

· · · · ·

In that same month, December 1992, Rabin and Chief of Staff Lt.-General Ehud Barak decided on the expulsion of 415 Hamas and Islamic Jihad agitators. The expulsion, which was provoked by some particularly bold and successful strikes by these militant fundamentalist organizations against Israeli army and police, did not have the desired effect. The outpouring of sympathy for the deportees by the world media and the pressure on Israel to allow them to return (to which Rabin soon succumbed) encouraged not only the Muslims but also the PLO (including Fatah, Arafat's own faction) to continue their terrorist activities.

By the end of March, Rabin found himself in a critical position. Fifteen months had passed since his election to the premiership, and though he had pledged to achieve an autonomy agreement with the Palestinians within six to nine months, there had been no progress on that front. The talks with the Arab delegations in Washington—begun by his predecessor Yitzhak Shamir in the wake of the Madrid conference of October 1991—had been suspended; increased terrorist strikes had made "Black March" one of the worst months in Israel's history; the Hamas deportees were becoming folk heroes; and his popularity in the polls was at an all-time low.

It was at this juncture that Rabin was finally informed about the Oslo negotiations. Instead of calling them off, he instructed that they be continued. Technically, this instruction was a violation of the country's law, which prohibited official contacts with the PLO except with cabinet approval. No such approval was given. The government ministers were not even aware of the negotiations.

At the end of April, Rabin decided to test the authority and clout of the PLO's interlocutors in Oslo by demanding of them that no official PLO representatives participate in the multilateral talks on refugees scheduled to be held (purely coincidentally) in Oslo. When his demand was promptly met, he was impressed. Why this should have been his reaction is puzzling. Obviously, a direct appeal from the Israeli Prime Minister was a more important sign of recognition to the PLO than the presence of its official representatives at the multilateral negotiations. Nevertheless, Rabin felt that the move proved he was dealing with the PLO's top echelon.

The media greeted the PLO concession with surprise, especially when the Palestinian representatives came out of the multilateral meeting beaming, and Abu Ala, although not a participant, announced to the TV cameras that it had been a great success. The reason for this elation was not only the recognition afforded the PLO by Rabin, but the fact that for the first time a high-ranking Foreign Ministry official—Director General Uri Savir—had become involved in the secret talks.

These talks now proceeded with Rabin's full acquiescence. From now on, they would be headed by Savir, an expert on U.S.-Israel relations (he had served as Consul General in New York) who knew little about the PLO, and Yoel Singer, an Israeli member of a prominent Washington law firm who would later become the Foreign Ministry's legal adviser. The secrecy was complete. In addition to the negotiators themselves, only Avi Gil, Peres's administrative assistant, and Shlomo Gur, Beilin's assistant, were privy to all developments. To ensure confidentiality, they handled typing, airline tickets, and other administrative details without benefit of secretaries. That nothing leaked to the press was extraordinary, particularly in light of the repeated PLO announcements that meetings at a high level were taking place. The world, accustomed to PLO prevarications and exaggerations, accepted the Israeli denials.

As Beilin recalls it, at the time they all still believed that the purpose of the negotiations was to draft a proposal that would be signed by the official delegations to the peace talks in Washington, which on the Palestinian side, of course, did not formally include the PLO. The Israelis thought they were getting a behind-the-scenes PLO endorsement, nothing more. Indeed, on August 15, only five days before the Declaration of Principles was initialed in Oslo, Rabin said at a government meeting that he hoped "Israeli elements" (a euphemism for "peace-camp" ministers and other dovish politicians) would not undermine Washington's policy of dissociation from the PLO.

On August 20, at the Norwegian government's guest house, Holst and a few Norwegian colleagues hosted Peres, Gil, Savir, Singer, Hirschfeld, and Pundik, who were joined by Abu Ala and his assistants, for the signing ceremony. The Israelis were there for one of the most momentous diplomatic moves in the history of their country—without having consulted a single military authority, a single intelligence officer, or a single expert on Arab affairs. To be sure, Rabin himself had gone over every word (though only later would he realize, as he admitted publicly, that the document had left "hundreds" of issues untouched; later still, he would declare that "the legal formulations of Oslo are rubbish" and that "what will be decisive are the facts on the ground").

Toasts were offered by Savir, Abu Ala, and Holst. Peres, in Oslo on an official visit, had sneaked out of his hotel for the ceremony, but he was still reluctant to take an active part in signing an agreement with the PLO. Savir and Singer initialed for Israel, Abu Ala and an assistant for the PLO. Hirschfeld was asked to add his signature, as a tribute to his contribution. As fortune would have it, on that day nine Israeli soldiers were killed on the Lebanese border.

· · · · ·

Rabin's approval of an agreement with "PLO-Tunis," as he had always referred to the organization's government-in-exile, amazed many. But Rabin, while he originally doubted that such an agreement would ever be reached, had also always deemed contacts with the PLO useful. Even in the days when he served as Minister of Defense in the national-unity government under Prime Minister Yitzhak Shamir, he would advise Shamir: let the local Palestinian leadership run to Tunis (an illegal act) as much as they want. They think they are putting one over on us, but in truth we are using them to get PLO approval for the agreement we must reach with the inhabitants of the territories. Without such approval, nothing will move. This way we can secure PLO sponsorship without having to accept the PLO's official presence or its participation in implementing the agreement.

But the PLO knew better. This would soon become clear when Rabin now applied much the same principle to the Oslo talks, explicitly announcing that "the test of the agreement is in its being signed by the delegations to the peace talks in Washington"—that is, not by the PLO. In a speech to the members of his government coalition he explained the tactic in detail:

> For a long time I believed that the Palestinian inhabitants of the territories would achieve their own ability to negotiate. But after more than a year of negotiations I reached the conclusion that they could not.... That is why the talks in Oslo were with Palestinians who are not necessarily residents of the territories. But the signing of the agreement will be between the delegations [to the peace talks in Washington].

Beilin, too, affirmed the separation between the Palestinian delegation in Washington and the PLO. Asked how Israel could sign such a declaration before the PLO abolished the clauses in its charter calling for Israel's destruction, Beilin answered: "The delegation [in Washington] is not the PLO, so the question is irrelevant." (This was in stark contrast to the Labor party's old accusation that the Shamir government had opened the door to PLO participation by negotiating in Madrid with a delegation that was "PLO except for its name.")

The original intention, then, in Beilin's words, "was to put the agreement on the table in Washington without exposing the fact that it had been negotiated with the PLO in Oslo." But at this point the story broke, possibly leaked by the Norwegians, who were approaching a parliamentary election. (Holst's party won.) Then, to the Israelis' surprise, the head of the Palestinian delegation in Washington, Haidar Abdel Shafi, clearly acting in coordination with the PLO, refused to sign the document. Let those who cooked this up sign it, he said.

Queried on an Israeli television program about what would happen to the agreement if Shafi refused to sign it, Beilin replied, "Pay no attention to him. We'll find someone who will sign it." But since no one in the Palestinian delegation would dare sign the document without the PLO's permission, there was only PLO-Tunis to do so. This elementary point seems to have eluded Rabin.

He was, it also seems, unaware that, on the eve of the Madrid conference, Faisal Husseini (the unofficial head of the Palestinian delegation who—being a resident of Jerusalem—had been disqualified as an official negotiator by the Shamir government) informed the then-Secretary of State, James Baker, that if an agreement were reached, only the PLO would sign it, not the delegation. (Husseini himself apparently leaked this information to the Hebrew daily *Ma'ariv*.)

So now Rabin had in hand a document which would not be signed by the only people he wanted to sign it: the representatives (albeit unelected) of the 1.8 million Palestinians living in the territories. He had to decide whether to let this "historic moment" dissipate or to enter into an agreement with PLO-Tunis, an organization which considered itself, and was considered by most of the world, the government-in-exile of the state of Palestine.

· · · · ·

Rabin, clearly feeling he had reached the point of no return, chose to sign. At this stage, to go back to his original policy would have meant that, having violated his vow not to deal with PLO-Tunis, he had emerged with nothing to show for it. This would have been a political disaster for him in Israel, and it was a price he was obviously not ready to pay.

To make final recognition of the PLO more palatable, however, he insisted on three minimal conditions, which even the most extreme Israeli doves had always said should precede negotiations with the PLO: Palestinian recognition of Israel's right to exist; the renunciation of terrorism by the PLO; and the cancellation of the clauses in the PLO charter calling for the destruction of Israel.

Only then did feverish negotiations begin, and during the next ten days they seemed to produce results. Israel and the PLO would officially recognize each other, Arafat would commit himself to changing the charter, and the PLO would both renounce and denounce terrorism. Ironically, had Shafi been willing to sign, nothing of this would have made its way into the agreement. Yet even so, the PLO, which had already achieved what it wanted most—namely, Israeli recognition—did not give Israel all it demanded.

Thus, Israel demanded that the PLO charter be declared "invalid." The PLO agreed only to a declaration that the offensive clauses "are now inoperative, and no longer valid." The difference was subtle, but enough to turn a determined repudiation into something that could be and, among Palestinians, would be read as a mere observation.

Israel also demanded cessation of "the armed struggle"—the standard PLO euphemism for terrorist activities, hallowed as a sacred means to a sacred end. The PLO adamantly and successfully refused. It also flatly rejected the Israeli demand to declare an end to the uprising, which the PLO calls "the blessed *intifada*." (A senior PLO source told the Hebrew daily *Ha'aretz* that the Israelis had not even asked for an end to the *intifada*, only to its more extreme manifestations.)

Peres insisted that the letters of mutual recognition to be exchanged by Arafat and Rabin include a pledge by Arafat to appeal to the Palestinian people to refrain from terrorism. But Peres was persuaded that it would be unseemly for Arafat to address his people through an agreement with Israel. Instead, the promise to make such an appeal was included in a letter to the Norwegian Foreign Minister, Jorgen Holst (who would die four months later).

Arafat's letter of recognition to Rabin also contained a pledge to punish members of the PLO who might disobey the order to suspend terrorist activity. This was demanded not by the Israelis, but by U.S. Secretary of State Warren Christopher, who felt he needed it to get the ban on the PLO repealed in Congress. (A curious last-minute attempt to acquire American sponsorship for the agreement was made by Peres during a quick trip to the U.S. But Christopher politely rejected the Israeli appeal: "The Norwegians are the sponsors," he asserted to the press.)

Once the PLO executive committee approved the Declaration of Principles, it was to be signed by Peres and the PLO's Abu Mazen at the State Department in Washington. But the PLO saw here an opportunity to get Arafat to the White House. The Clinton administration, hungry for a foreign-policy success, pounced on the idea with gusto. Rather than allow Peres to lead the Israeli delegation, it proposed to invite Rabin. At first Rabin said that he would not go. But when Christopher called him (at 6 A.M. on a Sabbath morning), he immediately changed his mind. This enabled Arafat—still officially a wanted terrorist in the U.S.—to appear in Washington as a head of government. Arafat must have been unprepared for the alacrity with which the U.S. accepted the idea. His plane, donated by Saddam Hussein and still boasting the Iraqi colors, had to be hurriedly repainted with Algerian colors, since Iraqi planes were banned in the U.S.

. . . . .

At six o'clock in the morning of September 13, Ahmed Tibi—an Israeli Arab gynecologist who is Arafat's political adviser (a breathtaking case of dual loyalty)—was awakened by a call from his boss. "I haven't slept all night," said Arafat, according to Tibi. "If the PLO instead of the official Washington delegation is not named as the representative of the Palestinian side in the agreement, I won't sign it."

Hearing of Arafat's ultimatum, Peres at first threatened to leave Washington. But within minutes, says Tibi, "a compromise was found": Abu Mazen would write "PLO" on the document where the words

"Palestinian delegation" appeared. In Tibi's account, when Arafat heard that Peres had accepted this "compromise"—in fact, an Israeli capitulation—he was incredulous. "Are you sure they agree?" he asked Tibi. "The man, Peres, is standing next to me," responded Tibi. "So I send two kisses on your head," answered Arafat, and Tibi rushed to dress for the ceremony.

The Israelis were promised that Arafat would not wear a military uniform or carry a gun to the ceremony. When he boarded the plane in Tunis he was wearing a uniform, and carrying a gun. At the White House, he appeared without the gun, but the military uniform remained. The Israelis called it a green suit.

The upshot was that, desperate by now for anything that would seem like a success, Rabin had become an easy mark. Simply by causing the negotiations to bog down and denying Israel a partner who could sign an agreement, Arafat got Rabin to break cherished taboos and cross hallowed red lines. He also got Rabin to accept promises that would be forgotten almost as soon as they were made.

For example, disappointed by the PLO's refusal to declare an end to the "armed struggle" and the *intifada*, Israeli officials rationalized it as Arafat's need to "save face"; the commitments to Holst, they maintained, meant in effect a total end to violence. Yet in numerous PLO messages to the territories, culminating in a January call to Gaza activists, Arafat would vow that the *intifada* would "continue and continue and continue." And indeed, following the agreement there was to be no slackening either of *intifada* activities or of terrorism.

Again, in his letter to Holst, Arafat promised that he would make his appeal against violence as soon as the Declaration of Principles was officially signed. Not unreasonably, the Norwegians, Americans, and Israelis all expected him to do this in his speech at the signing ceremony on the White House lawn. Waiting for the magic words to be uttered any moment, Ehud Ya'ari, the Israel Television commentator who covered the proceedings, used every break in Arafat's speech to announce, "Now he will denounce terrorism ... now he will say it ... now he simply has to say it...." Only after the last paragraph did Ya'ari give up: "He is not saying it," he reported, crushed.

Nor would Arafat set a date for implementing the changes in the PLO charter to which he had committed himself. Nor did it seem likely that the necessary two-thirds majority could be found in the PLO "parliament," the Palestine National Council (PNC), to ratify such alterations. And in any case, Arafat himself would go on to declare that he had no intention of asking for a change in the charter. As his colleague Ziad Abu Zayyad would put it: "Asking us to abolish parts of the charter is like us asking you to abolish the Bible."

．．．．．

Arafat was followed by the media throughout the day of the signing. What they did not report was that he made a broadcast to the Palestinian people through Jordanian television on that very day. In it, he mentioned neither a halt to terrorism nor peace or coexistence with Israel. Instead, he described the agreement as the first step "in the 1974 plan"— known by all Arabs as the "plan of phases" for the destruction of Israel.

He did not need to spell it out, for he could be confident that his audience would understand the implications: that the foothold the agreement had just given him would now open the way in short order to an independent Palestinian state in Gaza, Judea, and Samaria with Jerusalem as its capital; and that this would make it easier to continue the struggle for the "right of return" of between one and two million Palestinians to pre-1967 Israel, which they still regarded as their homeland.

Yet no Israeli government, not even the most leftist or the most dovish, would be able to accept such an outcome. Nor (despite the provision in the agreement of an interim period of autonomy) did the PLO have any intention of waiting for full sovereignty or settling for anything less. Therefore, the likelihood was that the deal would fall apart at an earlier stage, dashing the unrealistic expectations it had recklessly raised on both sides, bringing bitter and angry disappointment to Israelis and Palestinians alike, and leading not to peace but to a full-scale and very bloody showdown.

—March 1994

Douglas J. Feith

Land
for No Peace

T he 1993 Israel-PLO accord was supposed to bring on the new
dawn of peace that optimists contended could be Israel's for the
asking. Many Israelis, fatigued by decades of securing the land
and themselves against Arab threats, military and terrorist, had come to
regard the status quo as unbearable. Perhaps, they speculated, Palestinian-Arab leadership had evolved away from ideological anti-Zionism
toward a pragmatic willingness to share the land with the Jewish state
in peace. After the Soviet Union's collapse and the 1991 American-led
attack on Iraq for its seizure of Kuwait, Israel's strategic strength and
Yasir Arafat's political and economic weakness combined to make Israeli
officials think they could test that hopeful proposition without undue
risk.

The accord comprised, first, the Declaration of Principles (DOP),
which was concluded on August 20, 1993 and signed by Arafat and Prime
Minister Yitzhak Rabin at the White House on September 13, 1993; and,
second, the mutual-recognition agreement embodied in the letters dated
September 9, 1993 exchanged by Arafat, Rabin, and the Norwegian Foreign Minister. No one can doubt that these agreements are significant;
but what exactly do they signify?

The DOP provides for the withdrawal of Israel's military forces
from Gaza and Jericho and the transfer of governing authority for "education and culture, health, social welfare, direct taxation, and tourism"
to an Arab Council "empowered to legislate." The DOP is often called
the Gaza-Jericho accord, but this is misleading because the transfers of

governing authority are not limited to Gaza and Jericho. On the contrary: the Council's jurisdiction will cover "the West Bank and the Gaza Strip as a single territorial unit, whose integrity will be preserved during the interim period"—i.e., "a transitional period not exceeding five years."

The Council, to be established following general elections, will assume the responsibilities Israel is relinquishing, but in the meantime authority rests with the PLO. "Palestinians of Jerusalem who live there will have the right to participate in the election process for the Council," and Jerusalem is one of the "issues that will be negotiated in the per-manent-status negotiations."

Such Israeli concessions went far beyond the West Bank–Gaza Strip autonomy provisions of the 1978 Camp David accord signed by Israel's Menachem Begin and Egypt's Anwar Sadat. That accord designated the autonomy authority as an "administrative council" and withheld from it all legislative or proto-parliamentary powers. At Camp David, the Israeli government took care to specify that the aim was "to provide full autonomy *to the inhabitants*" (emphasis added) rather than to the terri-tories as such, let alone to all "the West Bank and the Gaza Strip as a sin-gle territorial unit." Begin considered this distinction between auton-omy for the inhabitants and autonomy for the territories important to prevent prejudicing the issue of Israel's right to assert claims regarding the territories in final-status negotiations. Israel did not, at Camp David, accept the PLO as an interlocutor. And it refused to make Jerusalem a topic for negotiation at any time.

Placing the 1978 accord side by side with the 1993 DOP highlights the historic and unprecedented nature of Israel's concessions in the lat-ter agreement.

· · · · ·

What of the PLO'S concessions? The Arafat-Rabin agreements were not the first time the PLO chairman had acknowledged Israel's right to exist, declared the PLO'S acceptance of UN Security Council Resolutions 242 and 338, and promised to renounce anti-Israel terrorism. Arafat did all of that in December 1988 to win the PLO its official, open dialogue with the U.S. government. (Eighteen months later, Arafat's unwillingness to repudiate a PLO terrorist attack compelled the Bush administration to terminate the dialogue.)

Nor was this the first time the PLO had announced that it would consent to accepting authority in whatever portion of the territories became available to it. The Palestine National Council originally did that in the summer of 1974, when it formally resolved to combine diplomacy with armed struggle. In what came to be known as the "phased plan," the PLO leadership agreed that its principles were not offended by the dismantlement of Israel in stages and through diplomacy, rather than all at once and solely by military means.

Wherein, then, lay the much-heralded "breakthrough to peace" on Arafat's side? In the view of those who perceived one, the breakthrough was that this time Arafat actually meant what he said. (One Israeli official was quoted to the effect that quarrels within the PLO over Arafat's peace pledges were a sign that the pledges were not tactical but reflected a deep ideological change.) Skeptics were referred to the fact that Arafat's promises were now formulated explicitly (as if an explicit statement cannot be false). Also, those promises now included an unambiguous commitment to delete provisions in the Palestinian Covenant rejecting Israel's right to exist. Furthermore, Arafat had formally agreed, directly with the Israeli government, to an autonomy timetable that was supposed to defer for years into the future any demand for Arab sovereignty in the territories. And finally, not only would the PLO's own anti-Israel violence end, but Arafat would cooperate in keeping Hamas, Islamic Jihad, and other overt rejectionists in check.

None of these PLO promises was kept.

To begin with, the PLO did not amend its Covenant. Though accepted by Israel as leader of the organization deemed "representative of the Palestinian people," Arafat proved unable to command the requisite endorsement of his leadership from the Palestine National Council, the body empowered to amend the Covenant, or even from many of the top officials of his own Fatah faction of the PLO. After a number of his top PLO colleagues resigned or otherwise protested the Israel-PLO agreements, Arafat dropped whatever plans he had to propose amendment of the Covenant.

Secondly, in violation of its agreement to defer the demand for sovereignty, the PLO insisted upon immediate moves toward that goal. Thus, throughout the negotiations that produced the May 4 agreement on implementing the DOP, Arafat pressed for an expansive definition of "Jericho" (far broader than the bounds of the town itself), exclusive PLO control over border crossings, immediate removal of Jewish settlements, and implicit endorsement of PLO claims to Jerusalem.

Thirdly, in the months after the DOP was signed, there was intensified violence by Arabs against Jews, some of it perpetrated by Arafat's own Fatah faction. Nor did the PLO crack down on Hamas and other non-PLO extremists. In fact, open collusion among them was evident, including the publication of joint declarations, participation in demonstrations together, PLO demands for the release of arrested Hamas personnel, and announcement of new PLO-Hamas understandings on cooperation to remove Israel from the territories. Though Palestinian-Arab terrorism had plagued the land for nearly a century, every new attack now evoked defensive explanations that the actual target was the "peace process." (This led one Israeli wit to call for an end to the peace process so that he could get some peace.)

. . . . .

Israeli government officials voiced frustration over this state of affairs, but they took pains not to sound accusatory. Shortly before the DOP was signed, Yossi Beilin, Israel's Deputy Foreign Minister, declared, "If there are problems on the way to implementing the agreement and if they cannot control their opposition and there is no order, we will say we can't go on." This reassuring theme was stressed repeatedly before the signing ceremony. On August 31, the *Washington Post* reported: "Peres told the Israeli parliament that Israel will not recognize the PLO unless it removes from its charter a call for armed struggle against Israel and halts violent attacks on Israeli targets." The next day, the *Wall Street Journal* reported:

> Mr. Beilin . . . also said that the DOP plan is conditional on the Palestinians being able to prevent Islamic fundamentalist groups who oppose the peace talks from carrying out terrorist attacks against Israel. . . .
> Mr. Beilin . . . said that a key part of the "Gaza and Jericho first" plan is the fact that it is reversible.
> Mr. Beilin continued, "As in any other agreement, there is the belief that both sides will be able to implement it and can be trusted, but if there is a clear violation, it will be more than understandable that we cannot adhere to it."

Nevertheless, when the PLO failed to control its opposition (and even its own elements), when there was terrorism and no order, and when the PLO otherwise violated the DOP and the mutual-recognition agreement, the Israeli government did not say, "We can't go on."

On September 13, the very day the DOP was signed in Washington, Jordanian television aired a speech by Arafat which, among other offensive features, explained his peace policy by reference to the phased plan:

O my beloved ones: do not forget that our Palestine National Council made the decision in 1974. It called for the establishment of national authority on any part of Palestinian soil that is liberated or from which the Israelis withdraw. It is the fruit of your struggle, sacrifices, and jihad. . . .

Brothers, beloved ones: Palestine is only a stone's throw away for a small Palestinian boy or girl. It is the Palestinian state that lives deep in our heart. Its flag will fly over the walls of Jerusalem, the churches of Jerusalem, and the mosques of Jerusalem.

They see the day indeed as a far-off event, but we see it quite near and we indeed are truthful.

This extraordinary statement was tantamount to Arafat's concluding his White House speech of conciliation with a loud and jeering "I take it back!" The Israeli government took it in stride, however, as it did the PLO's subsequent failure to amend the Covenant. Israel exerted itself to lure the PLO back to the table when the PLO walked away. Israel urged its U.S. supporters *not* to link PLO promises—for example, on the Covenant issue—to any waiver of various anti-PLO provisions of U.S. law. And Israel restrained itself and its U.S. supporters from pressing for a U.S. veto of the UN Security Council resolution condemning the massacre of Muslims by a Jew in Hebron, even though the resolution referred prejudicially to the territories as "Palestinian" land and designated Jerusalem as "occupied territory."

In light of the history of PLO terrorism and untruthfulness, and of Israeli defense-mindedness and distrust, it was stunning—one might even say disorienting—to see Israeli officials soliciting European and American financial support for the PLO, gesturing good will through the release of hundreds of suspected Palestinian-Arab terrorists, and muting their own and their public's outrage over continuing anti-Israel terrorism by the PLO. Students of military history are familiar with the fog-of-war phenomenon. Students of the Arab-Israeli conflict have, since September 13, 1993, come to know the fog of peace.

· · · · ·

What kind of strategy or rationale or theory underlies such a policy? The usual answer is "land for peace." But this longstanding concept has in important respects been transcended or shunted aside by the Israel-PLO accord and the implementation talks.

Israelis who view territorial withdrawal as the key to resolving the conflict between themselves and the Palestinian Arabs have generally done so on pragmatic grounds. The contention has been not so much that Israel lacks rights in the territories as that their retention, given the over-1.5-million Arab inhabitants, would swamp the Jewish state demographically. The classic formulation has been that holding on to the territories will ultimately destroy either the Jewish nature of the state, if the Arabs are given Israeli citizenship, or its democratic character, if they are not. Exponents of this view, most notably the present Foreign Minister, Shimon Peres, consistently maintained, however, that they would be willing to relinquish the militarily valuable territories to an Arab power only in return for peace and security.

But there was always a contradiction inherent in the demographic-bomb theory. If the Arab powers refused to grant Israel peace and security, would a proponent of that theory favor retaining the territory even though doing so would be suicidal, in that it would destroy either Israel's Jewish or its democratic nature? Clearly, underlying this position has always been a rationale not for trading territory for peace, but for unilateral withdrawal by Israel. The theory in effect tells Israel's enemies that they need not pay a price for the territories because Israel will either destroy itself by sitting tight, or up and leave for its own reasons, without demanding much (or perhaps anything) in return.

In the past, this contradiction was effectively finessed by the contention that the Palestinian Arabs (perhaps in confederation with Jordan) were in fact willing to offer Israel a secure peace if only the Israeli government, as a matter of policy, would agree to trade territory for it. Essential to a land-for-peace policy was a sequence of steps (and the order was important). First, Israel would renounce permanent control of the land, declaring its readiness to trade land for peace. Second, Israel's Arab interlocutors would make a credible and authoritative pledge of peace. And third, with this reliable peace promise in hand, Israel would effect the agreed-upon withdrawal.

This, in essence, was the policy the new Rabin government adopted when it came to office in 1992. In the so-called Madrid Process, the Rabin government, unlike its predecessor, made clear that it was willing to relinquish territory in return for peace. But after a year, the talks had produced no peace agreements. There was stalemate on all fronts. Mutual recriminations were rife. Anti-Israel violence was claiming numerous victims and provoking Israel into large-scale retaliations, such as the expulsion of 400 accused fundamentalist terrorists to Southern Lebanon in December 1992 and Operation Accountability in July 1993, which forced thousands of Arabs in Lebanon to evacuate their homes. Around the world, journalists and officials criticized these Israeli actions.

A land-for-peace policy had not produced the anticipated softening of Arab negotiating demands, and Israeli officials spoke with exasperation of their unhappiness that the Arabs refused to meet them halfway in the Washington talks.

If the Israeli government continued to insist on a credible and authoritative pledge of peace as a *precondition* of withdrawal, the prospect loomed that it would not be able, within its four-year term of office, to deliver to its citizens a new peace agreement or deliver them from the travails of the occupation. So the traditional idea of land for peace was set aside, and Israel concluded the deal embodied in the DOP.

It is noteworthy that the DOP was agreed upon and published by the Israeli government *before* the PLO and Israel had concluded the mutual-recognition agreement by which Arafat promised to respect Israel's right to exist; to renounce, prevent, and punish anti-Israel terrorism and violence; and to detoxify, as it were, the Palestinian Covenant. On September 1—that is, after the DOP was published but before the mutual-recognition agreement was achieved—Peres announced that Israel intended to implement the Declaration even if the PLO failed to make the peace pledges required for Israeli recognition: "The Declaration stands on its own legs. It doesn't need any further confirmation." The next day the *New York Times* reported: "Israeli officials say that if the two sides cannot agree on terms of mutual recognition in the near future, Israel would be ready to sign the accord anyway."

In other words, policy had evolved to the point where Israel was intent on beginning to withdraw from at least some of the territory *whether or not* it received a specific, authoritative promise of peace from the Arab side.

The deal, then, falls outside the traditional concept of land for peace. It treats Israeli withdrawals not as the reward, after the fact, for a clear-cut, credible, duly formalized, pacific change of heart on the part of an Arab interlocutor, as was the case in 1977 with Anwar Sadat, the President of Egypt. Rather, Israel is to withdraw in the hope that this will encourage such a change of heart and, if no such change occurs, then so be it.

· · · · ·

Though the case for unilateral withdrawal by Israel—now sometimes described euphemistically as a "divorce" from the territories—has greater internal consistency than the traditional land-for-peace idea, it puts Israel on a perilous course leading to grave disappointment and worse.

The traditional land-for-peace approach entailed danger for Israel because the land in question could serve as a staging area for terrorism, military attacks, or both, and because the promises given to Israel, even if sincere, would come from individuals who ruled undemocratically and could not commit their political successors. But the current approach of withdrawals-first-and-maybe-peace-later entails all these risks and more. For as the expression on Rabin's face made clear during the first famous handshake on the White House lawn, Israel can hardly take Arafat's credibility for granted. And even if it could, subsequent events have demonstrated that Arafat cannot win a reassuring margin of support for the deal from the PLO as a whole, or even from his own Fatah organization, let alone from the growing number of Palestinian Arabs who line up with Hamas, Islamic Jihad, and other non-PLO rejectionist groups.

Some Israelis dismiss these considerations. They believe that, even if the withdrawals do not resolve or even mitigate the Arab-Israeli conflict, Israel is better off confronting its future security problems without what they view as the encumbrance of the occupation. This is strongly implied when officials like Beilin refer to the territories as "a burden and a curse."

But unilateral withdrawal cannot produce the promised liberation from moral, military, or other problems. It will instead result in Israel's exchanging one set of problems for another. The material and moral burdens of the occupation—though not to be denied or belittled—are not a threat to Israel's existence. Neither, as 27 years of history attest, need they be fatal to Israel's democratic institutions or principles. They create strains, sometimes severe; but many democracies have suffered and survived strains from security threats, and Israel's commitment to a liberal rule of law remains robust.

On the other hand, territorial withdrawals that (1) reduce Israel's strategic depth; (2) deprive Israel of control over the Judean and Samarian highlands; (3) reduce Israel's time for mobilization in a crisis; (4) require greater reliance on preemption strategies; or (5) increase Israel's chances of being cut in half in a war will create problems of a far higher order. The often demoralizing psychological and economic burdens of the occupation will then be replaced by even more demoralizing psychological and economic burdens arising from physical insecurity and a hair-trigger national-defense posture.

It has been asserted that the Israel Defense Forces could easily handle any military threat Arafat and the PLO might pose from the territories. This is a reassurance that deserves to be credited—so long as current circumstances prevail. But if Islamic fundamentalist forces were to win additional political successes in countries like Egypt, Jordan, Syria, and Lebanon, and among the Palestinian Arabs themselves—hardly an inconceivable eventuality—the ability of Israel's enemies to exploit any territorial concessions made now to the PLO would increase substantially.

· · · · ·

There is yet another important issue in the negotiations: national rights. In debates over national-security policy, it is always useful to remind oneself of what one is aiming to secure. For a country like the United States or Israel, national security is far more than simply the physical survival of the citizenry. America is more than a land and a people: it is a society based on a constitution; it is an idea. Israel too is an idea. It is the fulfillment of the Zionist dream, the embodiment of the internationally recognized national rights of the Jewish people.

When contemplating a proposed concession by Israel, it is not enough to ask whether that concession would endanger the state's physical security. It is altogether proper for Israelis to ask themselves also whether the concession involves an undue relinquishment of national rights. This point was underlined for me by the comment of an Israeli friend—a strong proponent, by the way, of the Israel-PLO accord. He said:

> I have great sympathy for those Jews who value Hebron and Nablus, who have intense Zionist feelings about them. I personally don't share those feelings for those places, but I do share them for Jerusalem. If the Arabs were to say, "You Jews can have peace but you must give up Jerusalem," I would say that I'd rather have Jerusalem. If it ever got to the point where I would rather have peace than Jerusalem, I would move to the United States.

A statement like this reminds us that there is more at stake in the negotiations than peace and the physical security of Israelis. One cannot define the national security of Israel without reference to the principles of Zionism, any more than one could define the national security of the United States without reference to the principles of the U.S. Constitution. Though it is common for nations to trade assets with one another for purposes of commerce or to solve quarrels, there are some things that a nation can never trade away unless it is willing to change its basic character. Nations that try to buy peace with aggressive neighbors by trading national rights often wind up with neither sovereignty nor peace.

· · · · ·

Much has been made of the fact that the Arab parties are for the first time willing to negotiate peace with Israel openly. That is something; but does it establish that the Arab intent is peaceable? After all, every ambitious and aggressive dictator for the last 100 years engaged in highly publicized peace talks: Lenin, Stalin, Hitler, Saddam Hussein, and Slobodan Milosevic all participated in peace negotiations and used them to pursue belligerent designs.

Nor is there any guarantee that the follow-up negotiations will succeed in carrying the DOP into full effect. Notwithstanding the lengthy, complex, and bitterly negotiated May 4 implementation agreement, the overarching Israel-PLO accord of September 1993 could disintegrate, as have other diplomatic gossamers of the Middle East from the 1919 Feisal-Weizmann agreement to the 1983 Israel-Lebanon treaty.

Israeli withdrawal from the territories is beginning. Whether it can continue and to what extent are questions that hinge largely on Arafat's credibility and authority. Though the avant-garde of Israel's unilateral-withdrawal school may say to itself, "We will not let Arafat block our withdrawal, no matter what," the general Israeli public has been taught to expect reliable peace and security commitments in any trade for territory. It is crucial, then, that the PLO provide political cover: enough concessions from Arafat to give the appearance of mutuality; at a minimum, sufficient controls on political violence to allow Israeli forces to go on withdrawing from the territories without precipitating outbreaks of mayhem and killings; a decent interval.

Yet the more influential the unilateral-withdrawal school has appeared to be in Israel, the less Arafat has been inclined to make any concessions at all. Indeed, for more than half a year after he signed the DOP, Arafat devoted himself to taking back important concessions—for example, by raising issues like the settlements and Jerusalem. Given Arafat's record, traits, and various incapacities (including his lack of authority over even his core constituency), there remains a substantial possibility that the negotiating dynamics will ultimately produce not a final settlement under the Israel-PLO deal, but an unraveling.

If this unraveling should occur, Israeli advocates of unilateral withdrawal will lose the valuable cover provided by the peace process, but they may—in the open, as it were—succeed in winning their essential point. Perhaps Israel will make further withdrawals and additional concessions even without credible and authoritative moves toward peace by Arafat and the PLO. If it does, its Arab enemies may take this as confirmation that unremitting hostility and violence, having driven the Jews from the territories, can also drive them the rest of the way out of Palestine. In much of the Arab world, the Crusader analogy—two centuries were required to wear down and expel the Crusaders from the Holy Land, this analogy goes, and Arabs should be prepared to do the same with the Jews no matter how long it takes—is frequently invoked and is vivid and inspirational.

Israel may thus discover that the problem is not the intransigence or the flexibility of its own policies or the shape of its boundaries. Rather, the problem is whether its neighbors have the political leadership and the good will to sustain peace with a Jewish state on what, according to their religious and cultural convictions, is *their* land, *Arab* land—that is, anywhere in Palestine. If, contrary to all benevolent hopes, it transpires that those neighbors are not so willing, Israelis will have to tap into their Zionist heritage to find enough conviction and fortitude to defend themselves, for however long may be necessary, against hostility and violence, against *intifadas* and wars, if they are to preserve their state.

—June 1994

Dore Gold

Where Is the Peace Process Going?

Still another moment of transition is occurring in Israel as the government of Yitzhak Rabin moves toward implementing the next phase of the agreement it struck in September 1993 with the PLO in Oslo. As at earlier stages, the arrival of this moment has been beset by delays—for reasons that are not far to seek. Although incidents of Arab terror abated sharply in the months just prior to the deadline for this further extension of Palestinian self-rule, the previous year had been marked by a tremendous increase in anti-Israel violence, and within Israel itself the feeling had become widespread that the entire Oslo "process" had failed—indeed, had perhaps been misconceived from the outset.

That judgment was not limited to Rabin's parliamentary opposition and its supporters in the electorate. The Israeli military, normally extremely reticent about political matters, was quite blunt about the unfolding implementation of the Oslo accords in Gaza and Jericho. Thus, on May 3 of this year, Amnon Shahak, chief of staff of the Israel Defense Force (IDF), told the newspaper *Yediot Ahronot:* "The security situation in Gaza is far from being something to which one can give a passing grade." Shaul Mofaz, who as head of the IDF's southern command has operational responsibility for the Gaza area, told the same newspaper two weeks earlier that Arafat "has not met the conditions of the agreement he signed." In Mofaz's words, "Arafat . . . has failed, failed, failed."

The Israeli man in the street was no less outspoken. If ordinary Israelis had one main priority which they hoped their government would address in any peace settlement, it was personal security; in 1992, the Likud government of Yitzhak Shamir had fallen from power after a spate of knifing incidents that sapped public confidence. But whereas, during the worst years of the *intifada*, Israeli fatalities in terrorist incidents had ranged from 14 to 40 annually, in the past year Israeli fatalities shot up to over 80. Moreover, the sporadic knifings of the pre-1992 period were now replaced with a far more lethal form of terrorism: bus bombings. And these attacks were directed for the most part not at Israeli settlements in the administered territories but at the populace in the heart of pre-1967 Israel. (Some of the more spectacular terrorist incidents, like the kidnapping and murder of Nahshon Waxman, were in fact the work of Palestinians released from Israeli prisons after Oslo.) As two leading Israeli journalists concluded in mid-May: "From the start, Rabin marketed the Oslo agreement as an answer to a security problem. In this sense, the agreement has been revealed to be until today a failure."

· · · · ·

If such sentiments are justified, it bodes ill for the next stage of the Oslo agreement, no matter how warily Israel enters into it and despite temporary respites from terrorism. Are they justified?

To answer that question properly, one has to go back to the beginning of the process by which Israel got itself entangled in its almost-two-year-old agreements with the PLO. Until now this has not been easy to do, for the literature on the genesis of the process is, surprisingly, rather scant. Each of the other major turning points in the country's recent history—the 1978 Camp David accords between Israel and Egypt, the 1982 Lebanon war, the *intifada* that erupted in 1987—quickly generated a half-dozen or more books analyzing the political forces involved and the implications of the events in question. By contrast, the 1993 Declaration of Principles (DOP) between Israel and the PLO, probably the most important diplomatic agreement negotiated in Israel's short history and a story that begs for interpretation and insight, went relatively untreated except for a few memoirs by those involved.

Now, however, David Makovsky, the diplomatic correspondent of the *Jerusalem Post*, has come the closest to doing for Oslo what Bob Woodward and Carl Bernstein did in the United States for Watergate. Unlike the mass-market books that come out of the Washington press corps, though, Makovsky's *Making Peace With the PLO* is a work of scholarship. Makovsky is especially careful not to allow himself to get drawn into the pre-Oslo debate within Israel over whether peace with the Palestinians was possible, and he is equally careful to avoid the even more polarized debate that has taken place in Oslo's aftermath. He does not try to judge the Israeli government's decision-making process, only to understand and explain it.

Nevertheless, and despite its restraint, *Making Peace With the PLO* is fascinating to read, and it offers a vital resource to anyone wishing to reach his own conclusions about what exactly happened back in September 1993, and what it means.

The outline of the story Makovsky tells is well-enough known. A secret dialogue takes place in early 1993 between two obscure Israeli academics and the PLO in Oslo, Norway. The academics are connected with Israel's Deputy Foreign Minister, Yossi Beilin, a man whom Prime Minister Rabin had dismissed years earlier on Israeli television as the "poodle" of his arch-rival, Shimon Peres. Now, with Peres serving, ironically enough, as Rabin's Foreign Minister, the dialogue evolves into a full-blown negotiation that, with Rabin's apparent blessing and support, circumvents the official peace talks between Israel and the Palestinians going on simultaneously in Washington. With astonishing rapidity an agreement is concluded by mid-summer, and the DOP is rushed to Washington for signing. The full prestige of the Clinton presidency is mobilized to back the accord, culminating in the Rabin-Arafat handshake on the White House lawn.

Those are the bare bones; *Making Peace With the PLO* does much to flesh them out.

One thing that emerges with particular clarity from Makovsky's account is that the initial contacts between Israel and the PLO were put, fatefully, into the hands of people with a far greater interest in economics than in security, and with no experience or training as negotiators. That was certainly the case with the two academics, Yair Hirschfeld of Haifa University and Ron Pundik of the Hebrew University, who pioneered the Oslo channel. In a clear reflection of their interests and biases, the text of the DOP was full of references to economic-cooperation projects and joint-business ventures. And the Norwegian sponsors of the contacts were equally prone, as Makovsky notes, to invoke "the experience of the European Community in transforming political relations by institutionalizing shared economic endeavor."

Yet, on the assumption that the Rabin government was irretrievably bent on opening a channel to the PLO, there were other possible routes to go. Shlomo Gazit, the former chief of military intelligence who had been IDF coordinator for the territories back in 1967, had PLO contacts, as did Ephraim Sneh, a Labor-party member of the Knesset (MK) who once headed Israel's civil administration in Judea and Samaria. Either of these men would have brought to the discussions more military experience than what was on offer from Hirschfeld and Pundik. Or Rabin could have picked a loyal political appointee with a background in security and sent him to Norway along with the two academics.

As things stood, however, every major Israeli security organization—the Mossad, the General Security Services, Israeli military intelligence, as well as the IDF—was cut out of the loop; as Makovsky stresses, Oslo lay exclusively in the hands of the two academics from January until mid-May. On May 21, a week after Rabin had given his consent to the proceedings, the first Israeli official, Uri Savir, director general of the Foreign Ministry, joined the talks; yet Savir, although he could make a political assessment for his boss, Shimon Peres, had not participated in previous Arab-Israeli negotiations. Only on June 11 were the talks further strengthened on the Israeli side by the inclusion of Joel Singer, who had served in the advocate-general's office of the IDF and had provided staff work for military talks with Egypt in the late 1970's. But this left very little time for official input; the DOP was completed and initialed by both parties in Oslo on August 20.

In other words, the truly serious phase of Oslo was not more than six weeks in duration. In an interview with Makovsky, Joel Singer (who is now the legal adviser to the Foreign Ministry) conceded that what had gone before had made his job that much more difficult: "If someone who is not a doctor is performing an appendectomy and in the middle of the operation he turns it over to you, you cannot just start from scratch."

But the real problem with the two academics was not their lack of negotiating skills; after all, as Makovsky observes, they had "received only minimal instructions from Beilin" and certainly had not been given any mandate to reach an agreement. Their chief role, at least at first, was to test the PLO's seriousness and to ascertain its true position. But *just here* lay the weakness of the whole enterprise. Makovsky writes:

> Rabin was highly dependent for information regarding the Oslo negotiations upon the two men who were most intimately involved in the evolution of the Oslo process and therefore had the greatest stake in its success: Peres and Beilin.

And Peres and Beilin were dependent, in turn, on the two academics. All four of Rabin's "evaluators," in other words, were true believers in both the possibility and the desirability of a "dialogue" with the

PLO. For any one of them to have concluded, after initial discussion, that the contact with Arafat should be discontinued would have meant burying one of the central items of faith on the Israeli Left. In other words, Rabin, to say the least, did not have the benefit of impartial advisers.

. . . . .

What might such advisers have told him? One of the underlying assumptions of Oslo was that the PLO would have both the will and the capacity to fight the extremists in Hamas and Islamic Jihad, and hence protect Israel from terror. Makovsky quotes Joel Singer: "They [the PLO] kept saying all the time that Arafat could and would stop terrorism ... that Arafat would make the difference." After Oslo was signed, Rabin assured the Israeli public that the PLO would know how to take care of the fundamentalists, and, as he put it in his famously blunt manner, Arafat would not be hampered by the Israeli human-rights lobby and the Supreme Court. Yet independent analysis might have warned Rabin that this would not be the case. As Makovsky writes in one of his strongest judgments concerning the first months of the agreement's implementation, "This appears to be one of the big miscalculations of Oslo."

It is easy to reconstruct how the miscalculation transpired. Across the Middle East, from Algeria to Egypt, Arab nationalist regimes were facing a militant Islamic challenge. Most had not hesitated to unleash the full fire-power of their internal-security forces against armed fundamentalist factions. In the 1980's, moreover, Israel itself had created a South Lebanese Army to fight Hezbollah. Why could not something like this be recreated in the Gaza Strip, and later extended to the West Bank? Since the DOP was to be implemented in stages, Arafat would have built-in incentives for cooperating with Israel against Hamas—good behavior would mean getting the next chunk of territory under his control that much sooner.

But things did not work out as the architects of Oslo expected. Elsewhere in the Arab world, extreme Islamist forces had been challenging political establishments in place since the 1950's. Arafat, by contrast, was only getting started, and was immeasurably weaker than any Arab head of state.

Nor, more significantly, was Arafat's own calculus what the Rabin government imagined it would be. After the signing of the DOP, terrorist attacks were regularly followed by summit meetings at which Rabin would grimace, invoke the displeasure of Washington, and demand better performance by the Palestinian police. For Arafat, though, as unpleasant as these meetings could be, they were clearly preferable to the full-scale Palestinian civil war that a crackdown on the fundamentalists might have sparked.

Nor was even that all. It soon became evident that Rabin did not possess any real power of sanction against Arafat. To suspend the agreement itself—that is, to admit to failure—would be to incur an enormous political price at home that Rabin was clearly not prepared to pay. And even if the agreement *were* suspended, Arafat would not have lost much; the DOP, which he had negotiated in weakness, had gotten him Gaza and Jericho, and if the negotiations over the rest of the interim-status arrangements should be canceled, the possibility still lay open for jumping directly to final-status talks.

That, at least, is how things unfolded. What Makovsky's description makes clear is that any number of people might have told Rabin there was a good chance they would unfold in just that way.

· · · · ·

Other eventualities might have been anticipated as well. Makovsky does not get heavily involved in the economic assumptions behind Oslo—the area where the experts were supposed to enjoy a professional advantage—yet here, too, grave errors were made.

In particular, there was an expectation of a major cash windfall: international aid would rain on the occupied territories, and a new Singapore would arise from the sands of Gaza. As noted above, this scenario had political implications: with Gaza industrialized, thousands of new jobs created, and the standard of living on the rise, fewer young people would be attracted to the ranks of Hamas and Islamic Jihad. Or so at least the logic ran. Economic growth was seen as a good in itself, and also as a precursor of political and military security.

In reality, during the first six months of the Palestinian administration, the standard of living in the Gaza Strip did not rise—it fell by some 25 percent. Continued terrorist action forced Rabin repeatedly to close off Israel to Palestinian workers, and within Gaza itself nowhere near enough new jobs were created. Although some recent local investment by the upper strata of Gazan society has generated more construction activity, it has been of insufficient scale to affect any large number of the Gazan refugees. In the end, terror and security considerations have dictated economic conditions, not the reverse.

· · · · ·

Finally, Oslo would prove from the very beginning to have highly dele-terious effects on the status of Jerusalem.

Ever since 1967, Israeli governments had been prepared to discuss the rights of various religions to the holy places of Jerusalem. But no Israeli government prior to that of Yitzhak Rabin ever expressed an explicit and unqualified readiness to put Jerusalem itself on the table. This is what the DOP did in making the city a subject for negotiations with the opening of final-status talks scheduled (according to the origi-nal timetable) for May 1996.

Rabin's defenders might say there was a precedent for this: Yitzhak Shamir had gone to the Madrid peace conference in 1991 with the under-standing that all sides could bring any subject at all to the table. But how-ever reckless this might have seemed at the time, Shamir had no inten-tion of giving up control of the negotiating agenda, which in diplomacy is the first line of defense in protecting assets a nation does not want to concede. It was this outer line that fell at Oslo. Whether the Israelis real-ized it or not, the Palestinians certainly did, and celebrated the fact. In the words of PLO negotiator Nabil Shaath:

> [T]he Israelis up to this agreement never accepted that the final sta-tus of Jerusalem be on the agenda of the permanent status negoti-ations.... This [the DOP] calls into question the legality and final-ity of their annexation.
>
> Faisal al-Husseini was even more explicit: In the Oslo accords it was established that the status of Jerusalem is open to negotiations on the final arrangement, and the moment that you say yes to nego-tiations, you are ready for a compromise.

Of course, no more than Yitzhak Shamir did Yitzhak Rabin have any intention of giving up an inch of Jerusalem to the PLO. To the con-trary, he looked to the DOP as an instrument that would help protect Israel's position in the city—specifically, by allowing Jericho to evolve into an alternative administrative center for the Palestinians. But the PLO quickly installed two ministers of the Palestinian Authority (PA) inside Jerusalem itself. One of them, Faisal al-Husseini, now minister without portfolio, converted his family's property, known as Orient House, from an Arab-studies society to an administrative center at which major for-eign dignitaries were received. The PA also opened at least five other institutions in Jerusalem. The PA's security chief in Jericho, Jibril Rajoub, regularly sent his men into East Jerusalem to seize Palestinians and bring them to his headquarters for interrogation; by the end of June 1994, as

Rabin himself admitted in response to a parliamentary inquiry, some 200 Palestinian security personnel were operating in East Jerusalem. All these acts violated explicit clauses in the Oslo and Gaza-Jericho agreements, but Rabin did not combat them.

To judge by Makovsky's account, Arafat deserves high marks for successfully manipulating the Israeli Prime Minister over the Jerusalem issue. Essentially he pursued a double track, ordering the Palestinian delegation at the official peace talks in Washington to demand that the PLO be given some jurisdiction in Jerusalem already in the interim phase, while instructing his people in Oslo to take a more moderate position and agree to put off discussion of arrangements in the city until the beginning of final-status talks. Faced with a hard line in Washington, and seemingly greater flexibility in Oslo, Rabin gravitated toward the latter.

Arafat's Jerusalem ploy appears to have been behind Rabin's decision in May 1993 to upgrade the Oslo talks to the official governmental level. Indeed, one might say that an Israeli willingness to put Jerusalem on the table and at least theoretically envisage its future division is what finally made Oslo possible—surely not what Rabin had in mind, but just as surely something that cooler heads might have pointed out to him at the time, had they been consulted.

· · · · ·

In light of what Makovsky tells us, it is hardly any wonder that so many in Israel came to the conclusion by May of this year that Oslo represented a dead end. For the implementation of the DOP manifestly *had* failed to enhance Israeli security; failed to improve Palestinian well-being and hence reduce grievances; and failed to protect Jerusalem from the penetration of the PLO. Nevertheless, despite this general failure, the Rabin government persisted in its course, and made clear its intention of moving forward to the DOP's next stages. Why? The answer comes in several parts.

While the conservative portion of the Israeli political community has all along viewed Oslo as a fundamental if not a catastrophic blunder, some on the Left have stressed that, no matter how flawed it may be at any point in its implementation, it represents the correct strategic path. This has been implicit in Rabin's own rhetoric. After virtually each terrorist attack last year, he voiced his conviction that the only way to solve the Israeli-Palestinian conflict was through a "separation" of the two peoples. To that end, Oslo has been the means.

Many Israelis, indeed, Left, Right, and Center alike, are attracted by the notion that the Palestinians can be put behind some enormous fortification near the pre–June 1967 borders—a kind of Great Wall of China on the Green Line. For those on the Left who adhere to this view, the real barrier to success has been not the inability or the refusal of the PLO to adhere to the provisions of the DOP, but rather the existence in the territories of Israeli settlements built during the years of Likud rule—settlements which Rabin was, at least at first, reluctant to give up. As Makovsky writes, "In private discussions, Israeli negotiators in Oslo admitted that negotiating a quick divorce would have been their preference, but the refusal of Rabin to dismantle settlements at an early stage stood as an impediment." From this it would seem to follow that the way to deal with Oslo's failures is not to discard the agreement but, on the contrary, to *accelerate* the process of "separation."

In fact, however, all this talk of separation is just another way to avoid confronting Oslo's central problem. Separation is based on the principle that good fences make good neighbors. But Israel's history—indeed, the history of every nation in the world—shows that what is true is precisely the reverse: good neighbors make good fences. Where, as with Jordan, Israel enjoys such relatively good neighbors, fences supply security. Where it has bad neighbors, as in Lebanon, fences are wholly inadequate, and successive Israeli governments have had to introduce "security zones" to protect the country's border.

The architects of Oslo thought they could simply ignore the fact that every single one of the cruxes of the Israeli-Palestinian conflict—Jerusalem, borders, the fate of Palestinian refugees—remained unresolved. Instead, they proceeded to treat Arafat as though he were already the head of a neighboring state with which Israel happened to have a few, wholly containable, differences. As a thought experiment, this may have had something to recommend it; in reality, it foundered drastically on its own radically mistaken premise.

· · · · ·

Where, then, is the peace process going? Few would advocate that a future Israeli government should return to the Gaza Strip. But the current focus is on the West Bank, which, unlike Gaza, is right next to Israel's major population centers, as well as to 80 percent of the country's industrial capacity; whatever happens there bears on Israel's security, and indeed on its day-to-day existence, in the most direct way imaginable, and the perils are obviously enormous.

For one thing, as Yaakov Amidror, head of analysis for military intelligence, has acutely pointed out, the withdrawal of the IDF from West Bank cities, called for in the next phase of the agreement, may well *reduce* the PA's incentive to quell anti-Israel violence; terrorist organizations will no longer have to worry about local countermeasures by the Israeli military. But that is by no means all.

When the DOP was reached, it appeared that Israel had definitively abandoned its historic (under-the-table) alliance with Jordan, and from now on would give pride of place to its new relationship with the PLO. King Hussein himself stepped in to correct this distortion by completing his own agreement with Israel during 1994. Now, however, Israel appears about to place in power in the West Bank a political movement—the PLO—openly hostile to the Hashemite throne in Amman, thereby undermining both Israel's own interest and that of the United States in maintaining a moderate buffer state between the radicalism of the Fertile Crescent and Saudi Arabia's northwestern frontier.

One might have imagined an alternative course of action, and correspondingly different outcomes. Even today, when it is very difficult to envision a full-scale Jordanian role in the West Bank, one can still speculate whether many West Bank Palestinians might not prefer a tie with a strong, stable Jordan to one with Arafat's weak and chaotic Gaza. They might, indeed, have preferred such an arrangement even before the DOP, though it would have been impossible for them to say so. In light of what has occurred since Oslo, and what unfortunately appears likely to unfold in the next stage of implementation, is it inconceivable that West Bank Palestinians might yet begin to see their self-interest in more pragmatic and less ideologically charged terms?

For that to happen, however, and for all the interested parties in the region to be in a position to seek better alternatives than today's, the DOP would have to be permitted to lapse. But the chances of *that* happening, so long as the architects of Oslo are directing Israel's peace policy, remain slim indeed.

In the short run, therefore, one must look to other avenues. One thing that would have at least a somewhat salutary effect on the flawed Oslo agreements is a reordering of their priorities, giving primacy to the security needs of Israel in the next, crucial phase of implementation. Here, as David Makovsky's doleful chronicle reminds us, lies the heart of the Oslo "miscalculation." But it very much remains to be seen whether such a reordering will be put into place in the months ahead.

—August 1995

Hillel Halkin

The Rabin Assassination:
A Reckoning

As a voter for the Labor party and Yitzhak Rabin in the 1992 elections and a politically angry man for the past two years, I found myself growing angrier and angrier the week after his assassination on November 4, 1995. The angrier I grew, the more I argued with everyone around me, and the more I argued, the angrier it made me. Not, like everyone else, at the assassin and those said to have incited him, but at the Labor party, and at the Israeli Left, and even at the murdered man himself, who was certainly not responsible for the thick sludge of sentimentality, so far from his own personal style (though not from that of his speechwriters), in which he was being quickly shrouded. I must have seemed a very unpleasant person. I may seem one to you now.

A large part of the sentimentalization in the days after the Rabin assassination lay in the event's being treated as, above all, a violation of the Sixth Commandment. "How could such a murderer have come from our midst?" and "What Jew would kill a Jew over land?" were the two questions most often asked in Israel, while, when Ted Koppel brought his *Nightline* to Jerusalem the week after the assassination, he billed the special broadcast as "Thou Shalt Not Kill."

This is sentimental because, though murder is a frightful crime, large numbers of men and women whose right to live is as great as that of the Prime Minister of Israel are the barely noticed victims of murder every day. In Israel alone, the police blotters show that dozens of Jews are killed annually by Jews without *Nightline*'s paying attention. And what, if not land, has been the single greatest motive for killing in human

45

history? What, if not the struggle for land, has caused tens of thousands of Jews and Arabs to be killed in the Middle East?

Was it not a struggle for land that made Yitzhak Rabin join the Palmah, the elite fighting force of Jewish Palestine, as a young man, and thus begin the military career that led to his becoming Prime Minister of Israel? Was it not for the control of land that, as Prime Minister, he continued a military presence in Lebanon which in 1995 alone resulted in the deaths of over twenty Israeli soldiers? If land is never a legitimate reason for killing, every soldier who fights for the defense of his country is a murderer.

What made Yitzhak Rabin's assassination exceptionally atrocious was not its being a murder but its being a cataclysmic political blunder.

It was so, firstly, because—as Likud leader Benjamin Netanyahu put it—democratically chosen governments are changed by elections, not by assassinations. Break that rule once and democracy is imperiled—and an undemocratic Israel cannot prosper, no matter how much or how little land it commands.

And it was so, secondly, because what it most damaged was the public standing of the critics of the Oslo peace process, to whose extreme wing the assassin Yigal Amir belonged. Had Amir wished to deliver a crushing blow to these critics, he could not have found a better way. That is why a friend of mine in America, a far more unequivocal opponent of the peace process than I, faxed me the week of the killing: "I would gladly see the bastard hang who prevented the people of Israel from voting against Rabin."

· · · · ·

Equally sentimental was the instant mythologization of Yitzhak Rabin as a knight of peace in shining armor.

The day after the assassination I talked with a different friend, an Israeli Arab. "I'm sorry it happened," he said, "but you can't expect me to feel sad for Rabin."

"Why not?" I asked.

"Because," he said, "in the late 1980s I happened to be in Tulkarm [a city on the West Bank] one day at the beginning of the *intifada*, when Rabin, who was then Minister of Defense, gave his famous order to the army to 'break the arms and legs' of Palestinians. And what I saw in Tulkarm were broken arms and legs. Children's too. That order was not meant metaphorically."

Indeed it was not, as many Israelis who carried it out can testify.

It has been said that Yitzhak Rabin had a change of heart and came out of the *intifada* a different man, convinced of the need for a reconciliation with the Palestinians. That may be. But in the summer of 1993, after his conversion supposedly took place and Israeli and PLO negotiators were meeting secretly in Oslo, Rabin, now Prime Minister, launched Operation Accountability, a massive retaliatory artillery bombardment that caused great civilian destruction in dozens of Lebanese villages accused of harboring Hezbollah guerrillas. He was then what he had always been and remained until his death, several days before which he almost certainly ordered the murder of Islamic Jihad leader Fat'hi Shiqaqi in Malta—namely, a highly pragmatic soldier and politician who had no special liking for violence but no compunctions about using it when it served tactical or strategic ends.

．．．．．

I voted for Yitzhak Rabin in 1992 because, like many Israelis, I felt that the situation in the West Bank and Gaza had reached an intolerable point and that the Likud government was incapable of changing it. In terms of change, I was prepared to go farther than most Rabin voters. In an article published in *Commentary* over twenty years ago ("Driving Toward Jerusalem," January 1975), I had advocated, subject to certain conditions, the establishment of a Palestinian state along Israel's 1967 borders, and in 1992 I still held to this opinion. I still hold to it today.

Why, then, did I react with such anger to the Israeli-PLO agreement when it was announced in September 1993? Because it was obvious to me immediately that the Labor party had lied to the Israeli public; that it was either continuing to lie to it, or lying to itself, or both; and that all these lies were highly dangerous.

In its official 1992 campaign platform, Labor had declared:

> Israel will continue and complete negotiations with authorized and agreed-on Palestinians *from the territories occupied by Israel since 1967* [emphasis added].... There is a need for an agreement in a Jordanian-Palestinian framework ... and not a separate Palestinian state west of the Jordan.... Jerusalem will remain united and undivided under Israeli sovereignty.... The Jordan Valley and the western shore of the Dead Sea will be under Israeli sovereignty.... In any peace agreement with Syria, Israel's presence and control, both military and in terms of settlements, will continue [on the Golan Heights].

Let us set aside the question of the Golan Heights, even though Yitzhak Rabin's violation of his campaign promises in the course of his negotiations with President Hafez Assad was only partially compensated for by his announced commitment to holding a national referendum before signing a peace treaty with Syria. Let us speak instead of Oslo and the Palestinians.

The Labor party lied to the Israeli public because its 1992 platform clearly ruled out negotiations, let alone a comprehensive political settlement, between Israel and the PLO, which in 1992 was based not in the territories but in Tunis and which had been considered by all previous Israeli governments a terrorist organization not to be treated with. And since the PLO had stated repeatedly before Oslo, and continued to state after it, that its immediate goal was the creation of an independent Palestinian state in Gaza and the entire West Bank with East Jerusalem as its capital, there were only two explanations of Israeli thinking at Oslo. One was that Yitzhak Rabin and his government had secretly decided to acquiesce in the establishment of such a state, thereby reneging on the rest of their campaign pledges regarding the future of the occupied territories. The other was that they believed the peace process could be brought to a successful conclusion without yielding to the PLO's main territorial and political demands.

Let us first consider the second of these possibilities. In its final-stage negotiations with the Palestinians, supposedly set to begin later this year, can Israel simply declare: "Gentlemen, you are not getting a state and you are not getting Jerusalem and other areas, and you can either take or leave what we are giving you"?

In theory, of course, it can. In practice, the Palestinians, under the terms of the Oslo agreement, will by then have nearly 30,000 armed policemen in the West Bank and Gaza, close to the number of combat soldiers in Israel's standing army. Will Israel be prepared to risk engaging this force in armed conflict if a political impasse is reached?

This question, when put to supporters of the peace process, is met by a snort. It is absurd to think, one is told, that 30,000 policemen with rifles could offer serious resistance to a well-trained army with tanks and aircraft.

It is the snorters, however, who are being disingenuous if they imagine three divisions of Palestinian policemen will march on Jerusalem while the Israeli air force pounds them from above. These policemen can be divided into thousands of small cells of guerrilla fighters comprising five or ten members each. At the peak of the *intifada* there were probably never more than ten or twenty armed units of this size operating at any given moment in the occupied territories. Dozens of Israelis were killed by them. It took months to hunt down some of these bands; tanks and aircraft had little to do with the matter.

Would Yitzhak Rabin—who, we are told, was psychologically shaken to the core by the *intifada*—have been ready to expose Israel to a prolonged period of armed violence, possibly hundreds of times greater than that of the *intifada*, in order to keep his campaign promises regarding Jerusalem and the Jordan Valley, when he had already violated other key pledges in the same paragraph? Will his successor, Shimon Peres, be ready to do so if it should prove necessary?

· · · · ·

But, we are told, it will not prove necessary—because already at Oslo the Rabin government knew it was agreeing to the establishment of a Palestinian state in Gaza and the entire West Bank ruled from Jerusalem, and all its protestations to the contrary, at the time and subsequently, were not to be taken seriously.

"Honestly," said an Israeli to me during the week after the assassination, "you are being hopelessly naive. You yourself say that, 'subject to certain conditions,' you believe a Palestinian state is the solution. Do you really think that Labor could have been elected in 1992 had it openly said as much to a public that had been brainwashed against such an idea for years? And with whom could one negotiate such a solution *except* the PLO, an organization that Israeli voters feared and abhorred? No serious person expects politicians always to tell the truth. It is a leader's duty to get elected and lead, not to get permission for every step he takes."

Despite my own reputation among my friends as a cynic, such a view, which is almost universally held today on the Israeli Left, strikes me as cynical beyond bounds. Of course politicians frequently lie to the public, although those who lie least and with the uneasiest conscience are the ones who look best in the history books. But it is one thing to lie about ordinary matters of political expediency, another to lie about a momentous decision that will profoundly affect the future of one's country for as long as it continues to exist. If the question of Israel's borders, of their location and defensibility, of who lives and rules on either side of them, and of their relationship to the claims of thousands of years of Jewish history is not something about which to consult the Israeli public within the framework of democratic politics, what is democracy for?

Nor is it the case that Labor had to fool the voters in order to carry out its present policies. There were other alternatives. Having won the elections on the platform it ran on, Labor could have begun to prepare public opinion for the new direction it wished to take. It could have asked the PLO to help change the climate in Israel by declaring a moratorium on terror, or by repealing the provisions of the Palestinian Charter which call for Israel's destruction, or some other dramatic act. It could have begun tentative, noncommittal talks with the PLO and then revealed their content to the public. And having done any or all of these things, it could then have said:

> Citizens of Israel: now that you have seen how the PLO has changed and is ready to recognize the state of Israel and live peacefully alongside it, we are calling new elections in order to ask you for a mandate to commence negotiations with it that may lead to a Palestinian state.

Would that mandate have been given? It is impossible to say. But whether or not, the people would have spoken. And perhaps if the people had been allowed to speak, Yitzhak Rabin would be alive today.

· · · · ·

Or perhaps not? His murderer was a true believer in the Land of Israel, not in democratic procedures. Still, as has been frequently pointed out in the wake of the assassination, true believers tend to reach for their guns when they feel the rage of a wider public behind them—and the rage of many Israelis against Yitzhak Rabin dated to the day when, without asking or warning them, he signed an agreement with Yasir Arafat, a man regarded by them with revulsion, and shook hands with him on the White House lawn. Although those who in the next two years accused Rabin of betraying his country were speaking overheatedly, he did betray many of the voters whose ballots helped elect him Prime Minister by a narrow margin.

Rabin's turnabout has been compared by his defenders to that of Likud's Menachem Begin, who was elected in 1977 on a platform that never hinted he would return all of Sinai to Egypt. But there is a huge difference. When Begin submitted the accord with Egypt to the Knesset, it won overwhelming bipartisan approval, with an even higher percentage of Labor members than Likud members voting for it; had he called for new elections, he would have won them handily. By contrast, the Rabin-Arafat rapprochement split Israel in half, both in the Knesset and in the opinion polls. The Knesset's bitterly debated ratification of Stage 2 of the Oslo agreement, a month before the assassination, passed by a vote of 61 to 59. Minus the five votes of two anti-Zionist Arab parties that object to the definition of Israel as a Jewish state, the results were 59 to 56 against.

Granted, a parliamentary majority of two is as binding as one of 200. The question in Israel was never the Rabin government's formal legitimacy, it was its political and moral wisdom in pursuing a course that turned Israel ferociously against itself on a matter of the utmost historical gravity. But as Rabin followed this course, and was applauded by the same Left that in 1982 had denounced Begin's invasion of Lebanon for violating the principle that no Israeli government should go to war without a national consensus, he and his supporters scoffed at the proposition that a radically conceived peace demanded a measure of national unity, too.

Moreover, it was clear to many thinking Israelis that, even if the Rabin government had received the nation's backing to sign the accord reached at Oslo; and even if this accord led in a few years' time to a "final" peace settlement with the Palestinians, there was no certainty that its finality would be final. A Palestinian state, even one based on a complete Israeli withdrawal to the 1967 lines, would comprise only 23 percent of the area of British Mandate Palestine. It is no secret that many and probably most Palestinians, including the leaders of the PLO, hoped such a state would be the first stage in reclaiming more Palestinian land, possibly up to the 1947 partition borders and beyond.

Indeed, while it seemed obviously in Israel's interest that any Palestinian state be an economic and political success, the more successful this state was, the more Israel's own Arab citizens, of whom there are at present nearly a million largely concentrated in the Galilee, would be encouraged to want to join it. Given the current mood of disaffection toward Israeli society felt by most Israeli Arabs, whose sense of Palestinian identity has been greatly strengthened by the installation of the PLO next-door to them, a movement for *Anschluss* with the state of Palestine would be likely to develop among them in the future, plunging Israel back into a period of bitter internal Arab-Jewish strife that would probably draw into it not only an irredentist Palestine but still other Arab countries. The better the peace process went in the short run, therefore, the riskier it might turn out in the end.

Thus it was that, from the autumn of 1993 to the autumn of 1995, as the Oslo agreement was implemented and thousands of armed

Palestinian policemen arrived in Gaza and Jericho and began moving into the West Bank; and as some 150 Israelis died in Palestinian terror attacks which the PLO, while procrastinating about the Palestinian Charter, was not particularly vigilant in preventing; and as the Rabin government continued to keep secret from its own people what its aims were in the peace process, including the borders it planned to insist on and its conception of the fate of the tens of thousands of Jewish settlers living beyond them, much of Israel felt like passengers on a ship that had been hijacked by its own captain and crew, who were now piloting it through a dense fog and mined waters, with the consent of half of those aboard, toward an unrevealed and perhaps calamitous destination.

The emotions aroused by this were fear, helplessness, bitterness, frustration, and, as I have said, rage. All of them were channeled into the anti-government invective that mounted in volume and vituperation throughout this period and that was, so the Israeli Left now tells us, the finger that pressed the trigger that was Yigal Amir.

· · · · ·

I would not dispute this. Although Amir was apparently unaided on the night of the shooting, he was what is known in Hebrew as a *sh'liah avera*, a messenger of sin, for a large body of Israelis who would not have dreamed of doing what he did. This public, heavily represented in what is known as the "national-religious camp" and in the settlements of Judea and Samaria that are the most threatened by the Oslo pact, owes itself and the nation a reckoning for having allowed elements in its midst to be swept away by inflammatory rhetoric and bizarre rabbinical rulings that could have encouraged a Yigal Amir to think he was acting on its behalf

Such a reckoning, at least part of the Israeli Right is now making. The reckoning that is not being made, and of the need for which there seems to be no awareness among those who should make it, concerns the rhetoric and deeds of the Left, hardly any less inflammatory during the period in question.

Before me is the pro-government newspaper *Ha'aretz*, Israel's most respected daily, from March 26, 1995. Its front-page headline: "Rabin: Likud Is Collaborator With Hamas." The text of the lead article reports that "Prime Minister Yitzhak Rabin sharply attacked Likud yesterday [saying], 'The terror organizations are succeeding because Likud has become a collaborator with Islamic Jihad and Hamas.'" It goes on:

In inner consultations recently held at high levels of the Labor party, it was decided to step up attacks against the Right, especially against Likud and its leader. There is concern in Labor over polls, taken in the last several months, showing [Benjamin] Netanyahu with a large lead over Rabin.... Ranking members of Labor welcomed this changed line. One cabinet minister said he was happy that "The Prime Minister has decided to take off the gloves with Likud." A second minister, on the other hand, expressed concern that extreme language might cause the political arena to degenerate into verbal violence a year before the elections....

It would be interesting to know who the prescient second minister was. And it would be interesting to ask the first minister whether, if a left-wing assassin had killed Benjamin Netanyahu, he would now be saying that Yitzhak Rabin had "blood on his hands," as Labor has been saying of Netanyahu.

As it happens, Netanyahu and Likud have been specifically charged by the Left not so much with direct incitement as with failing to disown incendiary language and symbolism coming from extra-parliamentary right-wing groups—the prime example, repeatedly cited since the assassination, being the blind eye turned by them to a poster of Rabin in an SS uniform displayed by demonstrators at a Likud rally in October. This poster, it now appears, was commissioned and disseminated by Avishai Raviv, a right-wing extremist who was, however, acting as an agent for the Israeli General Security Service: i.e., the Rabin government itself

This does not exonerate the failure of the Right to react more strongly—but it is worth recalling that throughout the 1980s, long before it was employed by the right wing as a term of abuse, the word "Nazi" was often used by the far Left to describe the settlers and the Likud government that backed them. Perhaps the most egregious case was that of the late Yeshayahu Leibowitz, a well-known theologian and political polemicist, who invented the term "Judeo-Nazi" and who in 1993 was awarded the prestigious Israel Prize for intellectual achievement by Yitzhak Rabin's Minister of Culture, Shulamit Aloni. There was nothing wrong in calling Jews Nazis, it would seem, as long they were the right Jews.

Indeed, there was nothing wrong with calling the settlers many other names, too, which were routinely hurled at them by the Left in a systematic attempt to delegitimize them after they began organizing against the Oslo agreement: "enemies of peace," "religious fanatics," "dancers on the blood [of terror victims]," "Arab-haters," and

"Hamasniks" were some of the more common epithets. It made no difference that these same settlers, who for years had braved the daily dangers of the *intifada*, had been, in the name of the national security of Israel, assisted and encouraged to take up residence in their homes by previous Israeli governments, including the earlier 1974–77 regime of Yitzhak Rabin. Asked about one of their demonstrations, the same Rabin now declared that, for his part, "They can spin around like propellers for as long as they like."

Another example of right-wing incitement said to have provoked the assassination were the placards and shouts of "Rabin Is a Murderer" at many anti-government demonstrations, especially after Palestinian terror attacks. These were reprehensible—but the copyright on them, too, belonged to the Left. Such slogans first surfaced in Israel in 1982, at the huge Labor-party and Peace Now rally held in Tel Aviv's Kings of Israel Square (now Yitzhak Rabin Square) to protest the massacre of Palestinians by Lebanese Christians in the Sabra and Shatila refugee camps. There, signs proclaiming "Begin Is a Murderer" and "Sharon Is a Murderer" were held high by many demonstrators. I can vouch that no one asked for their removal because I was there holding a sign myself (although differently worded, as I recall).

But, protests the Left, there is no comparison: although we too may have sinned with words, nearly all the threats and incidents of political violence that Israel has witnessed in recent years have come from the Right. This is true. Right-wing extremism in Israel *has* been more violent; one reason for this is that, ideologically, the far Right tends to view conflict, rather than the resolution of it, as an inescapable existential imperative of Israeli Jews. And yet the Machiavellian use, by a secret service controlled by the Rabin government, of *agents provocateurs* like Raviv to foment and aggravate such violence as a means of discrediting the opposition to the peace process is no less frightening than the violence itself. Political thuggery is a grave threat to a democracy; employing a secret service to manipulate a country's political life in favor of its ruling party, let alone by paying hoodlums to threaten and assault people and destroy property, is far graver, reminiscent of some of the most unsavory regimes of our century.

In the end, perhaps, it is pointless to try to keep score in such a game of tit-before-tat. Indeed, although both the Right and the Left contributed generously to the acrimonious atmosphere that was created in the period after Oslo, it is on the whole remarkable, given the passions aroused by one of the most agonizingly fateful moments the Jewish people has ever lived through, that democratic forms have been so well observed in Israel up to the assassination. (Since the assassination there have been signs that the Labor government has embarked on a worrisome policy of using rarely invoked anti-"incitement-to-rebellion" laws in order to intimidate forms of protest and criticism that would be permitted, or at least considered less severe legal offenses, in most democratic countries.) In terms of the tone of the political debate, Dreyfusards and anti-Dreyfusards in France, pro- and anti-Vietnam-war demonstrators in the United States, were no more polite when arguing about much less. They, after all, were fighting only for the soul of their country; here the struggle is over the limbs of the body as well.

· · · · ·

One can point to the exact historical moment when the center dropped out of Israeli politics, leaving an overwhelmingly secular Left and a heavily religious Right facing each other across a discourseless chasm. But although this happened politically in September 1993 with the signing of the Oslo agreement, culturally it was a long while in the making.

In a deep sense, the processes leading up to this moment reflect the failure of the grand cultural project of Zionism, whose root assumption, once shared by secular and religious Zionists alike, was that it was possible to build a society that would combine a commitment to the modern world and its highest ideals with an allegiance, if not to the ritual forms, at least to the great texts and memories of Jewish tradition and their resonance in the physical landscape of Israel.

For most of this century, as reflected in literature, arts, popular culture, and politics, this project had every appearance of success. As late as the 1960s, the same Bible which, shortly before his death, Yitzhak Rabin referred to as "an antiquated land·registry" was still a living book in secular Israel. Here is Moshe Dayan, a product of the Labor movement and only seven years older than Rabin, speaking a month after the Six-Day war of 1967 placed in Jewish hands the portion of central Palestine that had been lost to Jordan in the unavoidable partition of 1948:

> We have returned to the mountainland, to the cradle of our people and the legacy of our fathers, to the land of the judges and to the bastion of the kingdom of the House of David. We have returned to Hebron, to Shechem [Nablus], to Bethlehem, to Anatot, to Jericho, and to the fords of the Jordan.

Today, when such language in the mouth of a Labor-party politician would sound hopelessly archaic, it is possible to see that Dayan's generation derived its own romantic attachment to the Bible and Jewish history less (as Zionist myth had it) from the vaunted contact of the native-born *sabra* with the soil of the land of Israel than from its East-European-born parents, themselves the products of religious homes; and that the apparent link binding Hebrew secularism to Jewish tradition was perhaps less a viable carrying forward of tradition than tradition's last gasp. What has happened with the final expiration of that gasp is well illustrated by the case of Moshe Dayan's daughter Ya'el, a left-wing Labor politician whose only known public reference to the Bible, made in defense of gay rights, has been to assert that David and Jonathan were homosexual lovers, and who has declared that she will be happy to visit Hebron on a Palestinian visa.

It was the Palestinians in the occupied territories, certainly, who hastened a polarization in Israeli life that would have taken place far more slowly and less painfully without them. For as the Israeli occupation of the territories lengthened, and the Jewish settlement movement grew, and with it the increasingly organized and violent resistance of the local Palestinian population, culminating in the *intifada*, the choice became a seemingly stark one. Either Israel relinquished its title to Judea and Samaria, the geographical core of the historical Jewish homeland, and so, by freeing the people living there from its yoke, took its stand (said the Left) with enlightened humanity; or else it pressed its claim to the areas and kept faith (said the Right) with Jewish memory.

This was a cruel dilemma. And it represented a great irony, for it meant that the Jewish state, which according to Zionism had come to heal the inner split between the human being in the Jew and the Jew in the human being, had now driven a new and terrible wedge into the breach.

Like a man in great torment who breaks psychologically in two, Israel thus went, or was dragged, to Oslo as two nations, each willing to risk what the other was not and unwilling to risk what the other was; neither able to communicate with or to understand the other but only to blame the other rancorously; thesis and antithesis, each half of the now-fractured personality of the Jewish people in its homeland.

I am not a believer in the view that tormented nations need psychiatrists rather than politicians. Only a wise politics can help to join again what a foolish politics has helped to sunder. But can one, in today's circumstances, imagine a politics wise enough?

—January 1996

Nadav Haetzni

In Arafat's Kingdom

On Sunday, July 28 of this year, a young man, diagnosed as brain-dead, was hospitalized in Nablus, a city on the West Bank under the rule of Yasir Arafat's Palestinian Authority (PA). According to the Palestinian security agents who brought him in, his name was Ahmad Sabah, and he was from Jenin, another West Bank town. For some reason, no one—no family members, no friends—came to look in on him.

To the medical staff of the hospital it was clear the mortally ill young man had undergone unspeakable suffering. His skull had been crushed by repeated blows, and every inch of his body was covered with reddish or bluish bruises. The severe burns on his chest and back told of torture by means of red-hot iron bars. Although the hospital made an attempt to find out what had happened, it was unable even to trace the man's identity.

Early the next day, a directive arrived from the security forces: the patient was to be transferred to a hospital in Ramallah, another town under the PA's jurisdiction about fifteen minutes by car from Israel's capital city of Jerusalem. There he was carried into the intensive-care unit, entrance to which was barred by four men armed with Kalashnikov assault rifles. Not even Bassam Eid, a well-known Palestinian human-rights activist who had been identified as a relative of the young man, was allowed in. Only that evening did a Nablus resident who was visiting a different patient in the hospital blunder by accident into the intensive-care unit, notice the clinically dead man, and recognize his features. Soon the story was out.

The pseudonymous youngster from Jenin turned out to be Mahmoud Jumayel, a leader of Fatah, Yasir Arafat's own movement, in Nablus. By the time his death was officially confirmed two days later, Palestinian riots had broken out in the West Bank. For the first time in history, however, these riots were aimed not at the Israeli but at the Palestinian "occupier"—Yasir Arafat himself.

Indeed, the final months of Mahmoud Jumayel's life throw into sharp relief the contours of a new Palestinian tragedy, just as they expose a deep sickness at the heart of the fledgling administration of the PLO chairman. At the signing of the Oslo peace accords in September 1993, the highest hopes were expressed by all parties for the new era that was about to dawn in the Middle East. Not only would peaceful relations at last obtain between Israel and its oldest antagonist, the Palestinian Arabs, but those Arabs themselves, liberated from the foreign occupier's yoke, would quickly reap the benefits of self-rule and democratic rights, and be enabled at last to develop the free civic institutions guaranteed them by the charter of the PLO. Less than two and a half years later, whatever the state of relations between the PA and Israel, it is all too clear that Arafat and his henchmen have brought to the lives of their fellow Palestinians a level of brutality and corruption reminiscent of some of the Arab world's most benighted regimes.

· · · · ·

Mahmoud Jumayel was not exactly an angel. As a leader of the Fatah youth movement he had taken an active role in the *intifada,* the violent uprising against Israel that began in the late 1980s. Later, during the twilight days of Israeli rule in Nablus, he prominently supported one of the most despotic local gangs (Tabuk) in its rivalry with Jibril Rajoub, head of one of the PA's notorious security agencies. So long as Israeli forces remained in Nablus, Rajoub could not prevail over his rivals; but with the accession of the PA in December 1995, Rajoub arrested Jumayel and one of his associates.

The two men were detained in a jail in Jericho. They were not interrogated, and no charges were filed. Though their distraught families knocked desperately on every door, and sent endless petitions to their esteemed leader in Gaza, no response was forthcoming; no one in a position of authority even consented to see them, and senior members of Fatah who inquired into the matter were told to mind their own business. And so Jumayel sat in prison for seven months. What happened to change things on July 27 is still not known—the PA has refused all requests for information—but upon his transfer from Jericho to Nablus,

Jumayel was handed over for some reason to investigators from the Palestinian naval command, who proceeded to string him up, crack his skull with blunt instruments, flog him with chains, and sear his flesh.

But as we have seen, the story did not end there. Apprised of what their stooges had done, PA officials compounded brutality with subterfuge, first hospitalizing their captive under a false name and then transferring him from hospital to hospital. When, finally, the truth came out, and public anger mounted, Arafat resorted—characteristically—to damage control: he announced the formation of a committee to investigate the cause of death. Whether such a committee was in fact ever formed is uncertain; if so, it investigated nothing. But, evidently alarmed by the intensity of the public protest, Arafat then undertook another characteristic initiative, convening a "state security court" in Jericho. This factitious body, composed of three military officers, conducted a hasty show trial of the officers who had tortured Mahmoud Jumayel to death. The men promptly confessed, and in the space of four hours, without benefit of substantive legal defense, they were convicted of all charges and handed lengthy prison sentences.

Scapegoats had been found, and more searching and decisive inquiries successfully avoided: who gave the order to interrogate and torture Jumayel; by whose authority had he been detained without trial for seven months, and why; who was responsible for the attempt to cover up the affair? Reporting on Jumayel's funeral, Palestinian newspapers highlighted the words of a eulogy said to have been delivered by his father over the open grave, unreservedly praising his illustrious leader Abu Amar (Arafat's *nom de guerre*). But Palestinian papers publish what the PA dictates; the fact is that shortly before the funeral procession began, Mahmoud's grieving father had spoken to reporters with exceptional harshness about Arafat. Either he was compelled under threat to deliver a prepared text at the graveside or the papers simply printed a eulogy that was never spoken.

· · · · ·

Thus the saga of Mahmoud Jumayel, as of mid-August the eighth detainee known to have been murdered by torture in a Palestinian jail. *Thousands* like him are being held behind bars without trial; thousands have been tortured; hundreds have been murdered for political reasons.

Who is behind these deeds? At the time of the Oslo agreement, the PLO command resided in Tunis, where it had ended up after long years of wandering from one Arab state to another. Arafat's troops, in particular those designated the Palestine Liberation Army (PLA), were scattered all over the Arab world—one unit in Iraq, a second in Jordan, a third in Egypt, and so forth. Enlisted men and officers, some veterans, others fresh recruits, did not exactly constitute a fighting force. Many of them had settled into the countries in which they were billeted, had taken jobs, and were merely collecting a salary from the PLO. They adhered to the norms of their adopted societies and had even begun to speak with an Iraqi or Egyptian accent.

Senior officers did not even know who their counterparts were elsewhere, or, for that matter, who was who in the PLO command structure. Inside the PLA, exaggerated attention was paid to matters of rank and hierarchy. There were stubborn rumors of corruption among officers, of mistreatment of subordinates, of cowardice in battle. Needless to say, this did not prevent anyone's advancement in the ranks; that depended on one criterion alone, namely, loyalty to the chairman.

The PLO's political officers were likewise scattered and likewise enmeshed in their local scenes, whether in Tunis, Amman, or Cairo. Educated at the feet of Arab despots, they maintained among themselves no orderly system of relationships; all lines led in one direction only, to Arafat. From grand strategy to trifles, everything began and ended with him.

Upon their entry into "liberated Palestine"—i.e., Gaza and Jericho—in May 1994, both the political officers and the PLA troops met up with and joined the top echelon of indigenous Fatah activists. There were two main criteria for appointing the latter to senior positions in the new military structures of the PA: personal closeness to the chairman, and length of stay in an Israeli prison. From the point of view of building a professional cadre, this was bad enough; much worse was what Arafat proceeded to do.

Far from attempting to transform the diverse units and their officers into a unified security force with a single hierarchy, the PLO chairman took the existing chaos and made it worse. As is well known, Arafat is congenitally suspicious of order and system, not to mention power consolidated in the hands of a hierarchy or any other center that might threaten his preeminence. In line with this, he established something like eight different security agencies with parallel and competing mandates. Though they bear impressive and comprehensive-sounding titles, they act as freewheeling militias or as gangs, each with its own detention centers and none accountable to anyone or anything, whether law court or legislative council. In effect, every ranking officer, and certainly every captain of a militia, is a king unto himself. In Gaza, even the fire-fighters maintain their own detention center, and freely arrest and imprison.

To this Turkish bazaar has been added the explosive issue of cultural difference. The population of the West Bank and Gaza spent 27 years under Israeli occupation—a lesson, among other things, in democracy. In those years it learned that even a man under "oppression" has rights. There is a law; there are avenues of public protest; and if all else fails there is a supreme court of justice. The encounter between the local graduates of Israeli-style democracy—even the Fatah members among them—and the new band of outsiders, violent, unrestrained, contaminated by Eastern ways, inevitably led to a collision.

· · · · ·

The problem could be contained as long as Arafat's forces were in control only in Gaza and Jericho. But by the end of 1995, when the second stage of the Oslo agreement was put into effect, men wearing the Palestinian uniform swarmed into the cities of Judea and Samaria—Ramallah, Nablus, Jenin, Bethlehem, and the rest—and the pot began to boil over. So far, the outsiders are prevailing.

In mid-July of this year, for example, one Nasser Masalmah arrived at his parent's house in the village of Bait Avva. One of many thousands of Palestinians who had cooperated with Israeli security forces in the years of Israel's administration of the territories, he had been given an Israeli identity card upon the accession of the PA and had moved into Israel proper. Now, coming home for a visit, he was picked up and brought in for questioning at a nearby Palestinian police station. (The interrogation was itself in violation of the Oslo accords, which forbid the arrest by Palestinians of anyone carrying an Israeli identity card; but such details have never troubled the PA.) At around 10:30 at night, Masalmah was released and made his way to his parents' house. An hour later, unknown persons burst in, raked the house with automatic weapons, and fled. One family member was wounded. Masalmah and his brother-in-law were killed on the spot.

No one took responsibility for the attack, but the trail pointed to Masalmah's interrogators from the Palestinian security organs: whoever released him no doubt also had sent the killers to deal with this man who had enjoyed good relations with Israel. And Masalmah is only one of hundreds of residents in the former territories who have been murdered on political grounds in the last two years. The victims are usually people considered to be "external" enemies, though not infrequently the passion for liquidation extends to members of rival security agencies.

Aside from such acts of deliberate violence, the last two and a half years have also claimed innumerable victims of official stupidity, light-mindedness, or a quick trigger finger. In April, Taysir A-Lozy, a twenty-three-year-old from Ramallah was returning from an outing with friends, and for some unknown reason their car was deemed "suspicious" by a Palestinian militiaman, who thereupon shot him in the head. As in the Jumayel case, the authorities next proceeded to cover their traces. Palestinian police attempted to kidnap the body from the local hospital in order to falsify the evidence, and then conjured up spurious charges against the young man and his companions, accusing them of drug-dealing, gun-running, and the like. The truth is that the militiaman responsible for the murder was simply acting in accordance with accepted norms—shoot first, ask questions later. No one investigates such incidents, and no one brings the perpetrators to justice.

· · · · ·

Which brings us in general to the subject of Palestinian justice.

In January 1995, a resident of Jericho by the name of Salman Jalayta, along with a number of his friends, was arrested and interrogated by men under Jibril Rajoub's command. After days of torture, Jalayta breathed his last; his body bore marks of treatment similar to that which would later be meted out to Mahmoud Jumayel (with minor embellishments—Jalayta's skin had been shredded by pincers). The other youngsters with him suffered similar treatment, though not to the point of death.

Jalayta and his comrades were publicly accused of having murdered a Jericho resident, a junior Hamas man, in a quarrel. (In what is by now a virtual convention, they were said to have collaborated with Israel.) They were also accused of larceny, lawlessness, and hooliganism. The charges were almost certainly false, but to this day none of them has been properly investigated, and Jalayta's associates are still behind bars; they have not seen a magistrate, or a written indictment. Only after relentless pressure from their families and human-rights activists did it emerge that in April of this year—that is, fifteen months after their imprisonment—the young men, unrepresented by counsel, had been tried by a military tribunal and convicted on the basis of a confession.

In early August, two Palestinian human-rights workers finally succeeded in getting hold of the young men's file. According to one of them, it was a fabrication through and through: all the documents it contained, including witnesses' depositions and the bill of indictment, were written in the same hand and bore the same date. Neither the indictment nor the "confessions" of the accused stipulated what had led to the events of which they were convicted. One of the convicted men, Rashid Fitiyani, managed to tell his mother how his signature had been procured: "When they got through smashing my bones and told me to sign, nothing mattered any more. I signed, and that was that."

The arrest and "trial" of the Jericho men illuminate some major features of the Palestinian system of justice. Prisoners are kept in jail for long months without trial, and sometimes without even an interrogation and without being told why they have been detained. When they are at last brought to trial, it is hardly ever clear under what provision of the law they have been charged, or why the trial is being conducted under one specific set of auspices rather than another.

In fact, there is no Palestinian law *per se*. Within the areas under the jurisdiction of the PA, at least four different systems are in place—Jordanian law, Egyptian law, British Mandatory law, and the revolutionary code adopted by the PLO in 1979—and no one knows which of them will be used when. Confusion reigns in the court system as well. For all practical purposes, civil courts can hardly be said to exist. There is a high court of appeals in Gaza, and another appellate court in Ramallah, but they compete in no clear-cut way with military or revolutionary courts whose very names are constantly changing. As for the military courts, they are mostly a kind of front, at the service of the regime when and as needed: a group of reliable officers is assembled, they set up an impromptu courtroom in some military installation or other, and hastily perform the task required of them by the chairman.

Lately a group of lawyers has turned to the appellate court in Ramallah demanding the release of ten students who have been held without a hearing since last March. The government prosecutor has responded that the appellate court lacks jurisdiction in the case. This confronts the magistrates with an exceptionally difficult dilemma. They must be well aware that if they rule against the prosecutor, not only will no one honor the ruling, but they may end up paying for their rashness. They have only to look to the example of Qusai Abdallah, chief justice of the supreme court of appeals in Gaza, who in early June dared to rule against the government prosecutor in the false arrest of the human-rights activist Eyad Sarraj. In short order the judge was forced to retire from the bench and put under house arrest.

. . . . .

If neither the military nor the judiciary can be trusted by ordinary Palestinians, what, then, of their representative institutions, or the media?

In late January of this year, voting took place for a new Palestinian Legislative Council. Former President Jimmy Carter, on hand for the occasion, duly pronounced the election democratic to a fault, and so did an international team of observers, cheered on by an Israeli government anxious to confer the tokens of legitimacy on its peace partner. Had the elections been properly inspected, however, a different picture would have emerged: not only were they undemocratic, they were not even proper elections.

For one thing, the Islamic resistance had condemned the exercise from the outset and for the most part refused to participate. For another, Arafat saw to it through the usual means that dissenting candidates would not be elected in any significant number, and he also winnowed his own Fatah list to make sure it was filled with yes-men. Here and there, it is true, he faced opposition—honest and brave men and women—but in general he was able to ensure himself a sweeping victory. The majority of those elected were drawn from the innards of his political apparatus.

The vote produced a council of 88 members whose job is to serve as a legislative assembly—a parliament, for all intents and purposes—but there can be no illusion that this parliament has teeth. It cannot influence, it cannot criticize, and it has not legislated a single matter of substance. Arafat freely ignores any action of which he does not approve, including the five proposals put forward so far for a proper constitution. At the end of July, when the subject of the constitution was about to be broached yet again, the chairman turned to the members, denounced them as "sons of whores"—and left the chamber. Whereupon the deliberations ended.

As for the administrative functions of government, though Arafat committed himself at Oslo to forming proper institutions—offices and ministries with orderly tables of organization, a professional bureaucracy, agreed-upon procedures for decision-making—no real thought was ever given to the matter, and from the start the executive institutions of the PA were staffed mostly with Arafat loyalists. A handful of Palestinian intellectuals, educated in Western universities, could be heard warning that a decade's imprisonment, or family ties to a given cabinet minister, or for that matter fanatic loyalty to Yasir Arafat himself did not necessarily constitute qualification for public office; what was needed were trained professionals, expertise, objective norms and standards. Nobody took the warnings seriously, and the results are evident for all to see.

Then there are the Palestinian press and broadcast media, an area in which Arafat's hand is especially evident. Most Palestinian papers of any substance are printed and published in the relatively protected environs of Jerusalem, the capital of the Zionist state. Yet despite this fact, and despite the shining model afforded by the unfettered Israeli press right next door, the PA has managed over the last year and a half to terrorize virtually every Palestinian publisher, editor, and journalist and turn him into a faithful parrot of the Arafat line.

Practically immediately upon the entry of the PA into Gaza and Jericho in mid-1994, for example, Arafat issued an order to close *Al-Nahar*, a daily newspaper which he accused of serving as a mouthpiece for King Hussein of Jordan. The paper's publisher, although he lived and worked in Jerusalem, did not dare defy the order from Gaza. Within 40 days of the shut-down, thoroughly broken, he agreed to accept Arafat's dictates and *Al-Nahar* began to appear again, as a now-dependable adherent of the "Palestinian national line."

In the days and months following, other editors and reporters received the personal attentions of Arafat's men whenever they dared write or publish something displeasing to the regime. One such incident occurred eighteen months ago, when a number of papers made the mistake of reporting the exact size of a rally held by the opposition. Summoned to a meeting, the editors were officially informed that henceforth they were authorized to publish only those texts and statistics given to them by Wafa, the Palestinian news service. Those failing to knuckle under, like the opposition paper *Al-Ummah*, were physically attacked: Arafat's security forces first confiscated the newspaper's press plates and then burned down its offices, which again were located in Jerusalem. (The Rabin government, which knew all about the incident, said nothing.)

These various actions had the desired effect, especially when combined with arrests. A journalist named Samir Hamatu, apparently suspected of having links to the Islamic opposition, has been sitting in jail in Gaza since March, unindicted and untried. Another, the night editor of *Al-Quds*, the largest Palestinian daily, having flouted an order from Gaza to headline some flattering remarks about Arafat uttered by a Christian patriarch, was kidnapped—yet again within Jerusalem—and held in prison for five days in Jericho until he learned his lesson.

On the radio, the "Voice of Palestine" has been docile from the start. Nevertheless, the station's most popular broadcaster, Danial Karim Halaf, was fired after she permitted a critic of the regime to express his views on the air.

· · · · ·

Helping to keep the PA enterprise afloat are corruption and graft, both petty and large-scale. On the level of the petty, which is what most Palestinians see every day, the practice among many PA officials is to help themselves to goods and services: when, for instance, the commander of one of the many security agencies operating in Bethlehem wants a haircut, his men block off the street and allow no one to pass until their chieftain has been served (gratis, naturally).

An intricate system of localized gangsterism and patronage has also sprung up. A resident of a village near Ramallah found himself in jail after accidentally hitting a car belonging to the son of a Palestinian cabinet minister; another resident, an engineer by profession, got two broken ribs after he declined to vacate the parking spot of the same minister's wife. On the other hand, if a local is lucky enough to have friends in high places, not even the legal rights of another Palestinian will hinder him from getting his way. Thus, in the Christian town of Beit Jallah south of Jerusalem, a woman fell out with two of her neighbors over a plot of land. Though the neighbors were from an important local family, and were in the legal right, the woman had an advantage: connections with the local police chief. Her adversaries were promptly seized and tortured until they agreed to sign away their claim to the disputed property.

As in most societies, events on the local level give a hint of arrangements at the top—in this case, the wholesale economic swindling of foreign donors and others by the PA elite.

In October 1993, at the height of the Oslo euphoria, a group of countries led by the U.S. agreed to contribute a total of $2.1 billion to the PA over a period of five years, as a token of support for the young democracy-in-the-making. Various conditions were attached to the gift, among them the establishment of an agency that would be responsible for absorbing and distributing the funds in accordance with strict accounting procedures. This agency was indeed set up, under the name Palestinian Economic Council for Development and Reconstruction (PECDAR). But the donor nations, instead of being rewarded with oversight and integrity in the handling of their money, have been treated to duplicity and obfuscation.

PECDAR was supposed to be wholly independent of the PA; its mandate was to ensure that the sums coming from abroad would flow especially to development projects. Today, the agency is entirely in the hands of Arafat, and most of the money that has already been contributed has gone not to development projects but to the establishment and maintenance of a growing military machine and a swollen government bureaucracy. At the same time, an impressive portion of the money—the gift of European and, especially, American taxpayers—has ended up in the pockets of senior PA officials. Arafat himself and his closest associates skim from the top, the former to subsidize his political activities, the latter to fatten their personal bank accounts.

It is not just foreign governments that are being ripped off. Private investors contemplating doing business under the PA can likewise expect to forgo hefty sums in graft and hush money. Muhammad Rashid, Arafat's economic adviser, is among those benefiting financially from every sack of cement, every carton of cigarettes, that comes into Gaza. One consequence of all this activity has been a marked rise in the quality of motor transport among PA officials. The astonishing number of luxuriously appointed Mercedeses adorning the streets of Gaza and the West Bank stands in stark contrast to the steadily shrinking economic prospects of ordinary Palestinians, many of whom—thanks to the failure or refusal of Arafat to curb terrorism against Israel—have been cut off from their source of livelihood by a closure of the territories and are on the brink of starvation. As the plight of the average Palestinian in the autonomous region worsens, the wealth of the PA political elite grows ever more conspicuous.

· · · · ·

How long can this go on? Lately, indeed, it has become possible to gauge the degree of dissatisfaction with Arafat's rule on the part of his subjects. In early August, as I noted above, popular riots broke out in two Palestinian towns, Nablus and Tulkarm. In Tulkarm, a mob of thousands gathered. Before things got out of hand, the angry crowd pulled down a giant poster of Arafat that hung in the town square (it had been paid for, under coercion, by a local publisher) and tore it to shreds. In the melee, some 50 to 60 detainees broke out of prison and managed to get away before police began shooting, killing one demonstrator.

This was six weeks after Benjamin Netanyahu's upset victory in the Israeli elections, an event that was greeted, ironically enough, by jubilation among many Arabs in Hebron and East Jerusalem, two

Palestinian strongholds which have yet to fall to the tender mercies of the PA. Some were open in expressing their joy; others whispered the hope that the new Israeli Prime Minister would yet rescue them from the clutches of dictatorship.

Around the same time, the lines outside the branch of the Israeli office of internal affairs in East Jerusalem began to lengthen. Most of the people there were anxious to apply, at any price, for an Israeli identity card. Throughout the PA, indeed, this blue card has become the most desirable commodity imaginable—a ticket out of hell.

But relatively few will receive a blue identity card, and relatively few will be able to save themselves. What then? Although the full scope of what is going on in the areas under the jurisdiction of the PA may not be known to the Western public, there is no doubt that interested Western governments have been apprised of every detail, and (like at least the previous Israeli government) have sedulously maintained silence. That silence is perhaps best explained by an offhand remark of the late Yitzhak Rabin, who once expressed his confidence in Yasir Arafat's ability to deal handily with his internal opposition, unhampered (in contrast to Rabin himself) by "the [Israeli] Supreme Court and [the Israeli human-rights organization] B'Tselem."

Rabin, in truth, had little interest in the human rights of Palestinians. What he cared about was the continuation of the political process initiated with Arafat at Oslo. So, too, the present administration in Washington; so, too, the donor nations of Western Europe; and so, too, those Arab countries which have declared their political support of the PA (Arab financial support has been minimal). Any effort to rein in this tyranny, to encourage the formation of real democratic institutions and a society of law, would have to come from those in possession of a stick—namely, the donors, and especially the U.S. Such an effort would bring untold benefits to the Palestinian people; but it would also clearly endanger the man, and the men, at the top. So far, and no doubt for that very reason, there is not the slightest sign of its happening.

—October 1996

Daniel Pipes

Israel's
Moment of Truth

I t might appear that things have never been going better for Israel,
or worse for those who wish it ill.

Consider: the Jewish state has signed peace treaties with Egypt
and Jordan, and five agreements with the Palestinian Authority (PA), its
"partner for peace." With Syria, high-level negotiations now under way
appear so promising that both sides have publicly predicted they could
be wrapped up within a few months. Other diplomatic ties are stronger
than ever: Israel has a powerful regional ally in Turkey, enjoys growing
links to such giants as India and China, and is generally shedding the
near-pariah status that hobbled it in the recent past. The connection to
the United States is warm, deep, personal, and reciprocal.

Should diplomacy fail for any reason, moreover, Israel can fall back
on its military strength. As the only country in the Middle East participating in the much-bruited "revolution in military affairs"—essentially,
the application of high-tech to armaments—it has built so great a lead
in conventional arms, including planes and tanks, that several Arab states
have basically conceded they cannot compete with it on that level. Instead,
they have directed their attention higher (to weapons of mass destruction) and lower (to terrorism). But even in those arenas, Israel is far from
helpless: it has a missile-defense system, the Arrow, in the works and,
for deterrent purposes, weapons of mass destruction of its own, as well
as formidable anti-terrorist capabilities.

Security matters hardly exhaust the list of Israel's advantages. Economically, it enjoys today a per-capita income of $18,000, placing it a bit

ahead of Spain and a bit behind Canada—in other words, in the big leagues. Better yet, it has shown a very impressive annual growth rate since 1990. Thanks to its "Silicon Wadi," Israel is a high-tech giant, with a computer and Internet sector larger in absolute terms than that of any other country in the world outside the United States. Demographically, the birth rate of 2.6 children per woman among Israeli Jews is one of the highest in the West, and the country also remains a magnet for immigration; with 5 million Jews, it is quickly gaining on the United States as the place with the largest Jewish population in the world.

Finally, there is the political scene. Unlike its neighbors and rivals, Israel benefits from a lively and robust civic culture in which everyone has his say, party lines are (notoriously) fluid, and no one defers to politicians. And yet, however colorful and argumentative the public forum, when it comes to key security issues the major parties find much common ground. In last year's elections, for example, the two candidates for the post of prime minister, Ehud Barak and Benjamin Netanyahu, differed on the tone and pace but hardly at all on the substance of the peace process: yes, they concurred, the Palestinians should do more to live up to their promises, but no, their failings in this area were not reason enough to cut off negotiations.

· · · · ·

By contrast, Arabs—and Iran, too—seem to be faring less well. Arab countries are, in the words of a UN official, "particularly exceptional in being the highest spenders in the world on military purposes": they devote 8.8 percent of their GDP to the military, versus 2.4 percent for the world as a whole. Nevertheless, despite all this spending, Arab conventional forces are in decline. To be sure, a few states (like Egypt) have access to advanced American arms, but their lack of technical proficiency means that they are nearly always consumers and not producers of military hardware, paying for completed goods that others have to teach them how to operate.

Allies? The Soviet Union is gone, and no one has come close to replacing it. The Arab states darkly suspect the United States of engaging in conspiracies against them, and these suspicions—as, most recently, in the case of the crash of an EgyptAir flight off Massachusetts—impede closer relations with the world's only superpower. Arabs also lack an effective counterpunch to the pro-Israel lobby in Washington, and have failed to respond to the growing cooperation between Turkey and Israel in a way that would advance their own interests.

Outside Israel, the Middle East boasts—if that is the right word—the world's highest quotient of autocratic regimes, not to mention an inordinate number of rogue states, including Iran, Iraq, Syria, Sudan, and Libya. A culture of deference and intimidation remains dominant everywhere; movements for democracy and human rights are feeble. Arab states are particularly vulnerable to Islamism, a totalitarian ideology in the tradition of fascism and Marxism-Leninism. While Islamists have suffered reverses in recent years, they are still the major opposition force in countries like Algeria, Egypt, and Saudi Arabia, threatening the stability of government after government.

Nor are Arab economies doing well. The recent jump in oil prices, however welcome to producers, cannot obscure some dismal realities, principally a per-capita annual income among Arabic-speaking peoples that does not rise to one-tenth of Israel's. Yes, Kuwait weighs in (just like Israel) at $18,000; but in Yemen the annual per-capita income is $270; more to the point, Egypt, Jordan, and Syria all hover in the neighborhood of $1,000. A paltry 1 percent of world equity flowing to emerging markets these days ends up in Arabic-speaking countries. When it comes to high technology, the Middle East is a black hole, with few sales and even less innovation. As the historian R. Stephen Humphreys has noted, "with the partial exception of Turkey and of course Israel . . . there is not one Middle Eastern manufactured item that can be sold competitively on world markets."

Demographically, the Arabs and Iran have too much of a good thing: a birth rate so high that schools cannot maintain standards, and economies cannot manufacture enough jobs. The demographer Onn Winckler has named population growth as the Middle East's "most critical socioeconomic problem."

Taken together, all these factors seem to suggest that Israel has at long last achieved a definitive edge over its historic enemies. Such, indeed, appears to be the view of Israeli leaders themselves. Thanks to Israel's position of strength, Prime Minister Ehud Barak now speaks confidently of an "end to wars" and of his country's being finally accepted as a permanent presence by its neighbors. These sentiments are widely echoed both in Israel and in Washington.

And yet—two trends suggest otherwise. The first has to do with Arab strengths, the second with Israeli weaknesses. In both cases, the phenomena I will be discussing are only partly material in nature, lying more in the realm of such elusive and intangible qualities as internal spirit and morale. But these are precisely the qualities that in the end can decide the fates of nations and peoples.

. . . . .

Some improvements in the Arab position, whether actual or imminent, have long been recognized: greater control over a huge portion of the world's oil and gas reserves, steady acquisition of weapons of mass destruction, movement toward economic modernization (notably in Egypt). Progress in any or all of these areas can seriously threaten Israel's qualitative edge and its security in the medium term—unless, of course, Arab enmity toward the Jewish state has dissipated in the interim. But just here is where the greatest reason for concern resides.

Historically, Arab "rejectionism"—that is, the refusal to accept the permanent existence of a sovereign Jewish state in its historic home-land—has been based on one or another local variant (pan-Arab, pan-Syrian, Palestinian, or the like) of nationalism, a European import into the Middle East. It has suffered from two disabilities: limited reach and factionalism. But in recent years, as the rejection of Israel has taken on a less secular and more Islamic complexion, it has also gained a deeper resonance among ordinary Arabs, with Israel's existence now cast as an affront to God's will, and has also benefited operationally from a some-what greater degree of unity (Islamists are surprisingly good at work-ing together). The net effect has been not to moderate but, on the con-trary, to solidify and to sharpen Arab antagonism to Israel—vocal rejectionist elements now include pious Muslims and Islamists, Arab nationalists, despots, and intellectuals—and to give fresh impetus to the dream of destroying it.

The point cannot be made often or strongly enough that, in their great majority, Arabic speakers do continue to repudiate the idea of peace with Israel.* Despite having lost six rounds of war, they seem nothing loath to try again. In one of the most recent in-depth surveys of Arab opinion, conducted by the political scientist Hilal Khashan of the Amer-ican University of Beirut, 1,600 respondents, divided equally among Jor-danians, Lebanese, Palestinians, and Syrians, stated by a ratio of 69 to 28 percent that they personally did not want peace with Israel. By 79 to 18 percent, they rejected the idea of doing business with Israelis even after a total peace. By 80 to 19 percent, they rejected learning about Israel. By 87 to 13 percent, they supported attacks by Islamic groups against Israel.

---

*For details, see my article "On Arab Rejectionism," *Commentary*, December 1997.

This is the view of Israel that dominates political debate in the Arab world and that is conveyed to the public in every arena from scholarly discourse to the popular media to nursery-school jingles. True, some Arabs think otherwise. The late King Hussein of Jordan spoke eloquently of the need to put aside the conflict with Israel and to get on with things; his son and successor appears to be of like mind. Some Arab army officers would undoubtedly prefer not to confront Israel's military forces any time soon. Kuwaitis and Lebanese Christians, sobered by occupation, now mostly wish to leave Israel alone. And there are business leaders who believe, as one Arab banker succinctly put it, that "the whole purpose of peace is business." But these elements, overall, represent but a minority of the Arab population, and have not shifted the underlying hostility.

An incident from the sports pages makes the point. Only a few months ago, Israeli athletes ventured on a first-ever official match to an Arab capital—the capital not of a front-line "confrontation state" but of the tiny and moderate Persian Gulf sheikhdom of Qatar. The experience turned out to be, as Agence France-Presse aptly characterized it, "a bruising ordeal." Forced to live in nearly complete isolation from other athletes, the Israeli champions had to enter and leave their hotel via a side door. Among the flags of the competing nations, Israel's alone was not raised in public. Huge crowds turned up to jeer at the Jewish athletes, and the media touted their presence as "an occasion to express the Arabs' rejection of all that is Israeli."

Twenty years of relations between Egypt and Israel since the treaty of 1979 testify bitterly to the same state of affairs. Formally there is peace, but Cairo permits, even sponsors, a vicious propaganda campaign against Israel that includes the crudest forms of anti-Semitism, and it is rapidly building up offensive military forces that could be deployed against the Jewish state. In effect, what Egyptian authorities are telling their people is this: for all sorts of reasons we have to be in contact with Israelis and sign certain pieces of paper, but we still hate them, and you should, too. In Jordan, where the government does not play this double game, things are in some ways worse: the best efforts of two kings have failed to induce in the Jordanian populace a more peaceable and friendly outlook toward Israel.

. . . . .

Fueling the dream of Arab rejectionists is the immensely important fact that within Israel itself (that is, within the old 1967 borders), the Jewish proportion of the population has fallen from a one-time high of 87 percent to 79 percent today, and is inexorably trailing downward. In 1998, of Israel's total population growth of 133,000, only 80,000 were Jews, with Arabs making up the bulk of the remainder. From such statistics, some demographers predict a non-Jewish majority in Israel by the middle of the 21st century.

But the Jewish nature of the "Jewish state" will shift in the Arabs' favor long before they reach majority status there. At present, were Israeli Arabs to be represented in the Knesset in proportion to their numbers, they would already hold 24 out of its 120 seats. Even with the seven seats they now occupy, as the analyst Eric Rozenman has noted,

> the Arab electorate and Arab Knesset members ... have helped override Jewish majorities on such vital matters as the creation of Prime Minister Yitzhak Rabin's coalition in 1992 and approval of the Oslo and Oslo II accords in 1993 and 1995 respectively. All seven Israeli Arab members voted for both agreements; the former passed 61 to 50, with nine abstentions, the latter passed 61 to 59.

These trends will undoubtedly persist, Rozenman writes, especially as Israeli Arabs become "energized by a new Palestinian state next door (and perhaps also by an increasingly Palestinian Jordan)." By the time the numbers of Arabs approach or even exceed parity with the Jews, "the state might still be democratic, but the civic atmosphere, the public culture, would not likely be Jewish in the tacit, general sense it is today."

The growing power and enfranchisement of Muslims in the United States provide further grounds for Arab optimism. Not only is the American Muslim community approaching the Jewish community in absolute size, it is also making strides in education, economic well-being, and political savvy. If the old pro-Arab lobby was hampered by its dependence on oil money, retired American diplomats, and left-wing Christian Arabs, dynamic new organizations like the American Muslim Council and the Council on American-Islamic Relations are another matter altogether. Although foreign policy is hardly their only cause, "Palestine" remains the single most mobilizing issue for American Muslims, and the position articulated by Muslim organizations on this issue is almost uniformly extremist—against negotiations with Israel or accommodation with it in almost any form.

Not only are these extremist Muslim organizations intent on making themselves heard, but the Clinton administration, at least, has openly welcomed them at the highest levels. At a dinner she hosted to break the fast of Ramadan this past December, Secretary of State Madeleine K. Albright told her guests: "I want to be sure that the legitimate concerns of Muslim-Americans are taken into account when shaping the programs, activities, and reports of this Department." Seated before her was a Who's Who of American Muslim radicals.

Is it any wonder that many Arabs, knowing such facts, or hearing such heady words from the lips of the American Secretary of State, should become newly imbued with a sense of confidence about the future? And that sense can only be bolstered by what they see happening on the other side, within Israel itself.

· · · · ·

Once renowned for its self-confidence, bravery, and purpose, Israel today is a changed society. Whatever the undoubted strength of its military machine, few in a position to know the heart and soul of the country try to hide the fact of a widespread demoralization, even within that military machine itself. As a retired colonel summed it up neatly, "the Israeli public is really tired of war."

Fatigue takes many forms in contemporary Israel. The pervasive feeling that they have fought long enough, and that the time has come to settle, leads many to express openly their annoyance with the need for military preparedness and the huge expense of maintaining a modern armed force. They weary of the constant loss of life, they want escape from the fear that terrorism imparts, they yearn to close down an atavistic tribal war—and peace treaties promise a quick way out. (As one Israeli put it to me, "My grandfather, father, myself, and my son have all fought the Arabs; I want to make sure my grandson does not also have to.") Among young people, draft evasion, hitherto all but unknown, has become a serious problem, and within the army itself, morale is hardly what it once was, as the IDF's decidedly unheroic recent record in Lebanon has revealed to all, including the Hezbollah enemy.

At the same time, Israel's soaring economy has given many citizens a taste for the good life that cannot be easily reconciled with the need for patience and fortitude—and, especially, sacrifice—in confronting a seemingly unchanging enemy. Middle-aged Israeli men are increasingly unwilling to go off and "play soldier" on reserve duty for several weeks a year when they could be at the office increasing their net worth or enjoying what that net worth makes possible. For those with an active social conscience, a number of long-deferred domestic problems—

persistent poverty, a faulty educational system, worsening relations between secular and religious—seem much more deserving of attention, and of state expenditure, than does grappling endlessly with Israel's opponents.

Finally, Israelis are tired of the moral opprobrium their country has long suffered—at the United Nations, in Western academic circles, and in editorial boardrooms. Indeed, in an extreme reaction to this ongoing moral ostracism, some of the country's foremost intellectuals have, as it were, defected: they have accommodated sizable chunks of the Arab side's version of the Arab-Israeli conflict, promulgating them as important new truths. Thus, to cite an especially influential expression of this line of thinking, the school of "new historians" in Israel argues that the Jewish state is guilty of an "original sin"—the alleged dispossession of Palestine's native inhabitants—and can therefore be considered to some extent illegitimate. Others, known as "post-Zionists," have characterized Jewish nationalism—Zionism—as, if not racist, then at best an outdated and parochial ideology, and one which should no longer form the basis of Israel's public life.

Such ideas, first incubated on the far Left and in the prestige universities, then spreading to students, artists, and journalists, are now the stuff of television documentaries and educational textbooks. As of the current Israeli school year, ninth graders no longer learn that Israel's war of independence in 1948–49 was a battle of the few against the many but, to the contrary, that the Jews enjoyed military superiority over the Arabs. They also learn that many Palestinians fled the country in those war years not to clear the way for invading Arab armies thought to be on their march to victory, but out of well-founded fears of Jewish brutality and terror.

In a front-page report on the introduction of these books into the schools, the *New York Times* rightly characterized them as marking a "quiet revolution." That revolution has by now reached the consciousness of politicians, business leaders, and even military officers; its impact can hardly be exaggerated. Thanks to the inroads of post-Zionism, as Meyrav Wurmser has observed in the *Middle East Quarterly*, Israeli society "is now facing a crisis of identity and values that strikes at the basic components and elements of [its] identity: Judaism and nationalism." Without those two components, clearly, little remains of the Zionist project.

· · · · ·

What are the implications, for politics and diplomacy, of Israeli fatigue, and of the intense self-absorption that is its corollary? What strikes one above all is how little attention Israelis are paying these days to their Arab neighbors. Sick of fighting, bent on building an Internet economy, they seem to have decided that Arabs feel the same way, and want the same things, they do. (In psychology, the term for this is projection.) According to a survey conducted by the Jaffee Center at Tel Aviv University, fully two-thirds of Israelis now agree with the following dubious assertions: that most Palestinians want peace; that signing agreements will end the Arab-Israeli conflict; and that if forced to choose between negotiations and increased military strength, Israel should opt for the former. Prime Minister Ehud Barak perfectly sums up this outlook in his repeated invocation of a peace that will "work for everyone," the unspoken assumption being that Arabs no less than Israelis seek to resolve their century-old conflict on harmonious terms.

Of course, at some level Israelis know full well about continued Arab rejectionism: the signs are too conspicuous for even the most ostrich-like to be truly clueless. But they have clearly chosen to de-emphasize or even ignore the phenomenon. How else to explain the absence of a single full-time Israeli journalist reporting from an Arab capital, or the fact that Hilal Khashan's meticulous survey of Arab opinion, with its thoroughly dismaying news, received no attention whatsoever in the Israeli press when it appeared last summer? "These are only words. Let them talk," is how Shimon Peres, speaking for many of his countrymen, has airily dismissed the undeniable evidence of Arab feelings and attitudes.

Peres's disdainful remark encapsulates a delusional but widespread Israeli assumption: that peace in the Middle East is Israel's for the making, and that if Israelis want to end the long-drawn-out struggle, they can do so on their own. They can "solve" the Palestinian problem by acceding to the creation of a state in the West Bank and Gaza; they can eliminate anti-Zionism by helping to funnel money to the Arabs, who will use their newfound affluence to become good neighbors (and never to amass more powerful arsenals); or—in the post-Zionist scenario—they can win Arab hearts by dismantling the Jewish attributes of the Jewish state.

Whatever the preferred tactic, the underlying premise is the same: that the key decisions of war and peace in the Arab-Israeli conflict are made in Jerusalem and Tel Aviv rather than—what is in fact the case—in Cairo, Gaza, Amman, and Damascus. Under the spell of this fantasy,

Israelis now seem prepared to execute what will amount to a unilateral transfer of hard-won territory—to Syria in the north, to the Palestinian Authority in the center of the country—in the hope that their troubles will thereby disappear. Indeed, they sometimes appear prepared to go to extreme lengths to induce their Arab interlocutors to accept the gifts they mean to confer on them.

Listening to the Israeli prime minister and the foreign minister of Syria as they inaugurated a new round of talks in December 1999, for example, one might have thought that Israel was the party that had instigated—and then lost—the Six-Day war of 1967, and was now desperately suing Damascus for terms. Barak spoke pleadingly of the need "to put behind us the horrors of war and to step forward toward peace," and of creating, "together with our Syrian partners, . . . a different Middle East where nations are living side by side in peaceful relationship and in mutual respect and good-neighborliness." By contrast, the Syrian foreign minister blustered like a conqueror, insisting that Israel had "provoked" the 1967 clash and demanding the unconditional return of "all its occupied land." The very fact that a prime minister had agreed to meet with a mere foreign minister, breaching a cardinal protocol of diplomacy, was signal enough; that the foreign minister of Syria lacks any decision-making power whatsoever further confirmed who in this encounter was the wooer, who the wooed.

When it comes to Lebanon, Israelis appear to have convinced themselves that the unilateral withdrawal of troops from their "security zone" in the south will cause their main Lebanese opponent, Hezbollah, to leave them alone, despite repeated and overt statements by Hezbollah leadership that it intends to continue fighting until it reaches Jerusalem and that it "will never recognize the existence of a state called Israel even if all the Arabs do so." More, Israelis seem persuaded that the prospect of their withdrawal from Lebanon is one of the things that have the Syrians worried, quite as if the best way to scare your enemy were to threaten a retreat.

On the Palestinian track, the ostensibly more muscular party—Israel—has pointedly refrained from requiring that the ostensibly more vulnerable party fulfill the many obligations it has undertaken since 1993, with the result that the PA has neither turned over criminals and terrorists, nor ceased its unrelenting incitements to violence, nor restricted the size of its armed forces. The PA's logo brazenly shows a map of a future Palestine stretching from the Jordan River to the Mediterranean Sea—a Palestine, that is, not alongside Israel but instead of it. To all this, the Israeli body politic appears to pay no heed.

The newspaper *Ha'aretz* reports that Israeli negotiators have already conceded in principle to the Palestinian Authority the day-to-day control of parts of Jerusalem. At the very end of 1999, when Prime Minister Barak took the unprecedented step of releasing two Palestinian prisoners who had killed Israelis, his action was met, predictably, not with Arab gratitude but with noisy demonstrations chanting aggressive slogans— "Barak, you coward. Our prisoners will not be humiliated"—and by the demand that Israel now let go all of the estimated 1,650 jailed Palestinians. No doubt, the demonstrators will eventually get their way. Israelis are on their own road to peace, and no "partners," however hostile, will deflect them from it.

· · · · ·

Today's Israel, in sum, is hugely different from the Israel of old. For four decades and more, the country made steady progress vis-à-vis its enemies through the application of patience and will, backed when necessary by military courage and might. From a fledgling state in 1948 invaded by five Arab armies, it established itself as a powerful force, overcoming oil boycotts, terrorism, and the enmity of a superpower. But by the time of the Oslo accord of August 1993, the signs of exhaustion were becoming increasingly manifest; by now they are unmistakable.

As recently as the 1996 national elections, a lively debate took place in Israel over Palestinian noncompliance with the terms of Oslo and over the wisdom of handing the Golan Heights back to Syria. By the time of the 1999 elections, with very little having changed on the ground, those issues had disappeared. Perhaps 10 to 15 percent of the population still adheres to the old Likud view that Israel should keep control of the territories until the Arabs have shown a true change of heart. Today, the main debate is over timing and tone, not over substance. Symbolic of the new consensus is the fact that the Third Way, a party that was exclusively focused on retaining the Golan Heights under Israeli control and that took four Knesset seats in 1996, vaporized in 1999, winning not a single seat. Even former Prime Minister Benjamin Netanyahu, the reputed arch-hardliner, signed two empty agreements with Arafat and, on the Syrian track, was ready to concede virtually everything Hafez al-Assad demanded. As Ehud Barak has correctly noted, "there are only microscopic differences between the things Netanyahu was willing to discuss and those discussed by [Shimon] Peres and [Yitzhak] Rabin."

Many who bemoan the weakness of current Israeli policy are tempted to place the onus on Washington. But (to put it symbolically) how can one become exercised over Hillary Clinton's advocacy of a Palestinian state when, only weeks earlier, Shimon Peres had already specified a date for such a state's inception? Israelis are perfectly capable of choosing leaders prepared to resist American pressure, and they have done so in the past. The collapse of a meaningful opposition party in 1999—Menachem Begin won two elections as prime minister in 1977 and 1981, but last year his son and political heir had to withdraw from the race because his support was so trivial—rebuts the notion that weak politicians are doing the bidding of Washington; rather, they are doing the bidding of their electorate.

No, it is inward, to the Israeli spirit, that one must look for the roots of the present disposition to ignore repeated Palestinian flouting of solemnly signed agreements, to turn the Golan Heights over to a still-fanged Syria, to withdraw unilaterally from Lebanon, and to acquiesce in huge American sales of military equipment to an unfriendly and potentially threatening Egypt.

Israel today has money and weapons, the Arabs have will. Israelis want a resolution to conflict, Arabs want victory. Israel has high capabilities and low morale, the Arabs have low capabilities and high morale. Again and again, the record of world history shows, victory goes not to the side with greater firepower, but to the side with greater determination.

Among democracies, few precedents exist for the malaise now on display in Israel. Imperfect analogies include the atmosphere of pacifism and appeasement that pervaded significant sectors of opinion in France and England in the 1930s, the United States during the Vietnam period, and Western Europe in the early 1980s. But none of these situations quite matches Israel's in the extent of the debilitation. Even more critically, none of those countries lived with so narrow a margin of safety. France succumbed to the Nazis, but was able to recover. England nearly succumbed, but had time to rally with American help. The United States lost a long, bloody war in Vietnam, but the nation as a whole was hardly at risk. In Israel the stakes are far higher, the room for error correspondingly minute.

This is not to say that the Jewish state is in immediate danger; it continues to have a strong military and a relatively healthy body politic, and democracies have demonstrated the capacity to right their mistakes at five minutes to midnight. But one shudders to think of what calamity Israel must experience before its people wake up and assume, once again, the grim but inescapable task of facing the implacable enemies around them.

—February 2000

Norman Podhoretz

Intifada II: Death of an Illusion?

"In my beginning is my end," wrote T. S. Eliot in words that are well suited to the Arab war against Israel. Although there is no end in sight to that war, the violence to which the Palestinians resorted in the wake of Ariel Sharon's visit to the Temple Mount on September 28 does at least mark the end of one act in this long and bloody drama. This was the act that began with the agreement at Oslo, which was then ratified on the White House lawn in September 1993 by Yasir Arafat, the chairman of the Palestine Liberation Organization (PLO), and Yitzhak Rabin, then the prime minister of Israel, with perhaps the most famous handshake in history.

So much diplomatic and political smoke has been blown in our eyes since that moment that a clear-sighted look at the act that opened then and is just now concluding requires us to step back and recapitulate. For even though we do indeed have here a near-perfect case of a beginning that was inexorably destined for the bitter end it has now reached, mighty efforts were made on all sides to persuade us that it would be otherwise.

In the early 18th century, the English theologian Bishop Joseph Butler said: "Things and actions are what they are, and the consequences of them will be what they will be: why then should we desire to be deceived?" About 200 years later, T. S. Eliot, to cite him again, gave us the answer to this breathtaking question when he observed in an entirely different context that "human kind/Cannot bear very much reality."

In this instance, the unbearable reality being evaded was that Israel's yearning for peace was shared neither by the Arab world in general nor

by the Palestinians in particular—that their objection was not to anything Israel had done or failed to do, but to the very fact that it existed
at all. Then, as time went on, and episode after episode occurred exposing the delusion of Oslo for what it was, more and more rationalizations
had to be invented, and more and more lies had to be told, to keep it
alive. Too much hope—and too much political capital—had been invested
in the "peace process" to allow any opening of eyes that had been blinded
and minds that had been closed by the dazzling mirage on the White
House lawn.

No doubt believers in the idea that the road to peace had at last
been found often directed these efforts to conceal the truth mainly at
themselves. But they were hardly the sole or the exclusive objects of their
own deceptions. On the contrary. The enthusiasm for Oslo—manifested,
among many other ways, in the awarding of the Nobel Peace Prize to
Yitzhak Rabin, his foreign minister Shimon Peres, and Yasir Arafat for
having brought it about—was worldwide. So universal was it and so
fervent that, with the ruthless unconcern of a tidal wave, it swept aside
all doubts about the wisdom or the viability of the agreement.

Not, to be sure, in the Israeli public as a whole, where such doubts
did continue to be harbored and, as we shall see, expressed from time
to time in the electorate's choice of political leadership; but certainly in
the major centers of opinion both in Israel and abroad, and wherever the
writ of contemporary liberalism extended. In that vast domain, any Jew
or for that matter any non-Jew (and there was a small brave band of
them, an unhappy few) who voiced skepticism about Oslo immediately
got stigmatized as an enemy of peace. This made him the moral equivalent, if not the de-facto ally, of Arab opponents of Oslo like the Muslim
terrorists of Hamas and Hezbollah. Having been thus morally delegit-
imized, critics of the now-sacrosanct process were derided as well for
their intellectual sins, accused of being too rigid to perceive that new
developments had totally transformed the conflict between Israel and
the Arab world.

. . . . .

There were two distinct though complementary interpretations of these
developments. One was the "realistic" analysis espoused by Rabin, the
other a "visionary" picture painted by Peres.

As Rabin saw it, the demise of the Soviet Union had completely
altered the old "strategic equation" in the Middle East by depriving the
"frontline" Arab states of the armorer they had previously depended

upon for engaging Israel militarily. In consequence, there was almost no likelihood that they would start any more conventional wars, as they had done several times in the past. This meant in effect that the Palestinians were now on their own; and while they could, on their own, assuredly make life miserable for Israel through terrorism, they were too weak to pose an "existential threat" to the Jewish state. The only serious such threat now came from the missiles of Iran and/or Iraq. To protect itself from that threat, Israel needed the help of the United States in building an effective system of antiballistic-missile defense.

In Rabin's view, then, the overriding strategic objective—merging military with political imperatives—was to ensure continued American support. How to do this? Well, the Americans were convinced (while not admitting it openly lest it arouse domestic political opposition) that giving the Palestinians a state of their own was the answer to unrest and instability throughout the Middle East. It followed that if Israel were to drop its "intransigent" resistance to this solution, relations with Washington would be more or less permanently shored up. This would in one stroke eliminate any future possibility that Israel might be denied the advanced military technology on which its survival now rested and that it could only get from the Pentagon.

My own guess is that Rabin in his heart of hearts was also motivated by the realization that Israel did not know how to deal effectively with the *intifada,* the new form of warfare that the Palestinians had now been waging for some six years. When the *intifada* first erupted in 1987, Rabin (then the defense minister under Yitzhak Shamir) had declared that he would "break the bones" of the Palestinian rioters. But breaking their bones did not avail, especially as the Palestinians—adopting a tactic that was at once brilliant and evil—were sending their *children* to throw stones at armed Israeli soldiers, most of all when TV cameras were present. In defending themselves and fighting back, even if only with rubber bullets, the Israelis inflicted casualties on these children, which inevitably tarnished their longstanding pride in their "purity of arms." In the end it was Rabin himself and a large segment of the Israeli people who were broken by the *intifada:* broken in spirit, broken in morale.

Prudently, Rabin never acknowledged anything like this in public. Nor did he ever make a speech explaining his overall strategy with respect to the United States. But it was no secret, having been spelled out in private to various friendly interlocutors. And others (in the course of trying to understand why Rabin was now crossing one "red line" after another that he had vowed never to cross) soon enough figured out what he had in mind. Of course, to understand the strategy did not necessarily entail agreeing with it. But disagreement, however carefully reasoned, had zero effect on Rabin and his battalions of cheerleaders.

Thus, it did no good whatsoever for critics of this analysis to observe that the United States was running into troubles of its own in constructing a defense against ballistic missiles. Admittedly, these troubles were more political than technological. Nevertheless, there was uncertainty as to whether the special aid from Washington on which Rabin was counting would ultimately be available.

Nor did it do the critics any good to pile up evidence that the State Department was flat-out wrong in its conviction that the Middle East would become more stable if a Palestinian state were to be established. As against the regnant cliché that the Palestinians were the "heart" of the region's problems, some of us pointed out that since Israel's birth in 1948 many wars had been fought among Arabs and/or Muslims over issues that had nothing to do with either the Jewish state or the Palestinians. Not only that, but the corpses produced by just one of these wars alone (Iran vs. Iraq) far exceeded the total number of casualties resulting from all those between the Arabs and Israel. Like every other argument we brought forth, this one too fell on deaf ears. Yet all by itself, it should have been enough to refute the dogma that "the key" to Middle Eastern stability was a Palestinian state under the despotic leadership of the PLO.

Moreover, there were many other grounds for expecting that a PLO state would breed more unrest and more instability than the present situation. To choose only the most obvious one, the fact that the majority of the population of Jordan was Palestinian could easily lead to a move by Arafat or his successors to take over that country, thereby creating the risk of an intervention by Syria (which had never ceased regarding not only Israel but also Lebanon and Jordan as "Southern Syria").

And none of this was even to mention the persistent refusal of the Palestinians themselves to surrender their claim on the entire territory lying within Israel's pre-1967 borders. (To this day, incredibly, despite at least three exultant announcements by Peres and Arafat that the articles of the Palestine National Covenant committing the PLO to the destruction of Israel had now definitely been repealed as mandated by Oslo, it remains unclear whether they actually ever were.) Nor did it touch upon the terrible problem that would arise with the million Palestinian citizens of Israel, some 800,000 of whom lived in the Galilee, where they constituted a majority. To which state would they remain loyal? Might they turn out to be a contemporary analogue of the German citizens of Czechoslovakia between the two world wars who became the pretext for Nazi Germany's phased conquest of that whole country?

· · · · ·

If there were deadly serious questions arising from the "realistic" analysis through which Rabin justified his embrace of Oslo, they were as nothing compared with the plain foolishness of Peres's vision of a "new Middle East." And if Rabin set foot on the path marked out by Oslo with misgivings and visible reluctance, Peres was so breathlessly eager that he fell all over himself in running toward it.

In the 1960's, a major slogan of the counterculture was "Make Love, Not War." Peres's vision of the new Middle East could be summarized in a variant of this catchy battlecry (and a battlecry, ironically, was what this pacifist slogan amounted to): "Make Money, Not War." Reading or listening to Peres, one might have imagined that a kind of vulgar-Marxist end of days had arrived in which the lion would not merely lie down with the lamb but go into business with it—both parties having discovered how much more pleasant it is to get rich than to fight, perchance to die.

To all appearances, the new faith Peres had adopted was not disturbed by the fact that, in the three or four years after Oslo, where the Arabs specifically pledged to renounce terrorism, about twice as many Israeli lives were lost to Palestinian suicide bombers than in the three or four years *before* the Arabs had presumably opted for money over war. Brushing off the grisly evidence of mangled corpses in the buses and marketplaces of Tel Aviv and Jerusalem—he and his supporters even took to characterizing the Jewish victims of these attacks as "martyrs to peace"—Peres went complacently on his visionary way. Though he never to my knowledge quoted Tertullian, the early father of the Church who declared of Christianity that he believed in it precisely because it was unbelievable, some such slogan could easily have become for Peres the spiritual complement, so to speak, of the materialistic "Make Money, Not War."

The complete fatuity of this notion was on vivid display at a 1994 conference in Morocco called by the Council on Foreign Relations (though I suspect the idea originally came from Peres). The purpose of the conference was to bring the nations of the Middle East together to formulate plans for cooperative economic development throughout the region. Here, if anywhere, was a chance for the Arab Middle East to signal that it had indeed arrived at a stage where it was more interested in making money by cooperating with Israel than in making war against it. Yet the delegation from Egypt—the first Arab country to have signed a peace treaty with Israel—showed up with a 90-page booklet containing a host of proposals in which the name of Israel was never once mentioned and illustrated by six maps of the Middle East on which the state of Israel did not appear. Meanwhile, in the military exercises of the Egyptian armed forces, Israel would continue to be cast as the presumptive enemy. So much for making money, not war.

Another component of Peres's vision of the "new Middle East," which dovetailed with Rabin's supposedly more hard-headed conception, was that the age of missiles had rendered territorial buffer zones obsolete. This assessment was intended to undermine the old conviction (once shared by all Israelis, emphatically including the younger Peres himself) that retreating to the boundaries in which Israel had lived before the Six-Day war of 1967, especially if a Palestinian state were left behind, was incompatible with the nation's security. But now, according to Peres, when land wars were becoming a thing of the past, so too was the notion of secure borders.

On this issue as well, abundant evidence to the contrary—most notably the Gulf war, which in the end had to be won (to the extent that it *was* won) by ground troops and tanks—was cavalierly ignored. Or else, like Palestinian terrorism, it was dismissed as just another hang-over from a past that would soon be disposed of by History in its own species of mopping-up operation.

Yet while Peres himself may have kept the faith, stubbornly continuing to insist that he would not give terrorists a "victory" by abandoning the "peace process," the Israeli voting public disagreed. Running for prime minister in 1996 after the assassination of Rabin, Peres was beaten by Benjamin Netanyahu, who had been a strong critic of Oslo and would presumably adopt a tougher policy toward the Palestinians.

· · · · ·

In the event, Netanyahu disappointed many of his supporters by deciding to honor the Oslo agreement even though repeated Palestinian violations provided him with a legally sound case for backing out of it. True, while running for election, he had all but openly suggested that he *would* stick with Oslo. Yet if Rabin, in running for election some years earlier, had sworn never to negotiate with the PLO and then proceeded to do the opposite, why should Netanyahu have been expected to hold to his own campaign rhetoric?

But there was something even more disappointing to the hawks who had looked to Netanyahu for salvation from a "peace process" that they regarded as suicidal. This was the hesitant and inconsistent manner in which he enforced what he had most definitely promised: namely, to take no further steps along the Oslo road unless the Palestinians "reciprocated" by fully honoring their part of the bargain.

To the dismay of many who had assumed that *this* promise would at least be kept, Israeli territorial withdrawals went on under Netanyahu even though Arafat and his minions continued calling among themselves (but never when they spoke in Western languages to Western ears) for *jihad*, or "holy war," against Israel; even though Oslo was characterized (but, again, only in Arabic) as merely a stage in a multiphased struggle to wipe Israel off the map; and even though Palestinian schoolchildren were still being taught that Israel was an abomination that had to be eradicated. (Israeli schoolchildren, by contrast, were daily being offered history lessons that bent over backward to present the justice of the Palestinian claims.)

Palestinian violations of Oslo were by no means confined to the spoken word, or even to terrorism. For Arafat's Palestinian Authority (PA) was also stealthily building an army. Oslo had authorized a 24,000-man Palestinian police force armed only enough to maintain law and order within the territory Israel was ceding to the PA. Bizarre as it seems, the arms had been supplied by Rabin and Peres on the assumption that the PA police would relieve Israeli soldiers of the unpleasant necessity of policing these areas themselves. With a cynicism understandably bred by the double standard always being applied to Israel in these matters, Rabin once even remarked that whereas the Israelis were constantly being berated by human-rights organizations for trying to keep order, the Palestinians could be as brutal as they liked without running into much trouble from those same organizations. About this, he turned out to be largely right.

But so far as we can tell from the record, what Rabin never foresaw was that the Palestinians would not rest content with only 24,000 policemen, nor with the rifles they happily took from Israel. As the years passed, the number of "policemen" would rise to at least 40,000, and the heavier weapons precluded by Oslo would be smuggled in from Jordan and elsewhere. What Rabin also failed to anticipate—and did not live to see—was that the guns he had agreed to give the Palestinians would wind up being turned against Israelis, and that the police who were supposed to control rioters would instead join in with and even lead them.

· · · · ·

The first time this happened was a kind of rehearsal for the violence we have just been living through. It occurred in September 1996, about three months after Netanyahu became prime minister, when a new exit was opened to an archeological tunnel in Jerusalem. Though work on this tunnel had been going on for years without objection from anyone, the new exit set off a Palestinian protest in Ramallah that soon spread through the West Bank and Gaza; and as it spread, it escalated. By the time Arafat had called a halt to the throwing of rocks and Molotov cocktails and the firing by Palestinian police on Israeli civilians and soldiers, who then fired back, 73 people were dead and some 1,500 injured.

Most of these were Palestinians, since in a firefight Israel still had a great advantage. To Arafat, however, this discrepancy in the number of casualties was more a source of pride than of regret. Had he not told the Palestinian police themselves only a week earlier that "our blood is cheap for Jerusalem"?

Besides, the whole incident could be and was exploited by Palestinian propaganda. According to the PA, the tunnel was intended by the Israelis to undermine the foundations of the al-Aqsa mosque on the Temple Mount, one of Islam's holiest places, and it was this nefarious enterprise that triggered the wholly justified rage of the Palestinians. Almost everyone in the world took the PA version of events at face value, and yet the most cursory glance at the situation would have shown that the allegation was blatantly false. As even the anti-Netanyahu editor of the *Biblical Archaeology Review* was constrained to acknowledge: "The tunnel is *outside* the Temple Mount. It threatens no religious sites. The al-Aqsa mosque is at the other end of the Temple Mount, as far away as you can get."

There were five lessons that should have hit home as a result of the tunnel episode. One was that the Palestinians felt no need to fulfill their main obligation under Oslo, which was to substitute negotiations for violence. This they more or less would do—if, that is, and only if, the negotiations were going their way. But if the Israelis did anything that displeased them, they would not hesitate to resort once again to force, even (or, with the media in mind, especially) if they themselves, and their children, were bound to suffer the heaviest casualties.

Was this enough to demonstrate that the critics of Oslo had been right all along in their belief that Israel did not have "a partner for peace" in Arafat? Not on your life. Rather than recognizing Arafat for what he was, and was not, much of the world decided that it was the Palestinians who did not have "a partner for peace" in Netanyahu. Having been denounced by his formerly most passionate supporters for refusing to abrogate Oslo, he now found himself vilified for sabotaging it. This charge was hurled at him by Jewish enthusiasts of Oslo within both Israel and America, as well as by the foreign ministries of virtually every country on earth, including the one in Washington, over which Bill Clinton, the allegedly "best friend" Israel had ever had, presided.

Yet all Netanyahu had done was to slow down the process a bit, and by means so trivial that after only a few years or even weeks no one could remember what they were. Even at the time, his political opponents and enemies had to go to almost comical lengths in drawing up an indictment against him. For example, in the words of one bill of particulars, his unforgivably major sins against the "peace process" consisted of (1) taking his time after being elected before deciding "to see Yasir Arafat"; (2) "making [Arafat] wait to travel in his helicopter within the West Bank"; and (3) "finally shaking hands with [Arafat] with a near grimace."

To this ridiculous list was added a number of more serious actions, but no hint was breathed that these same actions had also been taken by Peres when, in his brief tenure as prime minister after the assassination of Rabin, even he could not go on merely reaffirming his love of peace whenever another terrorist bomb exploded in Israel. (The main such actions by Peres were extending the deadline for a withdrawal from Hebron and sealing off the borders between Israel and the occupied territories.) Nor was there any mention of the things Netanyahu—eliciting even more furious disappointment among his old supporters—had done to mitigate or even reverse some of these policies he had inherited from Peres, like easing restrictions on the number of Arab workers allowed into Israel from the territories every day, and going through with the pullout from Hebron.

A second lesson of the tunnel episode, then, was that the term "peace process" was itself a fraud. It did not mean what the words normally signified: negotiations aiming at a yet-to-be-hammered-out agreement between parties previously at war. Rather, it was a deceptive euphemism for steady Israeli movement toward a predetermined end, which was the turnover of the West Bank and Gaza to a new Palestinian state. Any slowing of the pace for any reason was condemned as "foot-dragging," and even the slightest indication from the Israeli side that the Palestinians would not get everything they wanted was interpreted as contrary to the spirit of the peace process and a provocation that justified them in once again picking up the gun.

. . . . .

Which brings us to the third lesson yielded by the tunnel episode. Among the great achievements to which enthusiasts of Oslo and its aftermath proudly pointed was that Israel was becoming increasingly less isolated. Before Oslo, cooed the doves, Israel's only friend of any consequence had been the United States; and within the Arab world, only Egypt had been willing to make peace with the Jewish state, and only a "cold peace" at that. Now, however, Israel was ceasing to be a pariah. Even at the United Nations, which had for so long been viciously hostile, the atmosphere had grown warmer; and, more telling still, commercial and other relations were being established with some of the more moderate Arab states.

All true; but what the tunnel episode revealed was that every bit of this good will would vanish the instant Israel made a single false move—that is, a move that the Palestinians declared to be false. At the UN, a Security Council resolution condemning Israel over the tunnel incident passed by a vote of 14-0, with the United States under Bill Clinton—in a preview of what he would do in October of this year—abstaining when it might have exercised its veto.

As for the Arab world, even the states that had traditionally been least hostile to Israel now ganged up on it. The dovish *Jerusalem Report* summed up the situation:

> King Hassan of Morocco ... ordered a complete freeze on his government's relations with Israel.... The president of Tunis ... followed suit and ordered formal contacts between his country and the Netanyahu government severed. Oil-rich Qatar ... postponed the opening of [its] trade office in Israel and called off direct meetings with Israeli officials.

This report was supposed to prove that Netanyahu had done great damage to Israel. But what it inadvertently exposed was that any warming trend among the Arabs would turn to solid ice the moment they suspected that Israel might be stalling in its journey toward the only acceptable conclusion of the "peace process": complete withdrawal (with minor modifications) to the borders of 1967 and the recognition of a Palestinian state in the territories Israel had conquered in the Six-Day war of that year.

Even this, however, would not suffice—and here we arrive at the fourth lesson of the tunnel episode. In a moment of candor, Arafat himself admitted that he had started the miniwar over the tunnel to fight against "the Judaization of Jerusalem." The only acceptable "peace package," in other words, had to be stuffed with the gift of East Jerusalem as the capital of the new Palestinian state. No Jerusalem, no deal.

To this a codicil was added, and it represents the fifth and final lesson to emerge from the tunnel episode. If Israel would not deliver the right "peace package," the alternative was another war—a war not between Israel and the Palestinians alone but between Israel and the whole Arab world. Even Egypt, which had signed a peace treaty with Israel years earlier, and Jordan, which had just done the same, would participate in this war.

That a major war was in the minds of the Arab leaders became—or should have become—obvious during one of those hastily arranged meetings that Bill Clinton loves to call whenever another crisis erupts between Israel and the Palestinians. (Arafat, astoundingly, holds the record for the number of visits with Clinton by foreign leaders.) At the meeting to resolve the tunnel crisis, the late King Hussein of Jordan, that famous moderate, excoriated Netanyahu for having dragged the region to "the edge of the abyss." In spelling out his meaning a few days later, he had the impudence to bring up the Iraqi missile attacks on Israel during the Gulf war, when he himself had sided with Saddam Hussein to the point of providing targeting guidance to Iraqi controllers as their missiles—with the blessing of the "little king"—flew over Jordanian air space.

Having been forgiven, as he always was no matter what he did, thus spake King Hussein: "In the current situation, if we do not stride strongly forward to achieve peace, everything imaginable can happen, including a revival of 1991 when Netanyahu wore his gas mask on television. The alternative to peace is more awful than we can imagine."

And what of that other famous moderate, the Egyptian president Hosni Mubarak? Since he had recently described Israel as "a knife plunged into the nations of this region"—note the words "nations of this region" rather than "Palestinians"—it is not surprising that Mubarak should have refused to attend the White House meeting at all. Coupled with this refusal was a warning that the Palestinians would soon take up arms again, and through his former military chief of staff Mubarak also warned that Egypt and the other Arab states would be ready to rush into the battle with every expectation of victory: "The combined weaponry of the Arab states today exceeds that of Israel. If all these weapons were directed against Israel, the Arab states could defeat Israel."

Then we come to Hafez al-Assad, the late president of Syria. No one ever confused him with a moderate, but in spite of the "strategic decision for peace" he had supposedly made, Assad decided a few weeks after the White House summit that Israel was—in the words of one of his spokesmen—"preparing the region for a new war," and that the Arabs now had "to consider options other than the peace process." Note again that the war for which preparations had to be made was not between Israel and the Palestinians alone, but between Israel and the *Arabs*.

· · · · ·

When Ehud Barak of the Labor party, defeating the by-now much-battered Netanyahu, became prime minister of Israel in 1999, he was widely hailed as a disciple of Rabin who would put his martyred predecessor's policies back on track. And so he did—with a veritable vengeance. No one could accuse *him* of "dragging his feet" or of insisting on "reciprocity," and the only defect he could find in the Oslo "peace process" was that it was being implemented too slowly. In this he seemed to resemble Peres more than Rabin, raring to go, chafing at the bit, hardly able to wait before satisfying all Palestinian demands as quickly as possible—and to make a deal with Syria while he was at it. To judge both from Barak's statements and his behavior, the tunnel war might never have happened, so apparently oblivious was he of the lessons it had taught about the realities of Israel's situation and the intentions of the Arab world.

Accordingly, Barak cut immediately to the chase. Among the first things he did was to pledge an early withdrawal of Israeli troops from the security zone in Lebanon that, with the aid of local militiamen, they had been policing since 1982 in order to protect northern Israel from terrorist and other attacks by the Hezbollah—a pledge that he subsequently carried out under fire and ahead of his one-year schedule. Barak also indicated that he was willing to return virtually the whole of the Golan Heights to Syria in exchange for a peace treaty. And he declared himself ready to skip the type of interim steps and phased agreements with the Palestinians that were the progeny of Oslo. What he preferred was to discuss the terms of a final settlement. Which meant that precisely the *most* difficult problems—the status of Jerusalem, and what should be done about the Palestinians who had fled in 1948 and so many of whose descendants were still living in squalid refugee camps throughout the region—would be tackled now, and not (as formerly contemplated) be deferred to some later date when greater trust would presumably have developed between the parties.

So far did Barak's proposals go that in time they would even arouse the ire of Rabin's widow, Leah, who had previously anointed the new prime minister as her late husband's legitimate heir. But what had once been unthinkable, and unsayable even by Rabin and Peres, was by now so taken for granted that it practically went without saying at all: a sovereign Palestinian state would soon be established. The only remaining question was whether this would be delayed until its exact boundaries, the location of its capital, and a few other matters had been determined by negotiations with Israel, or whether Arafat would make good on his repeated threat to bring it into being unilaterally.

While letting slip one deadline after another for acting on this threat, Arafat found himself on the receiving end of offers that went beyond anything ever contemplated by any previous Israeli government. Although one would never have known this from the tenor of most reporting in the media, and certainly not from Palestinian propaganda about the onerous Israeli "occupation," 98 percent of the Palestinians in the territories were already living under the rule of the PA. With the Israeli army having withdrawn from most of those territories before he assumed office, Barak now proposed to turn over virtually all the rest to the new Palestinian state (with Israel left holding, on grounds of military security, only a small and largely unpopulated area). Barak even offered to leave the Jordan Valley, which had once been regarded by all sides in Israel as essential to the country's security.

Nor was this all. Barak—again conceding what had recently been unthinkable—would accept certain districts in East Jerusalem as the capital of the new state of Palestine, while turning over the holy places to international supervision. Finally, and in some ways most radically of all, he was willing to grant the "right of return" to some 100,000 Palestinian refugees and compensate the remainder with money that Clinton (a little too confidently) assured him would be forthcoming from America.

All this might have been too much even for Rabin's widow, but it was not enough for Yasir Arafat. He demanded a larger share of Jerusalem and complete control over the Temple Mount, the site of the al-Aqsa mosque and the Dome of the Rock (the latter repeatedly and mistakenly described in the media as a mosque). Under no circumstances would he entertain Barak's suggestion that a small sector of the Temple Mount be reserved for a synagogue. The Temple Mount belonged to Allah, and what Barak wanted was nothing less than a desecration and a blasphemy.

And so the stage was set for a replay of the tunnel war, one that would be bigger and more portentous than its predecessor. But before we can grasp what really happened, we must again clear the smoke away from several points that have—in the usual fashion of reporting on clashes between Israel and the Palestinians—been obscured either through ignorance or deliberate misrepresentation.

· · · · ·

For a start, take the issue of the Temple Mount itself. Because there is a place called Mount Zion in Jerusalem, many people are under the impression that *it* is the site from which—as Jews (quoting the prophet Isaiah) proclaim whenever they remove the Torah scroll from the ark of a synagogue—the law and the word of God will go forth unto the nations. But the Zion of this prophecy-turned-prayer is not Mount Zion. It is the Temple Mount, so named precisely because King Solomon built his Temple there in the 10th century B.C.E.; and when, about a century after the destruction of that Temple by Babylonian invaders in 586 B.C.E., a second one was built, it too was located on the same site until being destroyed by the Romans in 70 C.E.* And as if this were not enough, Jewish tradition also identifies the Temple Mount as the Mount Moriah of the Bible where God tested Abraham by commanding him to sacrifice his son Isaac and then stayed his hand.

In other words, the Temple Mount is the holiest of Jewish holy places, and has been so for at least 3,000 years—which means that the Jewish claim on it goes back over 1,500 years before there even was an Islam. Furthermore, whereas Jerusalem has been the center of Judaism since King David made his capital there in the 10th century B.C.E., the city is, by the Muslims' own reckoning, only the third holiest place in their religion. When Muslims pray, they do not face Jerusalem, as Jews do; they face Mecca.

In short, there is nothing in the least outrageous about the idea that the Temple Mount belongs to the Jews, though it was not even accessible to them during the years before 1967 when the Jordanians occupied Jerusalem. But in his notorious visit on September 28, Sharon was not even demanding that Israel physically take over the Temple Mount (which under Israeli sovereignty had long been administered by the Muslim authorities); all he was doing, as leader of the Likud opposition, was putting Barak *and* Arafat on notice that he would work against any agreement curtailing the right of any Jew to visit the Temple Mount whenever he wished.

---

*The Western Wall is a section of the retaining wall of the Second Temple. Though never part of the Temple Mount as such, it has nevertheless been sanctified by proximity as well as by the protective function it once served.

It is Arafat who has made it necessary to emphasize what ought to be a self-evident point. For just as much of the Arab world has joined the chorus of Holocaust deniers in the West, so with comparable gall does Arafat go around declaring that "Jerusalem is not a Jewish city, despite the biblical myth planted in some minds"; that the two Temples never stood on the Temple Mount; and that the Western Wall is not a Jewish but "a Muslim shrine."

Some think that in going to the Temple Mount, Sharon was also trying to upstage his main rival for leadership of Likud, the politically resurgent Netanyahu. But even if that is true, what difference would it make to the assignment of blame for the outbreak of violence by the Palestinians in response to a peaceful walk around the site—a walk, we have since learned, that a day earlier had been duly cleared with the head of PA security? In retrospect, considering how unlikely it is that the head of PA security was ignorant of the plan for an outbreak, and in the light of reports that he himself had a hand in fomenting the riots, one wonders whether he was setting Sharon up by assuring him that there would be no problem if he were to visit the Temple Mount.

· · · · ·

Be that as it may, we have also since learned that preparations for violence were already being made immediately before and during the summit between Arafat and Barak that Clinton had convened in July at Camp David. If, said a high-ranking PA security official quoted in an Israeli Arab magazine, the summit were to fail from the Palestinian point of view, a new *intifada* would follow:

> The Palestinian people are in a state of emergency against the failure of the Camp David summit. If the situation explodes they are ready for the next bloody battle against the Israeli occupation. The next *intifada* will be ... more violent than the first one especially since the Palestinian people [now] possess weapons allowing them to defend themselves in a confrontation with the Israeli army.*

---

*For this and most of the other quotations that follow from Arabic-language sources, I am indebted to the invaluable work of the Middle East Media Research Institute (MEMRI). Under the leadership of Yigal Carmon, a former adviser on counterterrorism to both Yitzhak Shamir and Yitzhak Rabin, MEMRI monitors the Palestinian media, as well as the press of other Arab nations, and issues daily translations into English of significant articles and interviews that are rarely, if ever, noticed in Western coverage of the Middle East. MEMRI's website is at www.memri.org.

Regarding those weapons, this PA official then went on a week later (that is, *two full months* before Sharon would set foot on the Temple Mount) to inform the same magazine that

> Popular recruitment in the PA territories has increased greatly and the popular Palestinian army has been established.... Weapons have already been distributed to citizens by the PA, which supervises training and preparation for a potential confrontation with occupation forces.

Finally, the commander of the PA police stated that "the Palestinian police will be leading, together with all other noble sons of the Palestinian people, when the hour of confrontation arrives."

When the summit did in fact fail, and when Clinton was perceived as blaming Arafat for turning down Barak's terms, which seemed even to the President extraordinarily generous, rocks and Molotov cocktails were at the ready, and the militiamen (or Tanzim) of Fatah, Arafat's own faction within the PLO, were lying in wait for an order from him to go on a rampage. In seizing on Sharon's visit as the right moment for such a signal, Arafat must have calculated that even though, as the leader of the Likud party, Sharon held no office within the Labor government, as a right-winger he was likely to be held responsible for the violence, exactly in the way the right-wing Netanyahu had been for the miniwar over the tunnel. And so it came about.

Despite the assurances of the PA security chief, violent disturbances broke out just moments after Sharon left the area. The Palestinian media and Muslim preachers immediately began spreading the word that al-Aqsa was in danger. The next day, September 29, in a sermon at the mosque itself, the mullah accused Sharon of the "slighting of Muslims' holy place," and asked: "Who will forbid the Jews from committing massacres today in al-Aqsa mosque?" The same kind of false, hysterical, and inflammatory rhetoric concerning al-Aqsa had been spewed forth over the tunnel, and it worked even more effectively in this latest battle against "the Judaization of Jerusalem."

So, too, did the tactic of taking casualties for the TV cameras to photograph. Echoing Arafat's statement of 1996 that "our blood is cheap for Jerusalem," the director general of the PA information ministry now wrote: "The only way to impose our conditions is inevitably through our blood. Had it not been for this blood, the world would never have been interested in us." Hence it was the "national duty" of the Palestinians to "continue to sacrifice our martyrs."

Palestinian and other Arabs had a lot of takers both in Israel and in the rest of the world for their assertion that it was Sharon who had provoked this latest outbreak of violence. But Barak was not among them. Partly, no doubt, because he had come to believe that his own political fortunes would be improved if he could persuade a reluctant Sharon to join him in a national-unity government, but also, surely, because he knew what he knew, Barak disagreed with the widespread condemnation of the visit to the Temple Mount. "We hold the Palestinian Authority responsible for the whole round of violence," he told Lally Weymouth in an interview in *Newsweek*.

. . . . .

What then lies ahead? As noted at the outset, it was to some degree because the situation that obtained prior to 1993 had involved Israel in the kind of guerrilla-cum-terrorist warfare it finally could not stomach that Rabin decided to enter into the "peace process" to begin with. Now, there has been a resurgence of precisely that kind of warfare. Will the Israelis be any more able and willing to stomach it this time around?

In trying to answer that question, we have to consider two opposing factors. One is that the Palestinians, as they have boasted, are far better armed than they were before and capable of inflicting more damage than they could in the first round. But as against that consideration, there is the balancing emergence of a new mood in Israel. By making as many concessions as they did—walking, as it were, the extra mile toward peace—and then being rewarded with violence, most Israelis, beginning with Prime Minister Barak himself, seemed to have been convinced for the moment that there was no corresponding desire for peace on the Palestinian side. If so, the delusory hopes that pushed them into the "peace process" and fed it for nearly a decade might give way to a greater readiness to face the grim realities of their own situation.

To illustrate, two examples should suffice. Shlomo Avineri, a professor at the Hebrew University and a former director-general of the foreign ministry, was among the earliest and most influential Israeli proponents of the two-state solution. But he now wrote in the *Jerusalem Post* that, in having persuaded themselves that a compromise with the Palestinians had become possible, he and his fellow doves were caught up in an "illusion":

> Last summer at Camp David, Arafat rejected the most generous offer ever made to a Palestinian leader by an Israeli statesman.... [Then] it suddenly dawned on us that we do not have a partner: only an enemy, who cannot even find a humane word when our people are lynched.... What came out—on the streets, among the

Palestinian elite on CNN—was sheer hatred, and a fundamental rejection of Israel.... [So] now we know: there is no such thing as a Palestinian leadership with whom an agreement can be reached. We are at war.

On a different level of the Israeli social spectrum, there was the mother of three in Jerusalem who was interviewed by the Associated Press. Like Avineri, she had been a supporter of the "peace process" from the start, but this woman (also like Avineri, and like almost all Israelis) was shaken to her toes by the murder and mutilation of two Israeli reservists who had mistakenly driven into Ramallah: "When I saw on television the Palestinian mob that lynched those two Israeli soldiers, I realized they don't want peace with us. There was such hatred in their eyes. They just want us out of the Middle East."

They just want us out of the Middle East. This is a fundamental truth that all Israelis once knew but that many either forgot or began to deny. Now they seemed to be remembering and relearning it; and in the nick of time. For they will need every ounce of spiritual and moral strength at their disposal to cope with the reality to which so many of them blinded themselves for so long.

That reality, to say it yet one more time, is summed up in the word—*jihad*—that Arafat and so many other Arabs have never stopped invoking when speaking among themselves in their own language. On those occasions, they have never bothered to pretend that the formula for peace is a "two-state solution." Nor have they had to pretend that this formula represents anything more than a temporary abandonment of the direct military action that failed in five previous wars, or a shift to a "strategy of stages" that will more circuitously and cunningly head toward the same ultimate consummation in the destruction of the Jewish state. Indeed, at this very moment, Palestinian and other Arab children are studying textbooks containing maps on which (as in the Egyptian proposals for regional economic development at the conference in Morocco) Israel is nowhere to be found. It is the making of such maps into a real picture of the Middle East that—to judge by their own words and deeds—remains the true objective of overwhelming numbers of Palestinians and their Arab brothers. Listen to a leading Egyptian cleric—and bear in mind that to him "occupied Palestine" embraces the whole state of Israel:

> *Jihad* in the path of Allah is a virtue that binds Muslims at all times, and it is an obligation on everyone who is able to carry it out....

Jihad to confront the enemy and liberate the pillaged land is an obligation on Muslims.... This is what our brothers are now doing in occupied Palestine.

When evidence was presented at his trial in Jerusalem that Adolf Eichmann, the former Nazi officer in charge of transporting the Jews of Europe to the death camps, had once said he would "die happy" because he had sent five million "enemies of the Reich" (i.e., Jews) to their graves, Hannah Arendt dismissed this as "sheer rodomontade." Is the exhortation to *jihad* by so many Arabs, from Arafat to the likes of this Egyptian cleric, sheer rodomontade? There is no more reason to think so than there was in the case of Eichmann.

A few years ago, Fouad Ajami of Johns Hopkins produced what may still be the best short article ever published on sentiment toward Israel within the Arab world—and perhaps the only such honest account by any Arab anywhere. "There has been no discernible change in the Arab attitudes toward Israel," he maintained in *U.S. News & World Report,* and went on to describe the genuine state of affairs in the world from which he himself (a Lebanese Christian by birth and upbringing) had come to the United States:

> The great refusal [to accept Israel] persists. A foul wind ... blows in that "Arab street" of ordinary men and women, among the intellectuals and the writers, and in the professional syndicates. The force of this refusal can be seen in the press of the governments and of the oppositionists, among the secularists and the Islamists alike, in countries that have concluded diplomatic agreements with Israel and those that haven't.

Only a few weeks ago, with the new *intifada* raging, Ajami observed that his original assessment still held:

> The circle of enmity surrounding Israel has not been breached— the young boys in the West Bank displayed their great refusal to come to terms with Israel's statehood; so did the demonstrators in Arab lands, from North Africa to the Persian Gulf, whose rulers had staked a claim to moderation. Diplomacy was shown to be a pretense and a veneer.

Some of us even thought for a while that this new *intifada* might be the start of the big war—the war with missiles and tanks and heavy artillery rather than rocks and gasoline bombs and rifles—we had always feared would result from the "peace process." Arafat and his subordinates seem to have thought so, too. "Palestinian blood [will] mix with Arab blood in defense of the legitimate rights of our people," Arafat announced on October 8 in Tunis. Another PA official was more specific:

> The continuation of the Palestinian bloodshed might push part of the Arab military to carry out military operations against Israel.... Also, Palestinian bloodshed will push parts of the Arab countries to launch missiles against Israel as the president of Iraq did in 1991.

Then, the very next day, Saddam Hussein himself actually threatened to take the lead in "putting an end to Zionism," or even to go it alone if the other Arab states held back.

Fortunately for Israel, and the world, most of the Arab states were not yet ready to engage Israel militarily. In late October, sixteen of the 22 member states of the Arab League met in Cairo to decide on what they should do about the current crisis. But while blasting Israel for its "crimes" and resolving to cut off relations of various kinds with it, they stopped so far short of declaring "holy war" that the Libyan delegates walked out in disgust at this "feeble" response, and the Iraqis were if anything even more contemptuous.

Meanwhile, demonstrations were being held all over the Arab world, demanding *jihad* and denouncing the Arab governments for being "too soft on Israel." For the time being, then, what Ajami calls "the peace of kings and pharaohs" still prevails. But how long can it withstand the pressures for war from every sector of Arab society?

. . . . .

As long, I would say, as the kings and pharaohs of the contemporary Middle East are deterred by the fear of Israel's armed might and the willingness of Israel to use it if necessary. About seven years ago, when the "peace process" was just getting under way, I gave a lecture in Jerusalem predicting that this process would lead not to peace but to another major war. During the question period, a leading dove amazed the audience by expressing total agreement with me. But, he added, "unless we convince our sons that we are doing everything possible to make peace, they will jump out of their tanks when the war comes."

He may have been right. From which one might conclude that the "peace process" was an exercise that had to be undergone if only to expose the main illusions behind it. Those illusions went beyond the idea that a compromise with the Palestinians had become possible. They extended to the notion that Israel bore at least as much blame for the Arab war against it as the Arabs did; that, if Israel were to reconcile itself to the establishment of a Palestinian state, the Arab world would reconcile itself to a Jewish one; and that it was in Israel's unilateral power to realize this vision of peaceful coexistence.

But the dream of wiping Israel off the map was not put into Arab heads by anything Israel did except enter into existence, and therefore it could not be canceled by anything Israel did except disappear. Neither the Palestinians nor their Arab brothers would remain satisfied with a Palestinian state living alongside Israel; what they wanted was a Palestinian state that would swallow up the Jewish state. And the only peace that could be achieved through the unilateral power of Israel was the peace of the grave that committing suicide would bring.

If they are finally learning all this, the sons of the older Israelis who had to relearn it themselves will not "jump out of their tanks" when the next major war erupts. But that alone could help avert such a war, by deterring the Arabs who had begun to believe, and not without good cause, that Israel was growing soft and would soon be ripe for the plucking. A strong Israel—strong not only in weaponry but in resolve and courage and the readiness to do whatever might be necessary to prevent the worst—could fend off the *jihad* that might otherwise be all but inevitable.

It could also fend off what the Israeli defense analyst Ze'ev Schiff thinks is the strategy for "bringing Israel to its knees" that Arafat has hit upon as a fallback or a prelude to *jihad*. This, according to Schiff, is "ongoing, low-level war that combines massive terrorism, guerrilla warfare, and the international media. . . . This strategy will expose Israel's Achilles' heel: an extreme sensitivity to loss of life and the kidnapping of its soldiers."

No corresponding sensitivity undermines the Palestinians. In an exceptionally objective piece, Jack Kelley of *USA Today,* describing a firefight in Ramallah in October, reported that "As darkness moves in, many of the television journalists, who had been filming on the Palestinian side . . . pack up their gear and leave. So do the youths." Kelley then, with no hint of a personal demurrer, quoted an Israeli officer on the spot: "The kids only want to die when the TV cameras are on so they can get the sympathy of the world. They'll be back tomorrow, as soon as the media arrive."

But why, asked Mark Helprin in his column in the online *Opinion Journal* of the *Wall Street Journal,* do not the Israelis—understanding full well that every youthful Palestinian casualty hurts them and strengthens Arafat in "the battle of public opinion"—use less lethal methods of riot control? To his own question, Helprin returned this answer:

> Because they cannot. . . . Every day, from the periphery and from within the rock-throwing and gasoline-bomb-tossing crowds,

automatic fire is directed at the Israelis, who are thus forced to use small-unit tactics and keep themselves dispersed. The Israelis cannot close with the crowds, using shields and batons, because to do so they would need to concentrate hundreds or perhaps thousands of men in these battles, soldiers who in such antiquated formations would be a vulnerable and irresistible target.

In sum, up to that point in the new *intifada*, the Israelis were doing what they had to do. Palestinian propagandists were having a field day proclaiming that the Israelis were "massacring . . . innocent children." But the complaint of many Israelis was that the army had been showing too much restraint on occasions like the gunfire attacks on a Jewish neighborhood within Jerusalem itself. On the other hand, as the officer whom Kelley accompanied during the battle that day said to him, with regret but without apology, and without the sense of guilt that had turned round one of the *intifada* into a victory for the Palestinians: "Since the first day, every time we shoot a person, it is because they . . . shot at us first. You don't want to shoot civilians and kids. On the other hand, you don't want your soldiers on the frontlines to be killed."

· · · · ·

Writing in late October 2000, I have no idea of what either Barak or Arafat will do in the next few weeks, or what might be triggered by this or that step one or the other might take. One such step by the Israelis might be toward "separation," about which the new *intifada* unleashed so much talk in Israel.

Why, it was said, could Israel not unilaterally draw its own borders and leave Arafat to his own devices on the other side, relying on deterrence to protect the country from terrorist or other forms of aggression? This, for Israel, would be a substitute for a negotiated settlement, still acceding to the birth of a Palestinian state though backing away from Barak's former willingness to recognize neighborhoods in East Jerusalem as its capital. (Amid all this talk about unilateral moves by Israel, Barak also warned the Palestinians that if *they* were to issue a unilateral declaration of statehood, he would annex parts of the West Bank. To which Arafat countered with a threat of an even wider state of war.)

Even at this early date, however, it can safely be predicted that no unilateral actions by Israel such as are simplistically contemplated by the repentant Shlomo Avineri and others would bring about what most Israelis envisage as "separation." As Ephraim Sneh, Israel's deputy minister of defense, commented to the *New York Times:* "People say, 'I don't want to see anymore the Palestinians,' ... but it doesn't work that way. The interdependence of the economies is such that you can't just detach them mechanically. We share water, electricity, electromagnetic space. It's not so simple."

Shlomo Gazit, a former general and government official, also quoted by the *Times,* brought up other difficulties attendant upon a real separation: "It means annexing the West Bank with its settlers, but also evacuating others." Gazit could not bring himself to state clearly, or possibly even to contemplate, that "evacuating others" might involve not only Palestinians in the West Bank but also Arab citizens of Israel, together with non-Israeli Palestinians who live in East Jerusalem. It is hard to imagine the Israelis undertaking so brutal an act of "ethnic cleansing," and still harder to suppose that the West would allow them to carry it through even if they made the attempt.

The upshot is that under present circumstances, there are no good alternatives, only choices that may be less bad than others. Still, present circumstances will not last forever. History could yet hit the Middle East with one of those unexpected surprises in which it specializes (such as the sudden collapse of the Soviet Union) and that would for the first time create a willingness among the Arabs to make their own inner peace with the permanent presence of a sovereign Jewish state in "their" part of the world. But unless and until such a change of heart cancels out "the great refusal," the change of heart in Israel that the new *intifada* seemed to have wrought in certain quarters will have to remain firm against the seductive temptations of a return to some new form of Oslo. It will also have to remain firm against the loudly intransigent insistence in other quarters that the "peace process" can and must be revived.

It is from those other quarters that the "post-Zionist" virus of self-hatred has spread in recent years, sapping the national morale and the old-time national resolve. To regain what they have lost, the Israelis will have to shake off this pathology once and for all; they will have to rely credibly once again on the deterrent effect of their military might; they will have to renew their conviction that their country has an absolute right to exist where it exists; and they will have to recapture the well-earned and well-deserved pride they used to feel in the miracle of that existence and the wondrous accomplishments that have followed from the Jewish return to Zion.

—*December 2000*

Ruth R. Wisse

On Ignoring Anti-Semitism

"Hitler is dead." In April 1945, a headline containing those three words might have heralded the collapse of Nazi Germany and the beginning of the end of World War II. In May 2002, appearing on the cover of the *New Republic*, the same words ridiculed the "ethnic panic of the Jews." In the lead essay, Leon Wieseltier, the magazine's literary editor, charged that American Jews, spooked by the history of Jewish persecution, were stoking unwarranted and apocalyptic fears by comparing the Arab war against Israel with Hitler's earlier war against the Jews. The first requirement of security, he advised his readers, was not to imagine the worst on the basis of historical precedent but to "see clearly" the situation of the present.

The article provoked a number of rebuttals, and also a number of strong defenses. In the words of the historian Tony Judt, one of its defenders, Wieseltier had "elegantly dissected those frissons of existential angst in which some in the American Jewish community are wont to indulge themselves." Wieseltier's call for clarity is thus as good a starting point as any to ask whether we have made much progress since Hitler in understanding the political phenomenon that he represented.

Not that Hitler was by any means the first politician in Europe to fulminate against the Jews; but it is certainly true that no one before him had ever organized so radical a political platform. Still, during the years that he was consolidating his power, the majority of European Jews, unwilling or unable to fathom what his policy signified, or how it would be implemented, did not seem to fear him *sufficiently*. Rather than manifesting the kind of "ethnic panic" that Wieseltier ascribes to their

American coreligionists today, they stand retrospectively accused by many historians of having minimized or ignored Hitler's menace until it was too late. Indeed, the same accusation has been extended to that generation's American Jews as well, who have been reproached for failing either to recognize the danger in time or to do what they could to help their beleaguered coreligionists.

We have, then, a variety of possibilities. It could be that the "panic" of today's Jews is an overcompensation for past negligence. It could be, contrarily, that the myopic Jews of the 1930s have finally been blessed with perfect vision, and that yesterday's Mister Magoo has become today's Ted Williams. Or it could simply be, as Wieseltier would have it, that Nazi anti-Semitism is so different in kind from the Arab variety that what would have been a proper response in the former case is improper in the latter. Since Wieseltier's article calls into question "the new recognition of the *reality* of anti-Semitism" (emphasis added), it would help to establish whether there is, today, a major threat to the Jewish people.

· · · · ·

The Arab war against Israel has been going on since before the Jewish state was established in 1948, but lately there have been significant changes in its scope, its nature, and the degree of international support it enjoys. Until fairly recently, Arab rulers who exerted despotic or autocratic control over their populations kept the lid on armed aggression issuing from their territory. Now, however, radical ideologies and terrorist tactics against Israeli Jews seem to be dominating Arab politics as never before, while in liberal and academic circles everywhere in the West, as well as in the chancelleries of Europe, blame for this state of affairs has fallen largely on the state of Israel itself.

The avant-garde of anti-Israel radicalism has long been the Palestine Liberation Organization (PLO), the bastard offspring of the Arab world's insistence that the Palestinian people be kept demonstrably homeless as permanent evidence of Jewish culpability. The terrorist groups constituting the PLO, and their multiplying rivals, were given unique license by their fellow Arabs to intimidate, to extort, and to kill. Over time, they served their handlers superbly well, doing far greater harm to Israel than all the Arab military assaults combined.

Unlike the Germans who unleashed their war against the Jews under cover of a wider European conflict, the Arab nations, through the PLO, placed the destruction of Israel explicitly at the heart of their mission.

The PLO's charter, a public document, defines the Jews as "not a people with an independent identity," branding them as colonial occupiers of land that belongs eternally to the Palestinian people, and their state as an illegitimate "entity" that needs to be eliminated. On these grounds, the PLO not only claimed the moral right to kill Jews but turned their murder into a sacred cause. And this, as the historian Michael Oren has pointed out, does mark one difference between German and Arab anti-Semitism, albeit a difference suggesting that the Arab variety is worse:

> For all the kudos discreetly given SS killers by the regime, Nazi Germany never publicly lionized them, never plastered their pictures on the streets, or openly encouraged children to emulate them. That kind of adoration for mass murderers can only be found, in abundance, among the Palestinians.

In the light of this adoration, indeed, it has become more and more difficult to maintain the distinction between anti-Semitism and anti-Zionism, with the latter defined as "merely" a political-territorial objection to the state of Israel as the homeland of the Jewish people. Rather, contemporary anti-Zionism has absorbed all the stereotypes and foundational texts of fascist and Soviet anti-Semitism and applied them to the Middle East. Every stratum of Arab society, from top to bottom, has been nourished on the myth of Israel's illegitimacy, and has been encouraged to express its loyalties through aggressive hostility to the Jewish people and its land.

The dissemination of anti-Jewish propaganda by and within Arab and Muslim societies has lately been swifter than the spread of the Internet. As anyone can discover by punching in the relevant keywords in any major library system, Arabic translations of all the major works of European anti-Semitism have been supplemented by an immense new body of original literature defaming Israel and the Jews. As long ago as 1986, Bernard Lewis could write in *Commentary* that certain Arab countries were the only places in the world "where hard-core, Nazi-style anti-Semitism is publicly and officially endorsed and propagated." Since then, Arab propagandists have been working hard to expand and revitalize the tradition. The sincerity and the steadfastness of this genocidal hostility, proliferating through the press, the visual media, literature, and the schools, are much greater in Arab lands than they ever were in pre-Hitler Europe—which had, after all, a contrary liberal tradition and at least the rudiments of a modern democratic culture. And now, thanks in part to Muslim immigrants, this same hostility has found its way back to the heartland of the very Europe where it originated.

Without citing all the other evidence that anti-Jewish politics is visibly on the rise in Europe, and even in scattered precincts in the United States,* I would therefore suggest that, on the question of the threat itself, Wieseltier has things backward. So obvious is this threat that we should ask why the reality had to wait *so long* for its "new recognition." But there is an answer to this question as well, and it leads directly to the real gravamen of Wieseltier's article.

· · · · ·

Palestinian bombings inside Israel and political/diplomatic assaults against the state's right to exist escalated dramatically after September 2000, when Yasir Arafat, unleashing the very kind of violence that under the Oslo accords he had solemnly undertaken to quell, launched the second Palestinian *intifada*. The first *intifada*, between 1987 and 1993, had claimed 160 Israeli lives. The second killed more than three times as many in twenty months, with thousands of wounded as a result of the explosives that had replaced the knives and stones that were the earlier weapons of choice.

But it was not until a year after the terrorist outbreaks in Israel that the American media and a significant proportion of American Jewry began to air anxieties about anti-Semitism. The reason clearly had to do with an intervening event: namely, September 11. President Bush set a new tone for the nation when he spoke before Congress of "a country awakened to danger and called to defend freedom." Although the president drew no analogy between the unprovoked assault on America and escalating Arab attacks against Israeli Jews, it was then that many observers began to think harder about the correspondence between the two types of terror.

At a Washington rally for Israel in April of 2002, said to be the largest pro-Israel gathering ever held in the United States, most speakers, Jewish and non-Jewish alike, linked solidarity with Israel to America's war on terror. Representing the government of Israel, Deputy Prime Minister Natan Sharansky saluted the president's determination to wage

---

*The evidence has been abundantly documented. In *Commentary*, see, for example, Hillel Halkin, "The Return of Anti-Semitism" (February 2002); Gabriel Schoenfeld, "Israel and the Anti-Semites" (June 2002); and Michel Gurfinkiel, "France's Jewish Problem" (July–August 2002).

a global battle against a common enemy. William J. Bennett, who in the wake of 9/11 had founded an organization called Americans for Victory Over Terrorism, pointed to the Holocaust Museum just a few blocks away and said: "What we are seeing today, what Israel is feeling today, was not supposed to happen again." Just as the attack on America had triggered memories of Pearl Harbor, the atrocities in Israel had begun to evoke the mass murders of European Jewry.

Drawing this analogy most insistently was the journalist and critic Ron Rosenbaum, who warned in the *New York Observer* of a possible "second Holocaust" at the hands of the Arabs should they ever get their hands on weapons of mass destruction. As for the origin of that ominous phrase, "second Holocaust," Rosenbaum traced it back to Philip Roth's 1993 novel, *Operation Shylock,* where a character opines that "Arafat's final solution is the same as Hitler's: extermination," and then urges Israelis to seek safety in a Europe where (in the judgment of this same fictional character) memory of the Holocaust still acts as a bulwark against anti-Semitism.

Roth in 1993 was only toying with this incongruous idea. But Rosenbaum, ten years later, finds Roth's dark fantasy much too optimistic. Europe's own recent outbreaks of anti-Jewish violence persuade him that there is likely to be another attempt to destroy the Jewish people; the question for him "is not 'whether,' but *when.*"

. . . . .

This was the trigger that set off Wieseltier's tirade. He describes the emotional condition of American Jews in the following language:

> The community is sunk in excitability, in the imagination of disaster. There is loss of intellectual control. Death is at every Jewish door. Fear is wild. Reason is derailed. Anxiety is the supreme proof of authenticity. Imprecise and inflammatory analogies abound. Holocaust imagery is everywhere.

As it happens, however, none of the evidence Wieseltier adduces in support of this claim can compete with the claim itself for sheer "excitability." Apart from the Washington rally and a number of other initiatives to advocate Israel's cause and help the victims of terror there, American Jews have been going about their business as usual, manifesting no more visible panic than has been apparent among American citizens in general in the long months after 9/11. When Boston's Jewish Community Relations Council scheduled a rally in May 2001 to coincide with the day of Holocaust remembrance, it drew only about one thousand persons in a city with a quarter of a million Jews. The Jewish press has reported no protest suicides, no burning barricades, not even a canceled vacation.

What, then, explains Wieseltier's own overreaction? Primarily, his objection to any analogizing of European and Arab anti-Semitism would seem to rest less on issues of accuracy than on issues of political utility. In his analysis, invoking the Holocaust is a means of exaggerating the degree of hostility to Israel, and this in turn promotes and justifies a hard line against concessions to the Palestinians. The Nazi analogy, in short, denies the possibility of the "peace process." As Wieseltier writes:

> If you think that the Passover massacre [of 28 Jews in Netanya, Israel] was like Kristallnacht [November 9, 1938, the night of multiple Nazi pogroms against the Jews of Germany], then you must think that there cannot be a political solution to the conflict, and that the Palestinians have no legitimate rights or legitimate claims upon any part of the land, and that there must never be a Palestinian state, and that force is all that will ever avail Israel.

Is Wieseltier right about this? Have the Jews fallen victim to a self-fulfilling prophecy, missing the chance for reconciliation with today's Arabs by insisting on portraying them as yesterday's Nazis? After all, if it were possible to temper Arab hostility by, for example, withdrawing from the disputed territories and encouraging the creation of an Arab Palestinian state, might this not go a long way toward reaching the "peace" that Israel says it has been seeking for many long years? Would not a more forthcoming Jewish policy induce a more receptive Arab policy in turn?

The argument is, alas, all too familiar. It is exactly what produced the Oslo accords, which were designed to lead to the very settlement between Israelis and Palestinians that Wieseltier now envisions as if for the first time. In 1993, a mere nine years ago, the government of Israel invited Yasir Arafat back from exile and transferred administrative power over parts of the disputed territories to a newly appointed Palestinian Authority, expecting it to become the nucleus of an independent Arab state. At that time, the majority of American Jews, Wieseltier assertively among them, hailed the Oslo accords as the road to peace, and many actively lobbied Washington on behalf of the PLO.

The most revealing section of Wieseltier's narrative is thus the one that is missing. No one reading his words about ethnic panic would ever guess that American Jewish celebrants of the peace process had so recently danced the hora in honor of Yasir Arafat on the White House lawn. If there has indeed been a "loss of intellectual control," it is not the one that Wieseltier attributes to today's nervous Jews, but that earlier orgy of hope, based as it was on political calculations that had no proven models and on trust in those who had least earned it.

Wieseltier's failure even to mention a seminal course of events at such extreme odds with his own recitation of recent history suggests less an oversight than a cover-up, an attempt to dodge responsibility for a catastrophically misconceived policy. This is no doubt why some diehard champions of the Oslo "process" have so eagerly seized on his *New Republic* article. "A Bracing Response to Current Hysteria," exulted the columnist Leonard Fein, a founding member of Peace Now and, for over two decades, an enthusiastic promoter of concessions to Arafat who has yet to account for the gap between his predictions and their results. Similar obeisance was paid by Tony Judt, who as an expert in modern European history has repeatedly likened Israel's occupation of the West Bank and Gaza to the French colonization of Algeria and attributed the lack of "credible Palestinian interlocutors" to Israel's own imperious behavior ever since its "hubris-inducing victory" of 1967.

To hold the Jews responsible for the aggression against them, as Judt does; to affirm the peaceful intentions of Arab terrorists, as Fein does; to transform American Jews who recently pimped for the PLO into paranoid hysterics of the Right, as Wieseltier does, is to disfigure political reality beyond recognition. Even if the Jews were the most rotten and misguided people on earth, they do not number 280 million in nationality (let alone one billion in religious affiliation); they have not organized *their* politics around the destruction of twenty-one Arab countries, or trained a generation of suicide bombers to achieve that goal; they have not used the United Nations as a medium for spreading a genocidal ideology around the globe, or their synagogues to preach "death to the Arabs!" Jews did not bomb America in the name of the Torah, or foment anti-Muslim sentiment throughout Europe.

It is certainly true that memories of the Holocaust and invocations of anti-Semitism can be used to justify militancy. They can also be used to justify pacifism, appeasement, and much else besides.

· · · · ·

Which brings us to another point of similarity between "then" and "now"—namely, the agitation among intellectuals not only over the relative significance of political anti-Semitism but also over the uses to which it is allegedly put by Jews themselves. During the 1930s, in the pages of the *New Republic* and elsewhere, a few Jewish intellectuals did track the danger to Jews in Europe and in Palestine, warning, in Ludwig Lewisohn's words, of "the pathological bloodthirstiness of the Nazi anti-Semitic campaign." But Lewisohn's was a minority voice. Most intellectuals urbanely mocked such apocalyptic scenarios, and some of the Jews among them worried lest their coreligionists exploit the whole issue either to further Zionist ambitions in Palestine or to resuscitate an "archaic" Jewish religion.

Today, too, when deadlier forms of anti-Semitism are on the rise, there is massive intellectual resistance to acknowledging the threat, and most political analysts still treat anti-Semitism like a hiccup that will soon give way to regular breathing. Tony Judt writes that the solution to the Israel-Palestine conflict is in plain sight: "Israel exists. The Palestinians and other Arabs will eventually accept this; many already do." He states this conclusion as though it complied with some obvious and inexorable logic, though he might as well be saying that fish will fly because they have fins and will eventually use them.

As a European historian, Judt presumably knows that the Jews of Europe also "existed," and that by 1939 many, if not most, Germans and Austrians "already" accepted their existence. Nevertheless, a dedicated minority of motivated idealists was able to cleanse their countries of the blight within an astonishingly brief period of time. Today's situation is once again arguably worse: one no longer needs to hold mass rallies in Nuremberg to spread the sort of genocidal anti-Jewish propaganda that Egyptian television carries nightly to millions of homes, and preachers who call for holy struggle against Israel are no less committed than Judt is to *their* sense of the inevitable. This is not to say that the Arabs will succeed, any more than that the Germans and Austrians had to succeed; it means that one cannot dismiss anti-Semitism just because it offends one's sense of rational possibility.

Nor, on similar grounds, can one dismiss the possibility of Israel's physical defeat by its Arab and Muslim enemies just because its military power is for the moment unmistakably preponderant. Even greater powers—the United States, for one—have been defeated in palpably unequal contests with lesser but more determined forces. The suicide bomber is a strategic weapon of immense effectiveness for those who feel they have expendable populations; more crucially still, the possession, imminent or actual, of weapons of mass destruction on the part of nations that have already declared their eagerness to use them against the Jewish state changes the regional balance of power definitively. And much as Israel may resemble the United States in other respects, it cannot lose a war to its enemies and necessarily expect to survive. Observers like Judt who point to Israel's defensive capabilities as evidence that it has little to fear from Arab aggression are playing a cruel game of loading up the donkey to see how much it can carry before it collapses.

Judt's views—I focus on them because they may be taken to represent the liberal academic consensus—are interesting in another respect as well: they illustrate how anti-Semitism makes inroads into the liberal mindset. In the years immediately following the creation of Israel, when Arab hostility was expected to give way "eventually" to recognition and acceptance, Israel was the beneficiary of widespread liberal sympathy. The question that Western liberals posed to themselves was: how long would it take before the Arabs came to their senses, relinquished their intransigence, and accepted the reality of a Jewish state? But the paradoxical truth is that the longer and more energetically the Arabs continued their aggression, the costlier it became for others—ideologically as well as politically or militarily—to defend Israel. As the hostility escalated, it turned neutral onlookers not against the aggressors but against their intended victims.

Anti-Semitism offends Western sensibilities because it is not amenable to the kind of reasoning that we believe is innate in human beings. ("Israel exists. The Palestinians and other Arabs will eventually accept this; many already do.") In attacking Jews, the anti-Semite also attacks, by proxy, the Western belief in tolerance, and the freedoms implicit in the Rights of Man. What is a good liberal to do? He knows hostility when he sees it, and he surely does not want it directed at himself. Since confronting Arab anti-Semitism would require confronting the entire Arab world, no less than confronting German anti-Semitism once meant confronting Germany itself, liberals and democrats find it much easier to blame the rising "anger" and "frustration" of the Arabs on *Israel's* intransigence, and to urge Israel to concede to them.

This helps explain why anti-Semitism began to be taken seriously only after the events of September 11. As long as Israel alone was being assaulted by terror and genocidal propaganda, there was little general credence in the idea that its destruction was the point at issue. But when nineteen homicidal Arabs coordinated a sophisticated attack on New York City and the Pentagon, it became harder to deny that something was afoot in the world that transcended "normal" international behavior.

Once one is prepared to acknowledge that a given act of aggression is incommensurate with any offense that may have been given, terms like evil—and anti-Semitism—become permissible.

In the case of the so-called Arab-Israel conflict, to permit the concept of anti-Semitism into the discussion is to acknowledge that the origins of Arab opposition to the Jewish state are to be located in the political culture of the Arabs themselves, and that such opposition can end only if and when that political culture changes. For some supporters of the "peace process," this post–September 11 realization hit with the force of a revelation, and it has led to much salutary rethinking of former positions. For others, alas, it clearly remains a bridge too far.

· · · · ·

"Is the peril 'as great, if not greater' than the peril of the 1930s? I do not see it," writes Leon Wieseltier. The determination not to see it is what has helped make the peril greater.

Consider the case of Michael Kamber, a correspondent for the *Village Voice* who had been reporting from Pakistan just before the disappearance of Daniel Pearl. When Kamber learned of Pearl's kidnapping, he knew for a certainty that Pearl would be murdered, and he was simultaneously shaken by the realization that he himself, being the son of a Jewish father, might just as easily have been the victim. After the murder was confirmed, Kamber filed a belated column, a kind of obituary-report about this land "where anti-Semitism flows as easily as water."

Kamber's column describes Pakistan as a country of 140 million inhabitants, 98 percent Muslim and 75 percent illiterate, all of whom seem to be obsessed with Jewish iniquity:

> In interviews conducted while I was there, government officials would occasionally veer off into long diatribes about the Jews; fundamentalist religious leaders, who educate hundreds of thousands of children in the country's *madrassas,* spoke of little else. In Islamabad ... an elderly mullah responsible for the education of hundreds of youngsters said, "To me [the bombing of the World Trade Center] seems the design of the Jewish lobby. The Jewish lobby wants to pit Islam against Christianity."

As Kamber tells the tale, Pakistan's uneducated populace, having no personal contact with Jews and no training in independent thought, takes its cues from religious and political authorities. Those authorities, unaccustomed to assuming any responsibility for the gross deficiencies of their society, blame the "Jews" for all that they need to explain away. No distinctions are made between Jews and Israel, or indeed between Israel and America—except when it is politically expedient to blame Jews for what is hateful about America, too. In such a climate, writes Kamber, now justifying his decision to hide his own half-Jewish identity, "to admit to being Jewish ... would have been unthinkable."

This is a very significant admission. If the effect of anti-Semitism on Michael Kamber was to inhibit any mention of his Jewish identity to others while he was in Pakistan, its effect on his published journalism, up until this final act of intellectual penance, was to inhibit any mention of a huge and central fact of life in the society he was writing about. Western journalists are paid to report accurately on reality. But the very enormity of anti-Semitism—the fact that in certain parts of the world, politicians and clerics turn abhorrence of Jews into an essential element of *their* reality—creates an inclination to turn away from it, if for no other reason than to retain the good will of the anti-Semites. Thus, in the name of maintaining "access," do American journalists affirm the power of dictators to control our putatively free and open press.

· · · · ·

The problem transcends the case of Michael Kamber, and is again not a new one. When Arthur Hays Sulzberger took control of the *New York Times* in 1935, he seemed far more afraid of having it thought that he ran a "Jewish newspaper" than of the rise of Adolf Hitler. He believed that the threat of anti-Semitism was being used by some Jews as a political cover for a kind of nationalism he abhorred, and he instructed his city editor not to give "too much space" to the efforts of the American Jewish Committee to aid European Jews. When Zionist leaders charged him with failing to present the news impartially, he blamed *them* for turning him from a non-Zionist into an "anti-Zionist." In 1942 he wrote to Rabbi Abba Hillel Silver, chairman of the American Zionist Emergency Council, "I am opposed to Goebbels' tactics whether or not they are confined to Nazi Germany," equating Nazi pressure on the Jews of Germany with Rabbi Silver's pressure on him.

The effect of this was to upend the stated editorial principles of the *Times*. Ostensibly, the family wanted the paper to remain evenhanded and free of bias, by which it meant that it would not allow its own Jewish origins to dictate favorable coverage of the Jews. But in practice the paper carried this to the point of *creating* bias: lest it be accused of favoring the views of one side, it banned all letters to the editor concerning

Hitler in the years that he was coming to power. The Ochs-Sulzbergers also believed that, since the Jews were not a people—the very claim that would one day be enshrined in the charter of the PLO—they were not in need of a Jewish homeland; and this, too, dictated a policy of minimizing anti-Semitism lest, by promoting sympathy for the Jewish plight, the *Times* play into the hands of Zionists.

Although the Ochs-Sulzberger families have since apologized for the "meager coverage" the *Times* gave to the Holocaust as it was unfolding, they have never made a connection between their prejudiced view of Jewish peoplehood and the paper's coverage of world news in general. They thus perpetuate the cycle of parochialization, as if the problem were one that affected only the Jews. But let us suppose for a moment that the publishers of the *New York Times* had acted truly without bias. They would then have responded to Hitler's virulent anti-Semitism as signaling a broader danger to everything precious to themselves and to America. They would have assiduously gathered information about Hitler's program of rearmament, as Winston Churchill tried to do once he became convinced that Hitler was planning to attack the West. They would have drawn daily attention to Germany's abuses of democratic freedoms, its perversion of the law, its abrogation of civil liberties. *And* they would have registered the way that Nazi anti-Semitism cloaked darker anti-democratic purposes behind an enmity directed against the Jews alone.

In brief, had the *Times* been truly neutral in reporting on Hitler's war against the Jews, it would have done a newspaper's proper job of ferreting out the painful but necessary truth about Hitler's war against the West. And the same holds true today, when embarrassment over Jewish causes still governs *Times* coverage of the Middle East and elsewhere, resulting in the same betrayal of professional standards. Had the *Times* been truly neutral and doing its proper job, it would have long since reported in copious detail on the unmistakable signs of growing Arab extremism, an extremism that erupted with spectacular force in the attacks on America of September 11. The reluctance to expose dangers to the Jews suppressed recognition of much that threatened, and still threatens, the West.

Not that the *Times* is alone in this submission to anti-Semitic regimes. The same pattern prevails everywhere today in the academic community, which if anything is even more sensitive than the press to questions of "access." Scholars who work in politically controlled areas of research are rewarded for their sympathies and punished for their criticisms, sometimes in bizarre ways. A professor of ancient Middle Eastern studies has told me that his German colleagues are embarrassed by Arabs in the places where they conduct research who congratulate them on what "they" did to the Jews; they dare not reveal their discomfort lest it prejudice their working relations with local personnel. More often, what begins as passive accommodation becomes active acquiescence. In American universities, the belief that Israel is to blame for the manifold failures of Arab society is by now such a corrupting feature of Middle Eastern studies departments that it has assumed the status of a natural condition, like smog in Los Angeles.

Arab terrorism against Israel has exacerbated this situation without raising a peep from university administrations. Citing the difficulty of securing proper insurance coverage, Harvard recently followed the lead of other American universities in forbidding travel to Israel on Harvard funding. A longstanding archeological dig in Israel had to be abandoned this past summer, and students and faculty had to cancel programs of study and research—this, at the very moment when Harvard is promoting a new commitment to study abroad as a direct way of learning about the world.

Meanwhile, Jewish students attending American-sponsored Arabic programs in Arab countries have been instructed not to reveal their Jewishness and have been provided with false identities: a concession to Arab anti-Semitism that has neither been officially protested by any academic official nor brought to the attention of the American public. Thus do universities casually accede to policies of genocidal hatred, all the while proclaiming their dedication to multiculturalism, pluralism, and anti-discrimination.

· · · · ·

What is it that, in the end, the record of anti-Semitism in Europe suggests? It suggests that the Jews are just the warm-up act to farther-reaching political ambitions. The ease with which Hitler was able to isolate the Jews, disenfranchise them, blackmail them, and begin persecuting them gave him the confidence to expand his conquests; he used the war against the Jews to encourage his followers to flex their muscles.

Anti-Semitism in this sense is not just a generic term for discrimination against Jews or even persecution of Jews. It is not just a means of scapegoating, though it is assuredly that. Nor is it merely a projection onto Jews of the desire to dominate the world. More precisely than any of these, modern anti-Semitism achieved its power as a political instrument through its opposition to liberal democracy itself—as personified by the Jews.

Wilhelm Marr created the League of Anti-Semites in the 1870s to save Germany from what the Jews represented. "We have among us," he said, "a flexible, tenacious, intelligent, foreign tribe that knows how to bring abstract reality into play in many different ways." By "abstract reality," Marr meant everything the Jews could be made to stand for, summarized in the freedoms—religious, political, economic—that undergird modern democratic culture.

Marr's perception of the Jews as incarnations of modernity harnessed ancient prejudice to brand-new fears in societies that were in the process of losing their religious certainties and shedding many aspects of their traditional way of life, including the sense of security provided by autocratic rule. What some Europeans were certain was progress seemed to others a mortal danger, and politicians found that they scored well when they concretized those fears in the image of the ubiquitous Jews—a small, highly adaptive people with arguably the largest image on earth, a people desperately seeking acceptance and targetable at no political cost.

As the Jews were the practice range for anti-democratic and anti-liberal forces in pre-Hitler Europe, so in the second half of the twentieth century the state of Israel took the brunt of the Arab/Muslim war against Western democracy. But, unlike the Jews of Europe, the Jews of Israel toughened under the assault, at least initially. Having acquired the means of self-defense, the Jewish state seemed to grow stronger the more it was attacked. And for a long time, in a reverse dynamic to the process I have been describing, the democratic West as a whole reaped the benefit.

"We may never know how much time Israel bought for us in our decades of negligence," writes William Bennett,

> how many American lives it saved by its long-kept refusal to negotiate with or capitulate to terrorist murder and extortion, its resolve to use every means to track down, confront, and undo those who captured and killed its citizens, its crystalline message of defiance. What we do know is that all over the world, especially in the Soviet gulag and in the prisons of Eastern Europe, captive men gulped great draughts of hope whenever word filtered through of an act of Israeli rescue and punishment: palpable and too rare signals in those dark decades [of the cold war] that evil was not everywhere triumphant, everywhere accommodated, everywhere appeased.

Bennett is surely right that, apart from America itself, Israel still stands as the world's brightest model of national self-liberation based on ideals of individual responsibility and human freedom. Israel's ability to withstand Arab attempts to destroy it in one of the longest and most lopsided wars ever fought serves as an indelible testimony to the strength of democratic culture.

Israel *had* to be gritty; otherwise it would not exist. Nevertheless, in the 1990s it too began to tire under the perpetual assault. In systematic and sustained terrorism, the Arabs discovered the first weapon that really works against a democracy, destroying the trust, the openness, of an open society, and exploiting its precious freedoms to expose its acute vulnerability. Here once again Israel has served as a test case. How well *can* democracies withstand this new form of all-out foreign aggression? We know from the past that the West paid dearly for ignoring Hitler's war against the Jews. One can only hope it will not pay as dearly for having ignored or underestimated for so long the Arab war against Israel and the Jews.

—*October 2002*

Fiamma Nirenstein

Israel's Last Line of Defense

Almost every other day in Israel, it seems, an ordinary waiter, store guard, or bus driver, a twenty-year-old soldier on leave or a fifty-year-old businessman, will seize a terrorist by the arms and, while his explosive belt is still ticking, push him away from the scene, simultaneously shielding bystanders with his own body. He may save dozens of lives, and may forfeit his own in the process. He is a new kind of citizen-defender, and Israel's last line of defense. The Jewish state begets many like him, but he is also a unique type—very much a local product.

As the world knows, the Israeli army and police force have not succeeded in creating a perfectly hermetic seal against the catastrophic terrorism that has hit the country over the past two years. Barriers, checkpoints, and occasional armed forays into the occupied territories function only partially to deflect the lone suicide bomber armed with TNT and hate. Since September 2000, this latest strategic weapon of the Arabs has claimed seven hundred dead and thousands of wounded, in a country of only five million Jewish inhabitants. Everywhere, you see children in wheelchairs and disfigured victims of every age, not to mention the legions of mourners for family members and friends lost in a moment's horror.

All this has changed the face of civil society in Israel, if not the very concept of civilian life itself. For now, the most effective protection against such attacks, aside from periodic incursions into Palestinian cities, is this spontaneous form of civil defense, the only thing that works even when the terrorists from Jenin and Nablus manage to get past the barriers and show up at a café in Tel Aviv or a gas station in the West Bank town of

Ariel. It seems to function naturally, on its own, but in truth it is a very strange phenomenon.

Noon. Emek Refaim, the long street that runs through Jerusalem's German Colony, where bougainvillea and jasmine hang down from the weathered three- and four-story stone buildings. By this hour the daily racket has already reached its height: bus and car horns, mothers yelling at their children not to cross in the middle of the street, the din of rock music blasting from car stereos. In among the old Arab houses and the buildings of the Knights Templar—the cemetery of that medieval Christian order abuts the local supermarket and Burger Ranch, the boughs of its trees extending over the stone walls—are dozens of cafés, upscale wine bars, boutiques, sushi joints, vegetarian and Chinese restaurants. It is impossible to find a place to park; the police who patrol the area seem to have accommodated themselves to the prevailing chaos. The cafés are full; chic girls and boys are out walking their dogs, pretending they are in Tel Aviv. The large glassed-in terrace of Caffit, where people sit sipping cappuccino, completely exposed to the street, is an open invitation to a terrorist.

Our hero, Shlomi Harel, twenty-three and a waiter, is dressed in a white shirt and dark pants. His eyes are puffy. He was up late the night before: being a waiter, a guitarist, a student, and popular with the ladies will do that. He wears a ring in his left ear and two studs in his right, sports a tattoo on his arm and spiky hair. How many lives has this boy saved? Around fifty, but it doesn't show.

"On March 7 at 1:30 I saw a big, fat guy trying to come into the place," he begins. "The guard had already stopped him, but I immediately rushed over. He was sweating a lot. I learned Arabic in the army so I asked him, 'What's your name? What do you want? Where are you going?'—anything to try and identify him, to try to understand. He had this lost look, he was sweating like crazy, and he said, 'I don't speak Hebrew,' in Hebrew. I pushed him into the corner, with the guard's help. I wasn't thinking about anything."

Shlomi has black eyes that his Iraqi-born mother might have painted on him with a paintbrush. He is well mannered, reserved though not exactly shy, and dead tired. He would not let me pay for the coffee I drank at the bar, allowing me instead to admire his method of carrying several cups and saucers in one hand. His coworkers and the bar's owners like to laugh about the great Shlomi, whom the international press has made briefly famous. "Oh, you're the real Shlomi, the one and only, the big hero," they exclaim. Everyone seems to adore him.

A civilian hero is deprived of the incidental benefits, such as they are, of armed combat: the adrenalin rush of anticipated battle, the comforting presence of commanding officers and mates. Instead, he is alone with a bomb, his hands clutching a crazy man bent only on killing and being killed. But Shlomi is very cool. From the instant he shoved the sweating and stammering stranger into a corner, he says, the rest of the event unfolded "like a machine."

"I pulled the backpack off his shoulders and it fell onto the floor. I opened the flap and saw the wires sticking out. It didn't explode because something must have been broken. I was lucky. I picked up the backpack, I was still on automatic pilot, and I took it away while someone else pinned the guy down until the police came. Why did I carry it away? I said to myself, 'If someone has to die, better one than many.' And then I thought, 'If it blows up, we'll all die and I'll really look like an idiot.' But it worked out, and so I became a hero."

When he got home, his mother screamed at him hysterically: "You idiot!" She was lying on the sofa, a glass of water in her hand. "I ran home to warn her before she heard the news on the radio," Shlomi says, "but she raised her hand to slap me, crying about how I could have been killed." He laughs, but his eyes are still a little frightened at the thought of his enraged mother.

Shlomi is something of a Zionist, as Zionists go in real life. He was not a big believer in the Oslo peace process, but he was a little believer in it. He likes the idea of peace, and terrorism scares him more than war. But what is the alternative? Slowly, the dirty cups still balanced in his hand, Shlomi offers his ex-post-facto philosophy: "It went well; that's a sign that life goes on. If the backpack had blown up, I wouldn't be here to talk about it. So," he lapses into Arabic, "*ya-Allah,* we have to live. We move around, we keep going, nonstop. People do their best, they're walking on eggs."

In Gilo, the Jerusalem neighborhood where Shlomi lives, the whole area was under nonstop bombardment a year ago. "When a shell landed in my apartment building it was really scary. There, it was hard to plan: if it hit you, it hit you. But when you can *do* something, things go a lot better." For having done something, Shlomi came into $5,000, a prize from an American philanthropist. "I'm saving it," he says.

· · · · ·

In the old days in Israel, heroism of the Shlomi type was both a national reality and a national ethic. It was part and parcel of the popular ideology of the ruling (mostly left-wing) elites, forged in the crucible of the 1948 war and, even earlier, in the age of the pioneering kibbutzniks and those who made the desert bloom. Driving it was a very anti-heroic dream: namely, the dream of a normal life in one's own land, among one's own people. This brand of valor had nothing to do with the outsized, myth-soaked heroism familiar to us from the propaganda and the statuary of fascism and Communism. It was not about gargantuan deeds by super-human champions; it was family- and home-oriented, and rather inti-mate in tone. It was celebrated in lots of sad and even rueful songs, but few marches.

No doubt to the astonishment of many, it is still alive, having sur-vived even the era of rampant consumerism and the good life. There are still many yuppies in Israel, but their roots would appear to run only a few inches deep. That there are also deep political divisions concerning the country's future goes without saying, some of them reflected in emi-gration figures and even in desertions from army service; but consider-ing the circumstances, these, too, are remarkably contained. As for the post-Zionist interpretation of Israel's history, which replaced the anti-heroic hero with a bellicose, aggressive villain—the mythically rapa-cious, colonialist Jew who first oppressed and then drove out the native Palestinian inhabitants of the land—this mendacious reading likewise seems to have failed to take hold in Israeli consciousness, at least to any-thing like the extent once feared. The classic Zionist personality has assuredly gone through more than a few permutations over the last decades, but the essential character seems to have remained largely intact. Which is perhaps not so surprising, since it is unfortunately grounded in an implacable existential reality.

And it is evidently contagious. On October 12 of this year, Mikhail Sarkisov, a thirty-one-year-old recent immigrant from Turkmenistan, saved the lives of about forty people who were sitting in the Café Tayelet along the oceanfront in Tel Aviv. Sarkisov had been a guard for three weeks, his training having consisted mostly of a stint in the Russian army. He was living in a trailer, without a bathroom or a refrigerator, his only items of luxury being a well-groomed moustache and a gold—well, maybe gold—ring. He had been issued a fake pistol because he did not yet have a gun license. When an Arab terrorist, his jacket bulging, approached, Sarkisov confronted him even as the metal detector started to go off.

"What do you have there?" he asked. "It's mine," the terrorist responded. "I didn't ask whose it was," was Sarkisov's swift retort. "I asked what you have there." As the Palestinian put his hand in his pocket, Sarkisov and two customers threw themselves at him and wrestled him down. "I understood that he was a terrorist because he spoke Hebrew very badly," says Sarkisov in a Hebrew flavored by a strong Turkmenistan accent.

Up until this day, Sarkisov had been treated very poorly by the company that hires guards for places like Tayelet and is linked to the worst criminal elements—whom it also recruits as guards. But now Sarkisov is smiling because they have given him a place to live. Also, he received $5,000 from the same American donor, and Prime Minister Sharon presented him with an honorary plaque. Sarkisov the hero is a man without social or personal resources: recently separated from his wife, he lives alone; as if in a Charlie Chaplin film, he found himself armed with a fake pistol and required blindly to act his part. But somehow he was prepared without question to give his life for his countrymen.

And how if not by some theory of positive contagion are we to understand the heroism of seventeen-year-old Rami Mahmoud Mahameed? This young Arab Israeli was at the bus station in Umm el Fahm in central Israel when he saw a Palestinian carrying a large black bag on his shoulders and wearing very dirty shoes. As the two were alone in the station, Rami politely asked to borrow the stranger's cell phone. Moving away, he quietly called the police. Then, instead of fleeing, he sat down next to the terrorist and waited. "I did what I wanted to do," Rami said later, as if surprised that anyone would find his actions peculiar. The police arrived in time to halt an arriving bus before it could enter the yard and grabbed the terrorist, who blew himself up. Rami was seriously injured. "Even if I had to die, I would have stayed there," Rami said later at the hospital, where at first he was under suspicion of having been an accomplice. "I thought to myself when I saw him, 'OK, if you want to kill yourself, go do it in Jenin.'"

· · · · ·

Of course, it helps that Israel's regular army, the IDF, is a citizen-army in the fullest sense, based on almost universal conscription and drawing much of its moral and cultural strength from a national mentality of preparedness and service that has been built up over the generations. It also helps, if in a grotesque way, that the enemy is so completely ruthless. "When I went into Jenin, I was astonished," says a reserve officer who participated in the operation in that West Bank city last April. "Under the beds, in the cabinets, in the kitchen, in the refrigerator there were explosives. The portraits of *shahids* ['martyrs'] were everywhere. It was sheer madness. Here were people who had built themselves a lovely city, who had been doing quite well financially, who had excellent rapport with their Jewish neighbors. We met a child carrying a bag of explosives. He must have been about seven years old." The terrible, sickening aggression of the enemy, the feeling of oppressiveness and rage that it induces in everyone who must face it, brings out a potent response. Besides, thanks to army training, the plain fact is that many people are *used* to reacting—when necessary, "like a machine."

A typical case is Eli Federman. If his family name is known in Israel, it is mostly on account of his brother, Noam, a former spokesman for Meir Kahane's extreme right-wing Kach movement, who has been arrested forty-five times. "My relationship with Noam is like my relationship with Yasir Arafat. To say we don't see eye to eye is an understatement," Eli asserts. On May 25, Eli saw in the distance a car driving much too quickly toward the Tel Aviv nightclub where he is a guard. With his imposing physique—he did his military service in a crack battalion—he started shoving people away and firing his gun. A bullet hit the oncoming terrorist, and the wildly careering car blew up.

Federman had lived in Thailand for a long time and had married there; that country holds a totemic place in the mentality of many young Israelis, whose post-army years often begin with a tour of the Asian hot spots. Today he lives with his family in a relatively leafy, lower-middle-class suburb. After the car blew up, he says matter-of-factly, he went over and "shot a few more bullets in [the terrorist's] head. We have to be as thorough as possible in the territories, not let them get as far as here." Benjamin ben Eliezer, then Israel's defense minister, inadvertently added a layer of complexity to the definition of the new Israeli hero when he hailed Federman as one "who deserves credit for defending the rights of people to get on with their daily routine and also have fun"—a hero who upholds a democracy's right to party.

I have not mentioned the bus drivers, who almost merit a category of their own as involuntary soldiers along Israel's civilian front line. They include Baruch Neuman, whose regular route runs from Petach Tikva to the Tel Hashomer hospital complex outside Tel Aviv. At the stop near Bar Ilan University, he saw a man trying to enter through the rear exit. This is forbidden for security reasons. He slammed the door in the passenger's face, causing him to fall back bleeding to the pavement. Terrified that he had injured someone, Neuman got off, together with a passenger who was a doctor, to inspect the damage. Opening the wounded man's jacket, they saw the explosive belt and, in a flash, pinned the man's hands. He tried to resist and was kicking hard.

"He was big and strong, and he could have managed to activate the bomb at any moment," Neuman recalls. "We started to shout: 'It's a terrorist! Run! Run!' My only thought was, 'Hold onto those big arms.'" All the passengers except for one old lady managed to flee in time. "As the minutes went by he gained more and more movement, and we also understood that the bomb could be activated from afar, like with a cell phone. We decided to get away, and on the count of three we started to run. He blew up, but by that point there was hardly anyone around.

"A hero knows what he's doing. I acted out of pure instinct," Neuman says in self-deprecation. "I was doing my job and I was responsible for the safety of my passengers; I see them every day, you know. Are my wife and children proud of me? Yes—especially of the fact that I came home in one piece."

On February 1 of last year, another bus driver named Menashe Uriel broke up a major bomb attempt by pushing away a young man who was trying to get on his bus strapped with explosives. He rolled onto the ground with him. "The boy was sixteen years old, and he held his bag tight. I was sure I was going to die, but the bus was jam-packed with kids going to the Love Festival and with soldiers heading north"— a postmodern mix if ever there was one—"so I did what I had to do."

· · · · ·

Not all who have done what they had to do have lived to talk about it. Yossef Twitto, the head of the response team in the West Bank community of Itamar, heard shots from a home one night last June but arrived too late to save the situation—three children dead, two wounded, all in the same family; when he burst in, the terrorist mowed him down, too. Another guard, Mordechai Tomer, nineteen, blond with a broad smile, was killed in Jerusalem when he stopped a car and asked to see identification papers; the driver blew himself up. And so it goes.

Sudden death, ever-present in the consciousness of Israelis, can lead to action, but also leads to a certain fatalism. Unlike in societies at peace, Israeli young people do not feel immortal. They live often to excess: dangerous trips, crazy nights, spur-of-the-moment impulses, exaggerated behavior punctuated by uncontrollable laughter and loud shouting. Beneath it looms the silence of death. "I knew perfectly well that he would have died to stop a terrorist. We'd discussed it many times," says the widow of Tamir Matan, forty-one, killed together with two young soldiers when the suicide bomber they were trying to stop blew himself up at a gas station.

This fatalism too is not new. In a 1947 novel by Moshe Shamir, *He Walked in the Fields*—a work much derided by later generations of intellectuals for its apotheosizing of the values of the old Zionist settlement in Palestine—the protagonist throws himself onto a bomb to save a comrade, even though his own girlfriend is pregnant with their child. Uri is a rural hero, torn between the dream of a quiet farmer's life and the ideal of service, of duty. For a man who would have preferred the countryside and love, duty wins out. He is like the boy in a famous ballad by the Zionist poet Natan Alterman, another self-sacrificing hero who gives his life to save his army buddies and does not even know why; or like the protagonist of another ballad about the terrible battle of Ammunition Hill in Jerusalem during the 1948–49 War of Independence, who "between the grenades and shots . . . ran and laid the explosive. I do not know why I got the medal of honor. All I wanted was to go home quietly."

. . . . .

Not too far from the King David Hotel, a sumptuous new hotel is being built; a suicide bomber blew himself up there, splattering blood onto the pale blue windows. A mere one hundred yards away, in a pedestrian mall, dozens of kids lost their lives to two suicide bombers as they sat drinking Coca-Cola and chatting while music wafted from the restaurant doorways. Not far from the Moment Café, where eleven young people were murdered in June, and from the Sbarro Pizzeria, where fifteen were blown to bits, lies the big Mahanei Yehuda market, and not far from the market is the large building that houses my gym. Everything is near everything else in a city as small as Jerusalem. After class one day, the gym instructor, soaked in sweat, her voice barely audible above the exercise music, shouted: "Good for you, girls, coming to gym even with the way things are."

Good for you? Whom was she talking to? What was she talking about? But as I looked around, at the Orthodox women, out of breath, carefully replacing their wigs or kerchiefs, at the rest of us pulling on our slacks before walking out the door to take our kids to school or shop in the supermarket or ride the city buses or sit and drink cappuccino as if mass murderers were not planning to murder us where we stood, my eyes welled with tears. Good for you. Really, well done.

—January 2003

Joshua Muravchik

Listening to Arabs

"Let him finish," called out Ruthie. The bell had sounded, but the class, at a summer institute in Greece, sat and listened as Gevara poured out his tale of woe. His mother had died in childbirth when her urgent passage to a hospital had been impeded at one of the scores of Israeli checkpoints dotting the West Bank. Then, not one but two of his brothers had died at the hands of Israeli soldiers—apparently, as best one could make out through Gevara's inexpert English, during the "Jenin massacre" in the spring of 2002. Nor was that all. His home had been demolished to make way for Israel's new security fence. And, only a few days previously, Gevara himself had been arrested as he tried to enter Israel for the flight to attend this very institute. Held for two days, he had missed his plane and been forced to find another, leaving from Jordan. Although the Israeli authorities finally released him, they had also summarily sentenced him to six months in jail, to be served upon his return.

As he spoke, Gevara—a nickname perhaps intended in homage to Fidel Castro's sidekick Che Guevara—began to cry. So did several of his listeners, including some Israelis. Afterward, one of them, the same Ruthie who had insisted that he be heard, contacted B'Tselem, an Israeli human-rights organization specializing in complaints about the treatment of Arabs, to see if she could secure help for him.

With this episode, the atmosphere at the institute lost some of its frivolity. Eighty-three students were participating in a three-week program in politics and economics on the island of Crete. Although some were Americans, most had been drawn from the Balkans and the

Mediterranean basin, including, by design, members of several nations in conflict: Greeks and Turks, Serbs and Albanians, Arabs and Israelis. I taught there every day for a week in August 2003, giving a series of lectures about democracy. It was one of several experiences in recent months that brought me into closer contact with Arabs than I had been before and left me with new impressions—new at least to me.

. . . . .

Until the Gevara incident, the mood had been about what one might expect in a gathering of college-age young people of both sexes on a Greek island far from home. Anticipation had built up weeks in advance through messages exchanged on an electronic bulletin board in the cyberslang that many of the youngsters seemed to know better than English ("congrats 2 u 2; c u soon"). An introductory posting from a Lebanese captured the high spirits: "Beirut isn't that terrible. Screw politics. We party till the morning. . . . About the readings [which the institute had sent to students well ahead of time], let's all agree on reading them after we get to Greece."

Having made acquaintances online, groups of students planned to link up in budget accommodations for a few days of sunshine before the start of classes. One such group comprised a Turkish girl and four boys—two Lebanese, a Syrian, and an American. Whether or not their parents knew of the arrangement, other parents, especially of Arab girls, had been more cautious about their children's itineraries. Once classes began, however, dorm life went on into the wee hours, and it did not center on assigned readings. Featured, rather, were such cultural exchanges as spin-the-bottle, a game the Americans obligingly taught the others to play.

But things had grown more serious after Gevara's terrible revelation, which occurred just before my arrival for the second week of classes. I heard it recounted many times, including, with great earnestness, by one of the other American teachers, a strong if soft-spoken partisan of the Arab cause who had once taught at the American University of Beirut. The tensions it fed between the Arab and Israeli students broke forth in my own classroom on the day I lectured about the state of democracy in the contemporary world.

In the course of our discussion, a shy girl from Jordan expressed her dismay at my assertion that her country was not a democracy. "But our king does so much for the people, and for the Palestinians," she protested. Hotter still were objections from numerous Arab students to my classification of Israel as a democracy. "How can you say that when they invaded us in 1967?" demanded one Syrian, revealing volumes about his education. What about Israeli "aggression," or the treatment of Israel's Arab citizens, or, especially, the occupation, asked others. My repeated explanation—that, the accuracy of their criticisms aside, a nation's political system does not necessarily determine the wisdom or justice of its policies—seemed to fall mostly on ears deafened by reluctance to hear anything positive about Israel, especially in a sphere in which the Arab states scored poorly.

A Palestinian-American boy, passionately devoted to the Palestinian cause but with a puppyish softness that bespoke his American upbringing, wanted to know how I could characterize a "religious state" like Israel as a democracy. Later, in the cafeteria, I explained that unlike the case of Christianity or Islam, Jewishness entails both a religion and a nationality. "Does anybody know this?" he asked finally, when he got the point.

Nor was Israel the only country whose standing as a democracy was challenged. An Egyptian girl pointed out that America could not be considered a real democracy because "no leftists are allowed to teach in American universities." I said that was mistaken, and after class informed her that so many American professors were leftists as to give rise to the complaint among conservatives that you could not teach if you were *not* one. Accepting the correction, she explained with a little embarrassment that she had only been repeating what she had heard from her professor—who was the daughter of former Egyptian president Gamal Abdel Nasser.

That evening, there was a dinner at which the students, grouped by country, exhibited or performed something of their native culture. When the Palestinians' turn came, Gevara led off. After showing an artifact of some kind, he picked up a fist-sized stone he had brought and said, "These are the stones we throw at our oppressors." Next came the Palestinian-American, who opened with the remark that "nothing is more important to us than family." At this point, Ruthie called out: "Not even your stones?" Evidently she was growing impatient with her Palestinian peers, perhaps because she had already heard back from B'Tselem that it had no knowledge of Gevara's family travails, even though it attempts to keep complete records of such things. For her outburst, she was forcefully shushed by the school's Greek director, who had sat silently through Gevara's presentation.

During the final days of the institute, after I was gone, a "peace lunch" was organized for the Arabs and Israelis, but several of the former, notably the Egyptians led by the girl who studied with Nasser's daughter, refused to take part. Earlier, bidding farewell to Gevara, I had invited him to look me up whenever he might get to Washington. "I think I'll be there in October," he replied to my surprise, this being August and his six-month sentence presumably lying ahead. "I'm going to a young leaders' conference that will be either in Washington or San Francisco."

· · · · ·

Wherever Gevara was heading, I was soon heading to Morocco to take part in a symposium on "Europe, America, and Islam." This was part of an annual cultural festival held in Assilah, a picturesque ancient fishing village and barebones seaside resort where inland Moroccans without the wealth to vacation abroad find refuge from the summer heat.

The event provided the familiar pleasures and frustrations that Americans face in small, poorer countries. We were transported in style—business class—but it had taken two dozen phone calls to get my pre-paid ticket issued, and when I finally picked it up in the Athens airport, I saw that it was one-way only. "You'll get the rest when you get there," I was assured. There were two other passengers on my flight headed to the same symposium, a Spanish academic and an Argentine newspaper editor. Met planeside in Tangier, we were whisked through passport control and customs. A waiting car then took us to a hotel in Tangier some twenty-five miles north of Assilah, our hosts deeming the accommodations in town to be unsuitable for the likes of us.

It was mid-afternoon, and the desk clerk told us that our rooms were ready but had not yet been cleaned. That was an understatement. Changing into my bathing suit, I took refuge by the pool; although the hotel abutted the beach, large signs warned that swimming was not advisable (apparently due to raw sewage). Many girls around the pool wore skimpy bathing suits, and I wondered how many of them were European, how many local.

Three hours later, when it was time to board the bus for the opening session, my room still lay in the filthy state in which I had found it. Our group of conferees was accompanied by motorcycle police, two of whom rode ahead, waving traffic off the two-lane highway so that our busload of deep thinkers could reach its destination unimpeded.

We were about thirty in number. As we seated ourselves around tables arranged in a large square, the chairman unexpectedly approached me and the other American present and asked if we would make opening statements. My compatriot's remarks were not very controversial, but I decided to speak bluntly about the three decades of attacks visited on Americans by Middle Eastern terrorists. These were not an expression of Islam, I stipulated; some of the attackers had come from secular Marxist-Leninist or nationalist groups. Rather, they were an outgrowth of an unhealthy political culture of violence and extremism that held sway in the region and that the United States was bent on altering by spreading democracy.

Various Arab participants sought the floor to rebut me. They were spearheaded by a professor of political science from the American University of Cairo who, unable to control her rage, shrieked that my remarks were "unacceptable" and, because they were being heard by such a large audience, also "dangerous." She pointed to the spectators, about two hundred townspeople seated amphitheater-style around and behind us. Each of her denunciations brought resounding applause from this gallery.

I began to wonder what I was doing there. "Unacceptable" and "dangerous" comments should be stopped, one supposes. Even if the crowd did not pose a physical threat, it occurred to me that I might just pick up and leave the next morning (until I remembered that I was still without a return ticket). But soon our official host, Mohamed Benaissa, Egypt's minister of foreign affairs, arrived to take the chair and announce that demonstrations from onlookers were out of order. As a sense of decorum was restored, I took the floor to protest my treatment. When the session adjourned and we were heading back to our bus, several of the Arab participants came up to express their friendly feelings and to say that the Egyptian woman's attack had been out of line.

· · · · ·

Was it a coincidence, I began to speculate, that here, as at the summer institute, the shrillest voices were Egyptian? Nor had these been my only recent encounters with Egyptian intellectuals of extremist bent. On several occasions I had had the chance to appear on talk shows on al-Jazeera, and been given an interesting taste of this Qatar-based station whose broadcasts have revolutionized television in the Arab world. Once I was paired with an Egyptian professor who opened with the remark that the last 2,000 years were one long story of unprovoked mistreatment of the Arabs by Westerners. (I parried this lightly, pointing out that, since my country had only recently celebrated its bicentennial, we Americans could not be held responsible for the first 1,800 of those years.) In a subsequent appearance on the same show, which al-Jazeera calls its equivalent of *Crossfire,* I found myself up against an Egyptian newspaper editor who made the professor look mild by comparison.

The subject was, "Can we trust the Americans about weapons of mass destruction [in Muslim countries]?" The moderator introduced the subject by using the word "lie" eight times, as in "the Americans always lie" and "everything they say is a lie." Then he turned the microphone over to the Egyptian, who spoke the word "lie" in a similar vein ten times in succession, for good measure throwing in two "Hitlers" as in "George Bush and the Americans are worse than Hitler." Before giving me a chance to say anything, the moderator then announced the first results of the station's call-in poll; lo and behold, on the question "can you believe the Americans?" fully 88 percent had responded in the negative.

Recent survey data suggest that my miscellaneous encounters may indeed be reflective of Egyptian public opinion. Zogby International asked people in a variety of countries whether they liked Americans. Usually, even in countries at odds with the United States, the answer to this question is "yes": for example, French respondents in Zogby's poll affirmed their liking for Americans by more than two to one. But more Egyptians responded negatively than positively, by a ratio of 47 percent to 35 percent. Asked their overall opinion of the United States, 86 percent of Egyptians registered themselves unfavorable and only 14 percent favorable.

Could it be that Egyptians feel so discomfited by their peace treaty with Israel that they strive to present themselves as the most militant of Arabs? At the Assilah symposium, one of the more conciliatory Arab participants told me that although the Egyptian woman had called me anti-Muslim, she herself was not a Muslim but a Copt. If the Egyptians feel driven to be the most Arab of Arabs, might a Copt have felt compelled to appear the most Egyptian of Egyptians?

Whatever the cause, my attacker had clearly overplayed her hand, and she failed to appear for the next morning's session. We Americans having already spoken, it was now the Arabs' turn to tell us what they thought. An adviser to the Moroccan king complained that "the U.S. has accused the Muslims very unjustly of terrorism," while several others, seconded by the Spaniard, offered excuses for terrorism on the grounds that all governments engage in it in some form and/or that it represents an understandable cry of despair. There was more, and worse. A jovial Sudanese listed in the program as a "penseur" explained that the United States had "fixed" the UN report on the Jenin battle of 2002 so as to deny that Israel had in fact committed a massacre. A famous Pakistani took a turn, prefacing his remarks with an apology for his inability to address the group in Arabic, a deficiency that he blamed not on his own lack of learning but on "the heritage of colonialism." A Paris-based Algerian intellectual expatiated on the problem that "there are no words in Arabic for mytho-history and mytho-ideology," leaving me to wonder what the English words for these notions might be. A bit later, my countryman, seeming to pander to the crowd, offered up the thought that we are all victims of distorted news media: "You have al-Jazeera and we have FOX."

· · · · ·

But this litany of victimhood, fantasy, moral equivocation, finger-pointing, and obscurantism was not the whole story, either. Despite administrative glitches, the Moroccans' hospitality was warm and generous. A hosted lunch at a seaside restaurant, for example, consisted of a large tossed salad topped with cold fish, or so I thought until salad was followed by a hefty paella and then, for the main course, platters overflowing with four or five species of fried fish.

On a substantive level, both within the sessions and outside, several Arab participants gave an impression dramatically different from the prevailing whine. I was approached by a young man from the audience, none too well groomed and dressed in a white *jalaba:* "I listened to you yesterday," he wanted me to know, "and what you said was painful to me, but I think we need to hear it." A Lebanese editor of a journal of international affairs interviewed me at length, for publication; although he did not appear to be buying most of what I was selling, he was interested and believed his readers would be, too.

On the bus, I had a long chat with a UN official based in Paris whose nameplate listed his country as "Palestine." It turned out he was an Israeli Arab. He shared with me his diagnosis of Arab ills, pointing to the lack of a work ethic and the preference for inherited over earned wealth. Emblematic of the problem, he said, was a poem still being taught in Arab schoolbooks in which the poet derides a rival because the man's uncle had been a manual laborer. As for the conflict between the Arabs and Israel, he had a proposal: get the Egyptian and Jordanian armies to police Gaza and the West Bank. It was not the most realistic of solutions, but it was based on a certain sympathy for both sides. At the end of the symposium, one of the Moroccan organizers expressed a sentiment in poignant contrast to the anti-American rage I had heard from others. "Don't think badly of us," she said on parting.

The most remarkable person I met at the symposium was Ali, an Iraqi exile living in Morocco. In the formal session, while others deflected responsibility or made alibis, he asserted: "Our societies have failed to move into the modern world because we have accorded no importance to the acquisition of knowledge." A writer, Ali let me see one of the few short stories of his to have been translated into English. Titled "Fear," it depicts a man who has had his tongue cut out and seems about to be murdered by uniformed figures while the narrator, who loves him, is too frightened to intervene. It was, of course, a parable about Iraq or perhaps the whole Arab world.

As a sideline, Ali translates American fiction for publication, so that Arabs "can see the human face of America." Soon after our meeting, he translated a newspaper essay of mine on the need for Arab democracy and got it placed prominently in Morocco's leading paper. He planned, he told me, to return to Iraq and use some of the money he has earned, enough to make him comfortable by Iraqi standards, on creating a library in his native village in order to give its children a better opportunity to learn.

Ali had·served as a critical reader of the draft of the second *Arab Human Development Report,* issued in October by the UN Human Development Program. The first such report, issued last year, was widely noted for its path-breaking criticism of the Arab status quo. Written by a team of a few dozen Arab intellectuals, it underscored three deficits in Arab life: freedom, knowledge, and women's equality. The new report, "written for Arabs by Arabs," elaborates on the knowledge deficit. Apart from its tediously familiar denunciations of Israeli "war crimes" or the "erosion of civil liberties" in the United States, it has much of genuine value to say and the courage to say it. The report decries the lack of "social and individual freedoms" that fosters "social and moral corruption [and] the absence of honesty" in the Arab world, and calls for "freedom ... of opinion, speech, and assembly." Its indictment of Arab intellectual failure is capped by this damning datum: in the two decades ending in 2000, the Arab states together registered 370 U.S. patents, while Israel, with less than one-fortieth the population, registered 7,662.

· · · · ·

Several members of the team that produced the *Arab Human Development Report* are Egyptian, which suggests that while that country produces an abundance of extremists, it also produces at least some liberals. This point was driven home to me at still another conference I attended recently, this one in Europe but attended mostly by Arabs. The Egyptians I met there—a newspaper editor, a leader of a human-rights group, a businesswoman, and others—could not have made a more vivid contrast with those I had encountered in Crete and Assilah and on al-Jazeera. They were democrats, pro-American, and believers in peace with Israel. The editor even informed me that he had appeared before a meeting of the Arab League to make the case for the war against Saddam Hussein.

At this conference I gave a talk similar to my opening remarks at Assilah but harder-hitting. Afterward many of the Arabs asked pointed but respectful questions; the only participants who clashed with me directly were an Iranian who accused me of attacking Islam and two Jewish Israelis. One of the latter, a prominent Labor-party leader, objected to my assertion that the roots of terrorism lay in a political culture of violence and fanaticism rather than in poverty.

If both this conference and the symposium at Assilah furnished some evidence of a liberal countercurrent in the Arab world, I even had similar hints in connection with my appearance on al-Jazeera. The day after the broadcast of the program featuring all the invective about American "lies," I received four e-mails from viewers. I had gone into the show reminding myself to keep calm, but my prudent intentions had disappeared as I got down in the street, rhetorically, and slugged it out with the moderator and the Egyptian guest. I may not have sunk to their level of abusiveness, but I did lose my cool and afterward regretted it.

One of the e-mails was from a young man named Khoury. "Someone should have told you that al-Jazeera's audience is not the notoriously ignorant American public you are so used to speaking to," he wrote. "I was left wondering whether you are a liar (which I know you are) or whether you really are that stupid. I assure you the Arab public is not." And he went on, in a threatening vein. (I wrote back telling Khoury he was choking on his own hatred of America. He replied, to my surprise, "I am also an American," adding the boast, apropos of who-knows-what, "Less than thirty years old, I am independently wealthy and don't have to work a day of my life.")

But the other three messages were of a contrary tenor. One was from Ali, who said, "you handled the debate very well. ... spectators were impressed by your dignity." Another, from a young Kuwaiti, assured me that my opponent was an extremist not typical of Egypt. The third was from an Arab Israeli journalist who wrote: "[The] style of answering and commenting you presented is the best way of attacking the bigotry we Arabs are suffering from. Those TV stations and their guests are reflections of the intellectual misery of the Arab world." Of course, a sample of four is of no statistical significance, but as anyone who speaks or writes on controversial topics can testify, a ratio of three to one friendly responses is very unusual.

As summer gave way to fall, my students from Crete were still bombarding each other with messages on the Internet bulletin board, many of them about the Arabs' relations with Israel and the United States. One Lebanese staked out a staunchly pro-American position, including on the war in Iraq. Another strove to address Arab-Israel issues with steadfast fairness and balance. But a third vituperated against Israel and added: "If only the Americans would leave us alone, what a euphoria." More extreme were the Egyptians, especially the girl who had studied with Nasser's daughter. In one message, she made a point of sending personalized greetings to the other students, country by country, conspicuously omitting the Israelis. In other dispatches, the vitriol was more direct.

One began: "Hi all, I would like you to read these two articles by an American writer." The articles, nearly 20,000 words in all, were by David Duke, former head of the Ku Klux Klan, and they gave a Nazi-like version of the role of Jews in American life, including the claim that it was really the Jews who bombed the World Trade Center. The Lebanese boy who strove for fairness reacted strongly: "I am ashamed of being associated with such an argument and wanted to assure everyone that no one in his right mind would advocate this bastard's ideas, nor would they listen to others who do." Once again the Egyptian girl was embarrassed. She had not known who Duke was, only that she liked what he said; in a private letter to me, she explained that she had been given the articles by "Dr. Asmat Abdel Magid, the former head of the Arab League and the former foreign-affairs minister of Egypt, the head of the negotiating mission in our peace agreement with Israel."

Other student postings presented more ambivalent sentiments. A Palestinian (not Gevara) wrote poignantly of his people's sufferings, then later spoke of having toured in Israel, commenting that "for a fifty-five-year-old country they didn't only make a great job, they made a miracle." In another message, after criticizing Israel and the United States, he wrote:

> I want also to say sorry for all the victims of the last attack in a restaurant in Haifa. . . . this is real terror and I am not afraid to say it as a Palestinian this is against Palestinians against every human being the stupid attack that also caused more than five Arabs killed and destroying property and also killing the peace process and innocent civilians I want to point out that also Palestinian are killed

in every attack not only Israelis sorry I am so nervous I cant express myself ... things will never be good again I am so desperate.

Then there was the Syrian who justified terrorism against Israel and even the September 11 attacks on America before sending warm personal greetings to Israeli students. As he put it, guilelessly: "Imagine [me] who has been overwhelmed by the idea of 'how to kill a Jew?' for eight years, now he has some Jews friend. This is something incredible." In another posting the same young Syrian dwelt on the source of his confusion:

> I really have a problem which makes me suffer. I feel that Ruthie, Yael (my dear friends) are very good people and I am proud of them and proud of th[e] great times at the [institute], but ... I have been taught that those people do not say what really [is] inside them.... I have known this for 25 years and it is very difficult to erase it within three weeks.

No doubt it is. What this young man has been taught for twenty-five years, the Arab world as a whole has been taught for a good deal longer, and few have had his opportunity, however brief, to get a different picture.

In the end, I take away two contrary impressions from this congeries of experiences. On the one hand, the dominant discourse in the Arab world continues to be even more fraught with hate and fantasy than we Americans consider it polite or politic to acknowledge, especially in light of our present need to stress that the war against terror is not a war against Arabs or Islam. On the other hand, a contrary current is beginning to make an appearance, exemplified by Ali, by the Egyptians I met in Europe, by some of my students in Crete, and at least in part by the scholars who have produced the *Arab Human Development Reports*.

That such an element exists gives cause for hope, although perhaps not for optimism. In the 1920s, liberal movements flourished in Germany and Japan and came close to remaking those two societies, only to be vanquished by the superior power of authoritarians and militarists who set the stage for World War II.

The liberal movement in the Arab world today is weaker than its predecessor in Japan, and much weaker than its predecessor in Germany. Even so, the prospects for war and peace in the coming decades depend, critically, on whether it can somehow achieve a better fate.

—December 2003

Efraim Karsh

Arafat Lives

No sooner was Yasir Arafat declared dead at the French military hospital to which he had been dramatically rushed in early November 2004 than a vast cohort of world leaders, from King Abdullah of Jordan to President Jacques Chirac of France, began to voice hopes for a quick revival of the Middle East peace process. "The best tribute to President Arafat's memory will be to intensify our efforts to establish a peaceful and viable state of Palestine," declared the European Union's foreign-policy chief, Javier Solana. At the same time, Solana unveiled a new plan to facilitate the so-called road map drafted in 2003 by the European Union, the United States, Russia, and the United Nations—but in "a less incremental manner": that is, by deleting the proviso conditioning progress toward the creation of a Palestinian state on a cessation of violence and terrorism.

Tony Blair, the British prime minister, echoed Solana's view. In 2003, in the run-up to the Iraq war, Blair had sought to pacify his domestic critics by urging on George W. Bush at least the appearance of "progress" between the Israelis and the Palestinians before confronting Saddam Hussein. As the war unfolded, and as his popularity at home and in Europe plummeted, Blair kept on repeating the theme. In October 2004, he told a Labor-party conference that he would make Middle East peace "a personal priority" after the U.S. elections; a few weeks later, he responded to Bush's reelection with an emphatic call for a renewed effort to resolve this "single most pressing political challenge in our world today." After all, said Blair, an agreement between Israel and the

Palestinians would help critically in "resolving the conditions and causes on which the terrorists prey."

Blair's conviction that the revival of the Middle East peace process would alleviate the situation in Iraq and reduce the threat of international terrorism struck a responsive chord in some quarters in the United States as well. "As Mr. Blair, the Europeans, and Arab states like Egypt constantly point out, the Israeli-Palestinian stalemate feeds Muslim anger and despair, giving a larger rationale to terrorist groups like al Qaeda and to the insurgency in Iraq," ran an editorial in the *New York Times*. "Before the Iraq war," the paper continued, "Mr. Bush had been told that 'the road to Jerusalem passed through Baghdad,' but with Iraq today a magnet for anti-Western fervor, it is increasingly believed in the region that the formula is the other way around." Former presidents Jimmy Carter and George H. W. Bush, who during their own terms in office had helped foster Arab-Israeli dialogue, hastened to add their separate articulations of this same idea.

Nevertheless, when he arrived in Washington on November 11 as the first foreign leader to visit the White House since the elections, Blair failed to persuade the American president either to endorse an international peace conference in London early next year or to appoint a personal envoy to the Middle East. "I'm all for conferences," the president told a joint press briefing, "just so long as the conferences produce something." He then proceeded to reiterate his commitment to the strategic vision he had outlined in June 2002—namely, that Palestinian democratization would have to precede rather than follow the creation of an independent state. While he promised "to use the next four years to spend the capital of the United States" on the creation of such a state, Bush made it eminently clear that the onus was on the Palestinians to ensure that this objective was achieved:

> It is impossible to think that the President of the United States or the prime minister of Great Britain can impose our vision. I think it's unrealistic to say, "Well, Bush wants it done," or, "Blair wants it done," therefore it'll happen.... If you choose not to be helped, if you decide you don't want a free, democratic society, there's nothing we can do. If you think you can have peace without democracy, again, I think you'll find that—I can only speak for myself— that I will be extremely doubtful that it will ever happen.

At the heart of Bush's words is an approach to the Arab-Israeli conflict fundamentally at odds with the one endorsed by most of the international community. In order to understand the role played by Yasir Arafat in creating the present impasse between Israel and the Palestinians, it helps to have some notion of what is at stake between these two contending visions.

. . . . .

The belief that Arabs and Israelis can be forced into a lasting peace by outside influence is based on a perception of Middle Eastern politics as an offshoot of global power politics. There is a long history—political, military, and diplomatic—behind this perception, which informed the actions of generations of modern policy-makers in Europe and elsewhere. Unfortunately, the perception is wrong.

Even at the weakest point in their modern history, during World War I and its immediate aftermath, local Middle Eastern actors were decisive in the restructuring of their region. It was not British officialdom but Hussein ibn Ali of the Hashemite family who drove the British to entertain seriously the notion of destroying the Ottoman Empire. Impressed by Hussein's promises to raise the Arabic-speaking Ottoman subjects in revolt, Sir Arthur Henry McMahon, the British high commissioner in Egypt, accepted his vision of an Arab successor empire and (tentatively) agreed to his main territorial demands. Hussein's and McMahon's initiative would have a considerable impact on the future shape of the Middle East. The emirate of Transjordan (later to be known as the Kingdom of Jordan), for example, was established in 1921 to satisfy the imperial ambitions of Hussein's second son, Abdullah, while in the same year the modern state of Iraq was created on behalf of and very much at the instigation of Abdullah's younger brother Faisal.

The bargaining power of local states was substantially enhanced during the cold-war era, when global polarization and the nuclear balance of terror constrained great-power maneuverability. For all their exertions, neither the United States nor the Soviet Union, the two powers that had supplanted the traditional European empires after World War II, had a decisive say in their smaller allies' grand strategies. Time and again they were powerless to contain undesirable regional developments, whether it was Egypt's defection to the American camp in the mid-1970s or the 1979 Islamic revolution in Iran, or were forced to acquiesce in actions with which they were in total disagreement.

It was on the cardinal issues of war and peace that superpower influence proved least effective. Just as the United States could not force its Arab allies and Israel to accept its position on a political settlement, so the Soviets failed to persuade most of their Arab partners to disavow their total rejection of Israel. Just as Israel launched the 1967 Six-Day war without Washington's blessing when it saw its existence threatened, so Egypt's war of attrition (1969–70) and October war (1973), Syria's military intervention in Lebanon (1976), and the Iraqi invasions of Iran (1980) and Kuwait (1990) took place against Soviet wishes and advice. Only in terminating hostilities did superpower intervention seem to carry any weight, if of a very limited kind and mostly where Israel was concerned. The Soviets failed to convince the Egyptian president Anwar Sadat to accept a ceasefire on the first day of the October 1973 war, or to force the Syrian president Hafez al-Assad to stop his offensive against the PLO in the summer of 1976.

This is not to say that the United States and the USSR slavishly followed the wishes of their junior partners. Rather, whatever success they had was due largely to the convergence of their own wishes with indigenous trends. In the late 1970s, it was the determination of Sadat and the Israeli prime minister Menachem Begin to end the longstanding enmity between their peoples that rendered American mediation effective. But when the Carter administration attempted to sustain the momentum and bring the Palestinians into the picture, it ran into the brick wall of PLO rejectionism. "This is a lousy deal," Yasir Arafat told the American Edward Said, who had passed him the administration's offer. "We want Palestine. We're not interested in bits of Palestine. We don't want to negotiate with the Israelis. We're going to fight."

Twenty-one years later, Arafat aborted two more presidential attempts to mediate peace with Israel by rejecting, in July and December 2000, Bill Clinton's proposals for the creation of an independent Palestinian state in 95 percent of the West Bank and Gaza Strip, with East Jerusalem as its capital. Even after Israel had confined Arafat to his Ramallah compound following the launch of his war of terror in September 2000, and even after President Bush had urged the Palestinians to substitute a new and democratic leadership for Arafat's corrupt and oppressive regime, there was little Washington could do to enforce this vision; Bush was forced to watch helplessly as his own preferred candidate, Mahmoud Abbas (Abu Mazen), was unceremoniously subverted by Arafat.

· · · · ·

Let us assume for the sake of argument that combined U.S.–European pressure succeeded in driving Israelis and Palestinians into a formal peace treaty. Would this, as Blair and others assume, eliminate violence from the wider Middle East or ameliorate the challenge of Islamic terrorism? Hardly—for the simple reason that the Palestinian question has next to nothing to do with either of these.

For one thing, violence was an integral part of Middle Eastern political culture long before the advent of the Arab-Israeli conflict, and physical force remains today the main if not the sole instrument of regional political discourse. For another, the Arab states have never had any real stake in the "liberation of Palestine." Though anti-Zionism has been the core principle of pan-Arab solidarity since the mid-1930s—it is easier, after all, to unite people through a common hatred than through a shared loyalty—pan-Arabism has almost always served as an instrument for achieving the self-interested ends of those who proclaim it.

Consider, for example, the pan-Arab invasion of the newly proclaimed state of Israel in 1948. This, on its face, was a shining demonstration of solidarity with the Palestinian people. But the invasion had far less to do with winning independence for the indigenous population than with the desire of the Arab regimes for territorial aggrandizement. Transjordan's King Abdullah wanted to incorporate substantial parts of Mandatory Palestine into the greater Syrian empire he coveted; Egypt wanted to prevent that eventuality by laying its hands on southern Palestine. Syria and Lebanon sought to annex the Galilee, while Iraq viewed the 1948 war as a stepping stone in its longstanding ambition to bring the entire Fertile Crescent under its rule. Had the Jewish state lost the war, its territory would not have fallen to the Palestinians but would have been divided among the invading Arab forces.

During the decades following the 1948 war, the Arab states manipulated the Palestinian national cause to their own ends. Neither Egypt nor Jordan allowed Palestinian self-determination in the parts of Palestine they had occupied during the 1948 war (respectively, the West Bank and the Gaza Strip). Palestinian refugees were kept in squalid camps for decades as a means of whipping Israel and stirring pan-Arab sentiments. "The Palestinians are useful to the Arab states as they are," Egyptian president Gamal Abdel Nasser candidly responded to an inquiring Western reporter in 1956. "We will always see that they do not become too powerful." As late as 1974, Syria's Hafez al-Assad referred to Palestine as being "not only a part of the Arab homeland but a basic part of southern Syria."

If the Arab states have shown little empathy for the plight of ordinary Palestinians, the Islamic connection to the Palestinian problem is even more tenuous. It is not out of concern for a Palestinian right to national self-determination but as part of a holy war to prevent the loss of a part of the "House of Islam" that Islamists inveigh against the Jewish state of Israel. In the words of the covenant of the Islamic Resistance Movement, better known by its Arabic acronym Hamas: "The land of Palestine has been an Islamic trust *(waqf)* throughout the generations and until the day of resurrection. . . . When our enemies usurp some Islamic lands, jihad becomes a duty binding on all Muslims."

In this respect, there is no difference between Palestine and other parts of the world conquered by the forces of Islam throughout history. To this very day, for example, Arabs and many Muslims unabashedly pine for the restoration of Spain and look upon their expulsion from that country in 1492 as a grave historical injustice. Indeed, even countries that have never been under Islamic imperial rule have become legitimate targets of radical Islamic fervor. Since the late 1980s, various Islamist movements have looked upon the growing number of French Muslims as a sign that France, too, has become a potential part of the House of Islam. Their British counterparts have followed suit. "We will remodel this country in an Islamic image," the London-based preacher Sheikh Omar Bakri Muhammad told an attentive audience less than two months after 9/11. "We will replace the Bible with the Qur'an."

This goal need not necessarily be pursued by the sword; it can be achieved through demographic growth and steady conversion to Islam. But should peaceful means prove insufficient, physical force can readily be brought to bear. As illustrated by the overwhelming support for the 9/11 attacks throughout the Arab and Islamic worlds, this vision is by no means confined to a disillusioned and obscurantist fringe of Islam. Islam's war for world mastery is a traditional, indeed venerable, quest, and it is far from over. In the words of Ayatollah Ruhollah Khomeini, the founding father of the avowedly imperialist regime in Iran:

> The Iranian revolution is not exclusively that of Iran, because Islam does not belong to any particular people. . . . We will export our revolution throughout the world because it is an Islamic revolution. The struggle will continue until the calls, "there is no god but Allah and Muhammad is the messenger of Allah," are echoed all over the world.

Within this grand scheme, the struggle between Israel and the Palestinians is but a single element, and one whose supposed centrality looms far greater in Western than in Islamic eyes.

. . . . .

This is not to deny that resolution of the Palestinian-Israeli conflict is a pressing issue. But the global ramifications of any settlement will be far narrower than is assumed by well-meaning statesmen like Tony Blair. Quite to the contrary, the best hope of peace between Arabs and Israelis lies in the *rejection* of the spurious "link" between this dispute and other regional and global problems.

The pretense of pan-Arab or pan-Islamic solidarity has long served as a dangerous elixir in Palestinian political circles, stirring unrealistic hopes and expectations and, at key junctures, inciting widespread and horrifically destructive violence. The sooner the Palestinians recognize that their cause is theirs alone, the sooner are they likely to make their own peace with the existence of the state of Israel and to understand the necessity of a negotiated settlement. Toward this end, a good place to start would be in eradicating the disastrous legacy of Yasir Arafat, the so-called "nation-builder."

With the exception of Haj Amin al-Husseini, the mufti of Jerusalem who led the Palestinian Arabs from the early 1920s to the late 1940s, Arafat did more than any other person in modern Middle Eastern history to *retard* the development of Palestinian civil society and the attainment of Palestinian statehood. Had the mufti led his people to peace and reconciliation with their Jewish neighbors, as he promised the British officials who appointed him to his high rank, the Palestinians would have had their independent state in a substantial part of Mandatory Palestine by 1948, and would have been spared the traumatic experience of dispersion and exile. Had Arafat set the PLO from the start on the path to peace and reconciliation instead of turning it into the most murderous terrorist organization in modern times, a Palestinian state could have been established in the late 1960s or the early 1970s, in 1979 as a corollary to the Egyptian–Israeli peace treaty, by May 1999 as part of the Oslo process, or at the very latest with the Camp David summit of July 2000.

But then, for all his rhetoric about Palestinian independence, Arafat was never as interested in statehood as in the violence attending its pursuit. As far back as 1968, he famously declared that "Palestine was lost in blood and iron, and it can only be recovered by blood and iron," and he never strayed from this track, though most of the blood he shed had little to do with the "recovery" of Palestine.

In 1970, Arafat nearly brought about the destruction of Jordan, which had generously allowed the Palestinians to use its territory for attacks on Israel. Five years later, he helped trigger the horrendous Lebanese civil war, one of the bloodiest conflicts in modern Middle Eastern history, which raged on for more than a decade and claimed hundreds of thousands of innocent lives. In 1990–91, he supported the brutalization of Kuwait by Saddam Hussein, at an exorbitant cost to the Palestinians living there, thousands of whom were murdered in revenge attacks and hundreds of thousands expelled after Kuwait's liberation.

In between these disasters, Arafat made the Palestinian national movement synonymous with violence and terrorism. Notwithstanding the PLO's rhetoric about "armed struggle," only a tiny fraction of its operations, both prior to the 1967 Six-Day war and later, were directed against military targets; most were aimed at innocent civilians. Palestinian terrorists planted bombs in public places, shelled population centers, and attacked villages and towns, taking hostages and murdering men, women, and children. In the late 1960s, the PLO introduced attacks on civilian air traffic—mostly bombings and hijackings—into the arsenal of international terrorism. In the 1990s, the Palestinians turned suicide bombings, hitherto an esoteric and rarely used method, into the most salient and effective means of modern terror.

And Palestinian statehood? In the late 1970s, Arafat told his close friend and collaborator, the Romanian dictator Nicolae Ceausescu, that the Palestinians lacked the tradition, unity, and discipline to become a formal state, and that a Palestinian state would be a failure from the first day. In the 1990s, once given control of the Palestinian population in the West Bank and Gaza as part of the Oslo peace process, he made this bleak prognosis a self-fulfilling prophecy.

Within a short time of its establishment, the Palestinian Authority (PA) had literally become the largest police state in the world, with one policeman for every forty residents. Backed by a dozen security and intelligence services, all answering directly to Arafat, these forces were ostensibly designed to enforce law and order and to combat anti-Israel terrorism. In reality they served as Arafat's tool vis-à-vis his Palestinian subjects, as an instrument of terror against Israel, and as guardian of the extensive protection and racketeering networks that sprang up in the territories under the PA's control. The largest of these operations were run by top security figures like Muhammad Dahlan in Gaza and Jibril Rajoub in the West Bank, but lower-ranking officials developed their own extortionist techniques, forcing landowners to sell them plots of land at marked-down prices, siphoning a percentage of land and property

sales, and coercing ordinary citizens to pay protection money for securing basic rights and services.

On a higher level, Arafat gave control of the Palestinian economy
to a group of cronies through a network of monopolies whose revenues
never reached the Palestinian population. Into secret bank accounts
abroad he siphoned hundreds of millions of dollars donated by the international community for the benefit of the civilian Palestinian population. The surrealist nature of this practice was starkly illustrated in Arafat's
last days when his wife Suha, whose sumptuous life in Paris was report-
edly financed to the tune of $100,000–$200,000 a month, and who was a
major shareholder in a number of large monopolies, would not release
her husband's body for burial before imposing her financial conditions
on his successors. These, for their part, hired the services of a detective
agency to try to trace their chieftain's hidden billions.

· · · · ·

Shortly before moving to Gaza in the summer of 1994 to take control of
the newly established PA, Arafat told an associate that he had signed the
Oslo agreement only because doing so would facilitate Israel's eventual
demise. "I know that you are opposed to the Oslo accords," this former
colleague has recently quoted Arafat as saying,

> but you must always remember what I'm going to tell you. The
> day will come when you will see thousands of Jews fleeing Pales-
> tine. I will not live to see this, but you will definitely see it in your
> lifetime. The Oslo accords will help bring this about.

In fact, Arafat never hid from his own people how he saw the Oslo
process: as a means not to a two-state solution—Israel and a Palestinian
state in the West Bank and Gaza—but to the substitution of a Palestinian state for the state of Israel.

As early as September 8, 1993, five days before signing the Israeli-
Palestinian Declaration of Principles (DOP), Arafat told an Israeli journalist who came to interview him in his Tunis headquarters: "In the
future, Israel and Palestine will be one united state in which Israelis and
Palestinians will live together"—that is, Israel would no longer exist.
And even as he shook Yitzhak Rabin's hand on the White House lawn,
Arafat was assuring the Palestinians in a pre-recorded Arabic-language
message broadcast by Jordanian TV that the DOP was merely an implementation of the PLO's "phased strategy" of June 1974. This stipulated
that the Palestinians should seize whatever territory Israel was prepared

or compelled to cede and use it as a springboard for further territorial gains until achieving the "complete liberation of Palestine."

During the next seven years, until the launch of his terrorist war in late September 2000, Arafat played an intricate game of Jekyll-and-Hyde. Addressing Israeli or Western audiences, he would habitually extol the "peace of the brave" he had signed with "my partner Yitzhak Rabin." To his Palestinian constituents, he would simultaneously depict the peace accords as momentary and transient arrangements. He made constant allusions not only to the "phased strategy" but to the "right of return," a standard Palestinian euphemism for Israel's destruction through demographic subversion. He also leavened his speech with historical and religious references, most notably alluding to the treaty of Hudaybiya, signed by the Prophet Muhammad with the people of Mecca in 628 only to be disavowed by Muhammad a couple of years later when the situation shifted in his favor.

Further to discredit the idea of peace with the Jewish state, Arafat's PA launched a sustained hate campaign of racial and political incitement, ongoing to this day and unparalleled in scope and intensity since Nazi Germany. Israelis, and Jews more generally, have been portrayed as the source of all evil; synonyms for iniquity, corruption, and decadence; and responsible for every problem, real or imaginary, in the West Bank and Gaza. Palestinians are not only indoctrinated in the illegitimacy of the state of Israel and the lack of any Jewish connection to the land, but also told of the most outlandish Israeli plots to corrupt and ruin them, wholly congruent with the medieval myth of Jews as secret destroyers and well-poisoners.

Arafat himself led the way in this campaign, charging Israel with killing Palestinian children to get their internal organs, masterminding the suicide bombings of its own civilians, and flooding the territories with weapons in order to precipitate a Palestinian civil war. The Palestinian Authority's minister of health, Riad Zaanun, accused Israeli doctors of using "Palestinian patients for experimental medicines," while the Palestinian representative to the UN's Human Rights Commission in Geneva charged that Israel had injected Palestinian children with the AIDS virus. The director of the PA's committee for consumer protection accused Israel of distributing chocolate infected with "mad cow disease" in the Palestinian territories. The PA minister of ecology, Yusuf Abu Safiyyah, indicted Israel for "dumping liquid waste … in Palestinian areas in the West Bank and Gaza." Suha Arafat famously amplified one such charge when, in the presence of Hillary Clinton, she told an audience in Gaza in November 1999 that "our people have been subjected to the daily and extensive use of poisonous gas by the Israeli forces, which has led to an increase in cancer cases among women and children." Little wonder that Arafat's death last November was quickly followed by widespread charges of Israeli poisoning.

Arafat also utilized the immense inflammatory potential of Islam to discredit his Israeli peace partners, if not the idea of peace itself. Week after week, Palestinian preachers used their pulpits to discredit the peace process and to instill hatred for Israelis and Jews. Worshippers have been taught that Jews are the "descendants of apes and pigs" and warned of Zionist machinations to divide the Palestinian people and spawn internecine strife. After Arafat launched his war of terror in September 2000, the Friday preachers embarked on an orgy of anti-Jewish invective and outright calls for the mass murder of Israelis and Jews wherever they were found.

Children have occupied a place of pride in the PA's hate campaign. Over the last decade, Palestinian children have learned about an evil Jewish persona, traceable to biblical times and supposedly accounting for the worldwide persecution of Jews through the ages. In particular they have been indoctrinated with the idea that Jews are, and always have been, implacable enemies of Islam. As they grow up, Palestinian children can join various youth organizations where they are further brainwashed with racist and anti-Semitic ideology. An extensive network of summer camps, modeled on the Nazi youth organization, Hitler Jugend, provides a carefully contrived mixture of ideological indoctrination and military training to thousands of Palestinian youth every year. The camps are named after "martyrs" or spectacular "acts of martyrdom" (i.e., terrorist attacks), and participants are thoroughly imbued with the virtues of death and "martyrdom."

Nor did Arafat confine himself to simply disparaging his peace partner. Making violence the defining characteristic of his rule, he built an extensive terrorist infrastructure in the territories under his control. He refused to disarm the terrorist organizations Hamas and Islamic Jihad (as required by the Oslo accords) and tacitly approved the murder of hundreds of Israelis by these groups. He also reconstructed the PLO's old terrorist apparatus, mainly under the auspices of the Tanzim, the military arm of Fatah (the PLO's largest constituent organization and Arafat's own alma mater). He frantically acquired large quantities of prohibited weapons, and, eventually, resorted to outright mass violence, first in September 1996 to discredit the newly elected Israeli prime minister

Benjamin Netanyahu and then in September 2000, shortly after being offered Palestinian statehood by Netanyahu's successor, Ehud Barak, with the launch of his terror war.

· · · · ·

But Arafat is hardly the only Arab leader to have used mass violence for political ends, to foster a cult of anti-Semitism, or to line his own pockets at his people's expense. He was a typical, if egregious, product of the ruthless Arab political system and a quintessential representative of a generation of cynical and self-seeking "revolutionaries." Nor have his main Palestinian associates been any better. While ordinary Palestinians have scrabbled for a livelihood, PLO officials have enjoyed a luxurious life in sumptuous hotels and villas, globe-trotting in grand style, acquiring properties, and making financial investments worldwide—all from the billions of dollars donated by the Arab oil states and, during the Oslo era, by the international community.

Neither was Arafat alone in his political philosophy. The rejection of the state of Israel and the need for its violent destruction have been constants within the PLO since the days of its hallowed founding document, the Palestinian Covenant, adopted in 1964 and revised four years later to reflect the organization's growing militancy. Having little to say about the Palestinians themselves, the Covenant devotes about two-thirds of its thirty-three articles to the need to destroy Israel, designating "armed struggle" as "the only way to liberate Palestine." Despite signing no fewer than five peace agreements with Israel during the 1990s, the PLO has failed to abolish its Covenant as promised and has in fact never shed its total rejection of the Jewish state.

Finally, such attitudes are by no means confined to "hard-line" elements within the PLO, like its "foreign minister" Farouq Qadoumi, but are a commonplace among supposed moderates as well. The late Faisal Husseini, widely considered a dove, famously likened the Oslo accords to a Trojan horse designed to bring about Israel's eventual demise. Yasser Abed Rabbo, a co-signatory to the 2003 "Geneva accords," persistently denied Jewish attachment to the Temple Mount, and by extension to the land of Israel, and vowed to regain "all of Palestine." So did Nabil Shaath, another supposed moderate and dedicated advocate of the Oslo process, and Ahmed Qureia (Abu Ala), chief negotiator of the Oslo accords. "We did not sign a peace treaty with Israel, but interim agreements that had been imposed on us," he said in June 1996. "When we accepted the Oslo agreement, we obtained territory but not all the Palestinian territory. . . .

We did not and will not relinquish one inch of this territory or the right of any Palestinian to live on it with dignity."

Even Mahmoud Abbas (Abu Mazen), after Arafat's death the acting chairman of the PA and perhaps the foremost symbol of supposed Palestinian moderation, has not shied away from denying the existence of the ancient Temple in Jerusalem (or for that matter, the legitimacy of the Jewish claim to Palestine) or from hinting at Israel's eventual destruction. In an interview with an Israeli newspaper in January 1996, for example, Abu Mazen gently restated the PLO's old formula of a democratic state comprising the whole of Palestine, expressing the hope that in the future Jews and Palestinian Arabs "will reach a state of complete mixture" in Palestine. This thinly veiled call for Israel's disappearance was repeated last October in a *New York Times* op-ed by the PLO's legal adviser, Michael Tarazi.

In one way, indeed, Abu Mazen is more extreme than many of his peers. While they revert to standard talk of Israel's illegitimacy, he devoted years of his life to giving ideological firepower to the anti-Israel and anti-Jewish indictment. In a doctoral dissertation written at a Soviet university, an expanded version of which was subsequently published in book form, Abu Mazen endeavored to prove the existence of a close ideological and political association between Zionism and Nazism. Among other things, he argued that fewer than a million Jews had been killed in the Holocaust, and that the Zionist movement was a partner to their slaughter.

In the wake of the failed Camp David summit of July 2000 and the launch of Arafat's war of terror two months later, Abu Mazen went to great lengths to explain why the "right of return" was a non-negotiable prerequisite for any Palestinian-Israeli settlement. "Peace will not be achieved without the refugees getting back their sacred rights, which cannot be touched," he argued. "It is the individual right of every refugee, and no one can reach an agreement in this matter without his consent." To dispel any doubt about the nature of this "right," he emphasized that "the right of return means a return to Israel, not to a Palestinian state."

· · · · ·

On the assumption that the elections scheduled for January 9 go as forecast, Abu Mazen's succession is thus no more likely to bring peace with Israel, or democracy to the Palestinians, than a new Germany would have been to arise after World War II with the accession of one of Adolf Hitler's erstwhile lieutenants.

It is true that during the past couple of years, Abu Mazen openly urged Arafat to scale down his war of terror and to return to the negotiating table. But this was a matter of tactics: Arafat himself had been amenable to negotiating so long as Israel proved sufficiently accommodating of his demands, while Abu Mazen never precluded a return to the "armed struggle" should circumstances so require. During his brief tenure as prime minister in 2003, he made no effort to disarm the numerous armed gangs in the territories as required by the Oslo accords, attempting instead to win their consent for a temporary suspension of hostilities that would bring about an Israeli withdrawal, something the Palestinians had failed to achieve by military means.

For all their markedly different personalities and political styles, Arafat and Abu Mazen are warp and woof of the same fabric: dogmatic PLO veterans who have never eschewed their commitment to Israel's destruction and who have viewed the "peace process" as the continuation of their lifetime war by other means. (A younger and more direct reincarnation of Arafat is Marwan Barghouti, the jailed Fatah terrorist with undisguised political ambitions.) As late as July 2002, Abu Mazen described Oslo as "the biggest mistake Israel ever made," enabling the PLO to get worldwide acceptance and respectability while holding fast to its own aims. Shortly after Arafat's death this past November, in his address to a special session of the Palestinian Legislative Council in Ramallah, he swore to "follow in the path of the late leader Yasir Arafat and ... work toward fulfilling his dream.... We promise you that our hearts will not rest until the right of return for our people is achieved and the tragedy of the refugees is ended."

One might have hoped that, eleven years and thousands of deaths after the launch of the Oslo process, the international community would pay closer attention to what the Palestinian leadership tells its own people and wider Arab constituencies. But that is evidently a hope too far. Even Bill Clinton, whose dream of brokering a Palestinian-Israeli peace was dashed by Arafat in the July 2000 Camp David summit and again in December of the same year, and who blamed the PLO leader for the collapse of the Oslo process, could suggest five months before Arafat's death that America and Israel had no choice but to resume negotiating with him. "Unless they ... seriously believe they can find a better negotiating partner in Hamas," he told the British leftist daily *Guardian*, "then they need to keep working to make a deal."

It is precisely here that the great importance of the Bush Doctrine lies. For while the EU seems all too happy to continue asking nothing of the Palestinians, as if they were too dim or too primitive to be held accountable for their own actions, Bush has tackled the issue of accountability head on. In his correct perception, it is the total absence of this factor from Middle Eastern political life that has allowed a long succession of local dictators, from Gamal Abdel Nasser to Saddam Hussein to Yasir Arafat, to inflict recurrent disasters and endless suffering on their peoples, and mayhem upon the world.

So long as the Palestinian territories continue to be run by men of this kind and by their terrorist organizations, there can be no true or lasting reconciliation with Israel. And so long as the territories continue to be governed by Arafat's rule of the jungle, no Palestinian civil society, let alone a viable state, can develop. Just as the creation of free and democratic societies in Germany and Japan after World War II necessitated, above and beyond the overthrow of the ruling parties, a comprehensive purge of the existing political elites and the reeducation of the entire populace, so the Palestinians deserve a profound structural reform that will sweep the PA from power, free the territories from its grip, eradicate the endemic violence from political and social life, and teach the virtues of coexistence with their Israeli neighbors. Until this happens, there will be no lasting peace in the Middle East.

—January 2005

Norman Podhoretz

Bush, Sharon, My Daughter, and Me

"Who are you?" my daughter Ruthie Blum demands as she greets me in the lobby of the King David Hotel, "and what have you done with my father?" I laugh appreciatively at this newest twist on her antic idea that I have been invaded by aliens—an idea that first began taking shape about fourteen months ago, during my last visit to Israel, where she has been living for about twenty-seven years now. And thereby hangs a long and complicated tale.

In late 2003, seizing as usual on a chance to see her and my four Israeli grandchildren, I had accepted an invitation to the conference on security held every year under the auspices of the Herzliya Institute. Though this was only the fourth such annual conference, it had by then developed into a major Israeli institution. And because everyone who was anyone felt obligated to attend, it had also increasingly become the place in which the nation's political leaders preferred to issue their most important public pronouncements. Hence it was at this fourth annual Herzliya conference in December 2003 that Prime Minister Ariel Sharon confirmed the rumors about his intention to put a "disengagement plan" into effect.

The plan had three components. The first was to accelerate construction of the security fence that had recently begun going up between "Israel proper" and the territories it had captured from Jordan on the West Bank in the Six-Day war of 1967. Already some eight hundred Israelis had been murdered by Palestinian suicide bombers who had infiltrated into the country from the West Bank, and the main (indeed, Sharon insisted, the only) purpose of the fence was to make it harder for these monstrous human missiles to do their grisly work.

The second component of the plan was to dismantle a number of Jewish settlements in Gaza and the West Bank. "I know," Sharon said, "you would like to hear names, but we should leave something for later." All he would divulge for the moment was that the settlements to be "relocated" would be "those that will not be included in the territory of the state of Israel in any future agreement." At the same time, however, he promised that Israel would "strengthen its control over those same areas in the land of Israel that will constitute an inseparable part of the state of Israel in any future agreement."

These formulations represented a reaffirmation of Sharon's acceptance of the "road map" implementing—or purporting to implement—George W. Bush's vision of (as Sharon now summarized it) "a democratic Palestinian state with territorial contiguity in Judea and Samaria and economic viability, which would conduct normal relations with Israel."

By now, Sharon's acquiescence in the establishment of a Palestinian state raised not a single eyebrow. This was in stark contrast to the response when he had first come out in favor of the "two-state solution." Then, there had been amazement all around. After all, Sharon had always been considered the most hard-line of Israeli hawks, and among the most determined opponents of Palestinian statehood. As a former general, he had opposed it on grounds of security—that is, because he believed that it would become a haven for terrorists and a launching pad for new military assaults on the Jewish state. But in addition to these considerations, he had also opposed it because, in his view, Israel had a solid claim on these territories.

Though not a religiously observant Jew, let alone an ultra-Orthodox one, Sharon often said (I heard him say it more than once with my own ears) that he was a Jew first and an Israeli second. It was, then, as a Jew that he always referred to the territories as Judea and Samaria, never as "the West Bank" and certainly never as "occupied." For how could the very heartland of the biblical land of Israel be considered foreign to the present-day children of Israel? And it was both as a Jew and as a military man that, through the various ministerial offices he held in past governments, Sharon had done so much to increase the number and size of the Jewish settlements in those territories that he became known as the "father of the settler movement." As he saw it, not only did Jews have an absolute right to live in Judea and Samaria, but by being placed along certain strategically located routes, they would form a protective barrier against invading armies.

· · · · ·

It was hard to say precisely when Sharon's conversion to the two-state solution occurred. But so far had he traveled from his old position that, shortly before the December 2003 Herzliya conference, he had even used the word "occupation" in speaking of the territories. There was, then, nothing new in Sharon's restatement at Herzliya of his commitment to the two-state solution.

There was, however, something very new indeed in the path he now laid out for getting there. The Palestinians, he said, had thus far failed to take the first step to which they had pledged themselves under the road map: namely, to "uproot the terrorist groups" and to "call a halt to incitement and violence." On the contrary: "the terrorist organizations joined with Yasir Arafat and sabotaged the process with a series of the most brutal terror attacks we have ever known."

This might well have been seized upon as a good and sufficient reason for Israel to renege on its own difficult obligations under the road map, which included withdrawal from a still unspecified swath of the "occupied" territories. And yet Sharon (who as a general had been famous for bold tactical surprises) went in precisely the opposite direction. Israel, he announced—and here was the third component of his disengagement plan—not only would stick by its commitments, but would do so even if the Palestinians were to persist in disregarding theirs. While he would still prefer "direct negotiations" with the Palestinian Authority (PA), if it continued "dragging its feet," Israel would within a few months act unilaterally on the new disengagement plan.

Some days earlier, upon arriving at the 2003 Herzliya conference, I had been uncertain about the value of the security fence. People whose opinion I trusted doubted that it could stop, or even significantly reduce, terrorist attacks; others were confident that it would. There was also the question of whether its real purpose, despite Sharon's strong denial, was to draw the de-facto border between Israel and the future Palestinian state, and if so, whether the proposed route conceded too much or too little. About these issues, too, I was uncertain.

And then there was the problem I had with the road map. George W. Bush was the first American president to come out openly in favor of a Palestinian state. But after being stuck for a while in old habits of thought, he clearly came to the conclusion that it made no sense to add still another state to those harboring and sponsoring terrorism, precisely at a time when he was fighting to rid the world of such regimes. This led to the historic statement of June 24, 2002, in which Bush declared that the United States would not support the establishment of a Palestinian state unless and until new leaders emerged who would begin building "entirely new political and economic institutions, based on democracy, market economics, and action against terrorism."

These conditions, like the Bush Doctrine out of which they logically flowed and of which they formed a part, constituted a rebuke to and a repudiation of the approach long favored by the foreign ministries and the foreign-policy establishments of virtually every country in the world, including the United States itself. At worst, the traditional approach had always been based on the demonstrably false premise that Israel was the main obstacle to a peaceful resolution of the war—both hot and cold—that had been waged against it by the Arab world from the moment the Jewish state was born in 1948; at best, the two parties were held (in the language of moral equivalence so dear to this mentality) to be equally responsible for "the cycle of violence." But on June 24, 2002, Bush effected a major change of emphasis.

To be sure, he did "challenge Israel to . . . support the emergence of a viable, credible Palestinian state" by freezing "settlement activity in the occupied territories," by "permitting innocent Palestinians to resume work and normal life," and by pulling its military forces out of areas heavily populated by Palestinians. But these demands were themselves made contingent upon Palestinian action against terrorism, and in any case they played a decidedly subordinate role to the imperative of Palestinian reforms "based on democracy, market economics, and action against terrorism." By beginning with that imperative, and by devoting most of his speech to spelling it out, Bush for the first time placed the onus on the Palestinians rather than on the Israelis. Moreover, he refused to accept the inevitability, never mind the desirability, of a Palestinian state run by the arch-terrorist and kleptocrat Arafat—or any other leader cast in the same mold.

Nor was that all. Instead of buying into the idea that the conflict in question was a struggle between Israel and the Palestinians alone—with Israel cast as Goliath and the Palestinians as David—Bush declared that the Palestinian people had for decades been "pawns" in a much wider war involving the whole of the Middle East and aimed at the destruction of the Jewish state. He therefore called on all the other states in the region to halt "the flow of money, equipment, and recruits to terrorist groups seeking the destruction of Israel—including Hamas, Islamic Jihad, and Hizballah." Specifically, "the shipment of Iranian supplies to these groups" must be blocked, and "Syria must choose the right side in the war on terror by closing terrorist camps and expelling terrorist organizations."

· · · · ·

All this had been sweet music to my ears. But a jarringly cacophonous note was sounded when the State Department took over the job of producing a blueprint that was supposed to put Bush's policy into practice; and to make matters worse, State then proceeded to join with the European Union, the United Nations, and Russia in what came to be designated in diplospeak as the Quartet. Had there, I wondered, ever been a better case of the fox being invited into the henhouse?

In due course the fox emerged from the henhouse with the road map—another diplospeak coinage—clenched between its teeth. According to a careful analysis of this document by David Makovsky and Robert Satloff, it represented not the fulfillment but "the antithesis of Bush's June 24 vision for peacemaking in terms of substance, sequence, and procedure."* This may have been going a bit too far; yet, leaving aside the technical details to which Makovsky and Satloff pointed, the very fact that the Quartet had no compunction about forging ahead even while Arafat remained in power certainly did conflict with Bush's vision.

Why, then, did Bush endorse the road map? The most plausible answer involved the British prime minister Tony Blair, who had been with him in his decision to invade Saddam Hussein's Iraq and who was still with him in the difficult effort to plant the seeds of democracy there now that Saddam was gone. Since Blair believed that nothing was more important than resolving the Israeli-Palestinian conflict, Bush had promised to repay his support on Iraq by devoting more attention to that conflict. Even so, was it really necessary for Bush to play along with the fiction that the new leadership he had called for had materialized in the person of a prime minister appointed and controlled by Arafat?

Here, I thought, the answer lay in what I had come to see as Bush's characteristic *modus operandi.* Thus, just as he had challenged the UN to enforce its own resolutions on Iraq; just as, far from "rushing into war," as his opponents charged, he had waited many months before taking

---

*See also, in *Commentary,* Daniel Pipes, "Does Israel Need a Plan?" (February 2003) and Abraham D. Sofaer, "The U.S. and Israel: The Road Ahead" (May 2003).

action without the blessing of the Security Council; and just as he would later do in backing the negotiations aimed at keeping Iran from developing and North Korea from deploying nuclear weapons—so in this instance he was giving his critics every chance to show that they could attain the goals they claimed to share with him by means other than the use of force, or at least without rocking every boat in sight.

It was because I had come to place so much faith in Bush that I was able to overcome my misgivings about the road map. And it was partly because Sharon was also putting his money on Bush that I was ready to bet on Sharon. Unlike most Israelis, Sharon seemed to understand that the Bush Doctrine was already changing the entire context in which the Arab/Muslim war against the Jewish state had always been waged, and that in this new context, there were things Israel could do that it would have been too risky to do before.

As Sharon spoke that night at the Herzliya conference, it was not yet clear that the disengagement plan would entail a complete Israeli withdrawal from the Gaza Strip. But so far as my daughter was concerned, the dismantling of any settlements whatsoever meant giving in to the terrorists, and it therefore clashed rather than dovetailed with the Bush Doctrine. There were those who objected to the disengagement plan mainly because of its unilateralism. But not Ruthie. Along with some of her political friends and allies on the Right, especially those who (unlike her) were religious, not even reciprocal concessions could justify throwing Jews out of the homes they had been encouraged to build by successive Israeli governments—and most of all by Sharon himself.

Ruthie took it for granted that I would be on her side, and so, I soon gathered, did other opponents of the disengagement plan whom I ran into during the breaks between sessions at the Herzliya conference. These were people who remembered me for my early and relentless criticism of the Oslo agreement. They were right: even before it was formally announced, I had laced into this rumored agreement in a lecture in Jerusalem, attacking its assumption that the Palestinians had given up their dream of wiping Israel off the map, and predicting that it would lead not to peace but to war. For the next seven years I would persist in this vein in my own writings, while also, as editor of *Commentary*, opening the magazine's pages to the handful of intellectuals who had the stomach to endure being excoriated as enemies of peace. Then, when war finally came in the form of the second *intifada* launched by Arafat in September 2000 in response to an Israeli offer of statehood on 95 percent of the occupied territories, even many on the Israeli Left who had worshipped at the shrine of Oslo finally acknowledged that its viciously reviled critics had been right all along.

Having always been proud of me for playing this role, Ruthie was now amazed to discover that on the whole I supported Sharon's disengagement plan—more amazed even than she had been by Sharon himself for announcing it. No doubt explanations could be found for Sharon's turnabout, but there was simply no accounting for mine. Desperately searching for something, anything, that would explain it away, she hit upon a happy inspiration. Like the "pod people" in the movie *Invasion of the Body Snatchers*, I had been taken over by aliens who were using me to mouth opinions that her father—the real "pod(horetz)"—could not conceivably hold.

· · · · ·

The joke would prove to be a godsend, making it possible to avoid nasty arguments as, in the months ahead, the gap between us would widen with further adumbrations of Sharon's disengagement plan. Now here we are at the end of January 2005, and if at Herzliya Sharon had refused to specify which settlements he meant to uproot, by this point he is proposing to withdraw every last Israeli—some 8,000 in all—from the Gaza Strip, and to dismantle at least four settlements in Samaria.

By this point, too, Arafat has died and Mahmoud Abbas has been elected to succeed him as president of the Palestinian Authority. This is the same man who two years earlier served a brief and hapless term as prime minister under Arafat. Hastily embraced then by Sharon and Bush as the kind of new leader demanded by the president's June 24, 2002 statement, he turned out to be the instrument of yet another of Arafat's con games. Now Sharon is accepting him once more as a "partner for peace," and there is even a photograph of the two of them shaking hands in a gesture that inevitably conjures up the image of Rabin and Arafat going through the same motion on the White House lawn the day the Oslo agreement was signed. No wonder Sharon seems to his opponents to be entering into Oslo II—though they also seem unable to decide whether this is better or worse than his unilateral "surrender to terrorism."

As for the fence, it has proved a far greater success in cutting down on terrorist attacks than even its most enthusiastic proponents had expected. On the other hand, its proposed route has kept changing and its completion has repeatedly been delayed by rulings of a supreme court that makes even the most liberal members of our own Supreme Court look like strict constructionists and models of judicial restraint.

This is why Ruthie and other Israelis of her persuasion fear that the fence will wind up sitting on the insecure borders that enclosed Israel before 1967; that all of Judea and Samaria—and even East Jerusalem—will be handed over to the Palestinians; and that, because the whole world (including many Israelis) takes as axiomatic the Arab position that a Palestinian state must be *judenrein,* the roughly 240,000 Israelis currently living in Judea and Samaria, like the settlers in Gaza before them, will in their turn face the prospect of being dragged out of their homes by the Israeli army and packed off to "Israel proper." If, she now says to me—her eyes ablaze with indignation—any such thing were to be done to Palestinians, or to anyone else, it would be called "transfer" or "ethnic cleansing" and condemned as a crime against humanity. But with Jews as the victims, it is being transmuted by a malignant political alchemy into nothing less than an act of justice.

Ruthie is absolutely certain that her father would have been the first to understand and protest against all this. But the aliens have invaded him, and the aliens have other ideas.

TUESDAY, FEBRUARY 1

On this occasion, I have come to Israel as part of a small group associated with the Hudson Institute. We are here to receive a series of "briefings," mostly from the political Right, on the current state of affairs in the country, the first of which is being given today by A.*

Knowing that A. is a great admirer of Sharon, I am not surprised when he launches into a strong defense of the disengagement plan. But there are two unexpected wrinkles in his presentation.

One is his description of the pullout from Gaza as a "shortening" of Israel's defensive lines—not in the military but in the political sense. This formulation is new to me, though on reflection I realize that it does not differ all that much from how the new Palestinian leaders interpret the disengagement plan. Their take on it is that Sharon is withdrawing

---

*Not having taken notes, I feared that I might misquote the speakers who briefed us. I also wanted to avoid saddling them with the responsibility for my own paraphrastic summaries of what they said. For these reasons I have withheld their names and disguised their identities in other ways as well. In addition to scrambling the dates on which we met with them, I have sometimes amalgamated points made by several different speakers and assigned them to a single one, and in other cases I have taken points made by a single speaker and distributed them among several. I have done my best, however, to present an accurate account of the points themselves and of the general arguments they serve.

from Gaza only to get American permission for a "land grab" in the West Bank, and they cite the projected route of the fence as proof that Sharon intends to maintain control over anywhere from a third to a half of the occupied territories.

Be that as it may, to judge by everything I have been reading and hearing in recent months, A.'s description of the disengagement plan is not the usual argument Israelis make for it. As that argument goes, the only way Israel can remain democratic is to stop ruling over the Palestinians; and (because the Palestinians have a higher birthrate than the Israelis) the only way it can remain Jewish is to separate itself from them.

This line of thought originated on and was once largely confined to the Left. But no longer. The second *intifada,* and especially the horrific new weapon of suicide bombing that it introduced into the terrorist armory of the Palestinians, drove most Israelis to the despairing conclusion that there was simply no living with these people. As one participant at the 2003 Herzliya conference said to me in a private conversation: "Why should we keep trying to negotiate peace with people who want only to murder as many of us as they can? Instead of going on with this charade, the best thing we can do is cut ourselves off from them with the fence, and then let them stew in their own juices."

He was putting the case more bluntly than most Israelis would have been comfortable with, but it seemed clear that this sentiment was very widely shared and that, more than any other factor, it lay behind the overwhelming degree of support then being expressed for Sharon's disengagement plan.

Today, however, it is equally clear that Sharon has much less support than he did fourteen months ago. Since then—with the death of Arafat, the election of Abbas as his replacement, and Sharon's decision to accept him as a "partner for peace"—the unilateralist component of the disengagement plan has been dropped and the "charade" of negotiations has been resumed. In tandem with these developments, second thoughts about the price and the risks of his plan have come into play. By now, opposition to Sharon from within his own ranks has hardened to the point where former supporters and admirers are certain that the Palestinians have him exactly wrong, and that, far from aiming for a "land grab" in Judea and Samaria, he intends to pull all the way back to the '67 borders.

Nevertheless, Sharon, who (to my great surprise) has turned out to be as brilliant a politician as he was a general, has managed by adroit tactical maneuvers to fend off the opposition bred by these second thoughts.

Having exhausted all the parliamentary means at their disposal, the opposition has now invested all its hopes in forcing a referendum on the pullout from Gaza—and it is in connection with this issue that I encounter the second unexpected wrinkle in A.'s briefing. Proponent of the disengagement plan though he is, A. thinks Sharon is wrong to resist holding a referendum. For one thing, he believes that Sharon would win it, and that this would silence the opposition and unite the nation behind him. And if he were to lose? A.'s answer is to shrug.

Whatever the merits of the debate over a referendum, I gather that the chances of holding one are very slim. At this stage, moreover, it is impossible to tell whether the pullout from Gaza will presage a large-scale evacuation of Judea and Samaria, or whether it will strengthen Israel's case for maintaining its hold over large chunks of those territories.

WEDNESDAY, FEBRUARY 2

Visiting a special facility set up by the police to monitor the Old City of Jerusalem and the area around the Temple Mount, I am reminded that the army is not the only instrument Israel has used in fighting the second *intifada*. With the help of cleverly located cameras, the police have been able to spot and catch a number of suicide bombers before they could blow themselves up. But I am also reminded of the amazing job the army has done under Sharon's direction.

Everyone said that terrorism could not be countered by military means, and that it could only be stopped by a political solution. But as is so often the case in such matters, everyone was wrong. Until June 24, 2002, Bush had not yet fully freed himself from the "cycle of violence" paradigm under which Israel's retaliatory strikes against terrorist attacks, and even such strictly defensive measures as checkpoints, were, and still are, equated with and even blamed for the attacks themselves. But once he realized that this way of looking at things clashed with his general attitude toward terrorism, Bush gave Sharon a tacit green light. No longer having to worry about jeopardizing his relations with the United States, Sharon was finally able to go all-out with the strategy he had hit upon: a combination of defense (the fence, which made it harder for suicide bombers to get through) and offense (targeted assassinations that decapitated the terrorist leadership, plus incursions into and sweeps of their strongholds).

So well did this strategy work that suicide bombing has by now been largely eliminated from the terrorist arsenal of the Palestinians. And even though there continues to be sporadic shelling of several towns and villages within range of the homemade Kassam rockets favored by Hamas, it does little damage. All in all, then, it can be said that the second *intifada* has been defeated.

If I had entertained any doubts about this, they would have been dispelled by the stroll we take with B. through the Old City after leaving the police station. Only a short while ago, he tells us, it would have been foolhardy for any Jew to walk these ancient streets, but today, as we can see for ourselves, there is not so much as a hint of menace in the air: no threatening posters, no hate-filled looks, nothing but beckoning smiles from the Arab shopkeepers in the densely crowded marketplace. They were, B. says, hit very hard by the loss of business they suffered as a result of the *intifada,* and they understandably long to see Israeli bargain-hunters and tourists from abroad streaming into the Old City once again.

THURSDAY, FEBRUARY 3

C., another expert on the Palestinians who briefs us today, is less sympathetic toward them than B. seemed to be. Make no mistake, he warns us: Abbas and the others represent Arafatism without Arafat. The stubble may have been replaced by a clean shave and the kaffiyeh by a coat and tie, but Abbas himself is cut from the same cloth as the man he has replaced.

True, Abbas believes that terrorism has become counterproductive, and that the second *intifada* has ended in failure. But he does not oppose terrorism in principle, and he will not use force to disarm Hamas, Islamic Jihad, or even the al-Aqsa Brigades associated with Fatah, the party of which (like Arafat before him) he himself is the head. In other words, he will not comply with the demand made by both Israel and the United States that he "dismantle the infrastructure of terrorism."

This means that the latest ceasefire—whose terms include a pledge by Israel to refrain from any further targeted assassinations—will only give the terrorist groups a much-needed breathing space. And as they exploit this welcome chance to rearm and regroup in preparation for their next systematic campaign, they can also resort to sporadic attacks whenever they feel that the "peace process" is going too well.*

Nor, C. goes remorselessly on, does Abbas's own willingness to observe a ceasefire and enter into negotiations with the Israelis signify

---

*This prediction would be borne out by the suicide bombing in Tel Aviv on February 25, 2005—the first in more than three months.

that he is genuinely interested in a peaceful resolution of the conflict. If nothing else, his continued insistence on the "right of return" flatly contradicts his professed commitment to the two-state solution. For if such a right were ever granted to the Palestinians, the demographic threat to the Jewish character of Israel would be impossible to fend off, and the end result would be not two states living side by side but a single state with a Palestinian majority.

Asked how the Palestinians see the disengagement plan, C. offers a smile that is simultaneously cynical and wan. Yes, he replies, Abbas and his colleagues do recognize that the second *intifada* failed in its objective—which was to disrupt Israeli society, demoralize its people, and cripple its economy. Nor do they credit the *intifada* with driving Sharon out of Gaza. But ordinary Palestinians are a different story. They have no doubt that Sharon's decision to get out of Gaza—exactly like the decision of his predecessor Ehud Barak to abandon the security zone Israel had established in Lebanon—is another proof that the shelling and bombing of Israeli civilians is the way to go.

But what about the Bush Doctrine? This time, C.'s smile is more cynical than wan. It is all very well, he says, to deliver pretty lectures to the Palestinians about democracy. But Bush is fooling himself if he thinks that the Palestinian people are any less opposed to the existence of Israel than their leaders are. C. does not deny that ordinary Palestinians have been repressed and oppressed by the thuggery and corruption of those leaders. And yet, after years of unremitting indoctrination by the textbooks they study in school, the newspapers they read, the television programs they watch, and the sermons they hear in the mosques, the Palestinians are so imbued with hatred of Israel, and of Jews everywhere, that most of them can hardly imagine living in peace with so great an evil.

Is there, then, no hope at all? Here, to my surprise, C. shies away from the logical conclusion to which his entire analysis points. Suddenly turning into an economic determinist, he allows that internal reform along the lines of Bush's June 24 statement might be possible, but only if it is made a precondition of any further financial aid to the Palestinian Authority. Yet Bush now proposes to give the new crowd an immediate down payment of $350 million. In the absence of a stick, C. is sure that a goodly chunk of this carrot will wind up in the same Swiss banks as all the other millions before them. As for the rest, instead of being used to improve the lot of the Palestinian people, it will in all probability be spent on illegal arms.

· · · · ·

I agree with just about every word C. has uttered. I still see no evidence that "the Abu's"—as Ruthie sardonically mimics the post-Arafat leaders' swaggering preference for their *noms de guerre* as terrorists—have experienced a change of heart. Abbas (Abu Mazen) and his prime minister Ahmed Qureia (Abu Ala) were Arafat's loyal henchmen from the start. As such, they either acquiesced or played an active role in the long series of terrorist atrocities perpetrated by the PLO.

And why not? Far from having been punished for following this path, the PLO under Arafat achieved recognition by the "international community" as the "sole and legitimate representative of the Palestinian people," and was ultimately embraced even by Israel and the United States, both of whom had pledged never to deal with it. Even then, and even after Arafat was awarded the Nobel Peace Prize, he went on sponsoring terrorist attacks without losing any sympathy or support—not from the world at large; not from the United States (under the administration of Bill Clinton, he was invited to the White House more often than any other foreign leader); and not from Israel (under the Labor governments of Yitzhak Rabin, Shimon Peres, and Ehud Barak, and, if reluctantly, under the Likud government of Benjamin Netanyahu as well, he continued being treated as a "partner for peace").

Things began to change only in 2001, when Sharon, deciding that enough was enough, refused to have anything further to do with Arafat, and finally penned him up in his compound in Ramallah. At first Bush had permitted himself to be influenced by the State Department's knee-jerk disapproval of this move. But then the Israelis intercepted the *Karine A*, a ship trying—in violation of a ceasefire that had been brokered by an American envoy—to smuggle arms into the hands of the Palestinians. Questioned over the phone by Bush, Arafat claimed that he knew nothing about any such ship and accused Israel of trumping up the incident as an excuse to break the ceasefire.

This was exactly the kind of con game Arafat had been playing with perfect success ever since assuming his new persona as a pursuer of peace. But like practically everyone else in the world, Arafat had "misunderestimated" George W. Bush. Not only did Bush refuse the sucker bait, but—aware of the overwhelming evidence proving that the *Karine A* had been a PA operation from start to finish, and disgusted by being told so blatant a lie in a one-on-one conversation—he now joined Sharon in refusing to have anything to do with Arafat.

It was the isolation of Arafat, combined with the launching of Sharon's new strategy and the green light Bush gave to it, that turned the tide against the second *intifada*. And as things grew worse for the Palestinians, Abbas and a number of other Arafat loyalists correlatively grew more and more convinced that the deliberate murder of Israeli civilians was losing its usefulness as a tactic and becoming both militarily and politically counterproductive.

I agree, then, with C. in doubting that there has been a real change of heart on the issue of terrorism among Arafat's successors. As for their embrace of the two-state solution, C.'s insistence that it is tactical rather than principled fits very well with my own take on the situation. Thus, I have long been convinced that the war against the Jewish state can be ended only by those who have been waging it since 1948, and that the Arab/Muslim world will make peace with Israel only after it makes peace with *itself* over the existence of a sovereign Jewish state in its midst, wherever its boundaries might be drawn. Until, that is, the day comes when the peoples of the greater Middle East, and their Muslim brethren elsewhere, can find it in their hearts to acknowledge the right of the Jewish people to a state of their own in the land of their forefathers, any peace treaty will amount to nothing more than a temporary ceasefire in an ongoing campaign to wipe Israel off the map.

At the same time, on the assumption that in the affairs of men nothing is forever, I could not rule out the possibility that this wondrous day might actually come. Which brings me to George W. Bush, and to where I disagree with C.

I have no great quarrel with him when he questions the wisdom of sending more money to the Palestinian Authority before Abbas has earned it by cracking down on the terrorists and taking serious steps toward democratization. But surely the money is only a gesture, and is in any event a trivial matter as compared with what Bush has done to the context in which the Palestinians are now forced to operate. Under the Bush Doctrine, terrorist acts are no less evil when committed by Palestinians than when perpetrated by al-Qaeda; and the PA is just another one of the despotic regimes in the region that the United States has set about to replace with governments committed to the establishment and expansion of political and economic freedom.

Of course, the PA, unlike all the other regimes targeted by the Bush Doctrine, is not a full-fledged state. But there's the rub. If Abbas and his colleagues want a state of their own, the price they will have to pay is both a serious commitment to democratization and a break with Arafat's policy of professing to accept Israel while waging a terrorist war against it for which he brazenly disclaimed any responsibility. Arafat got away with this game until he tried it on George W. Bush; if his successors are foolish enough to reach into the same bag of tricks, they stand to lose a great deal more than a few hundred million American dollars. For unless I completely misread him, George W. Bush will not be put off by the rit-ualistic condemnations of terrorism or the revolving-door arrests of the Arafat era; he will not be bamboozled by lies ("I never authorized this"); and he will not tolerate excuses ("I don't have the power to stop it").

The upshot is that the Palestinians are now as subject as all the other regimes in the broader Middle East to the great new force that Bush has set into motion throughout the region. Moreover, the velocity this force has acquired since the elections in Iraq on January 31 strongly sug-gests that the Bush Doctrine will have proved itself so decisively by the time its author leaves office that it will be next to impossible for his suc-cessor to change course. Hence, if the Palestinians are hoping to wait Bush out, the odds are that they are hoping in vain.

All in all, the plain fact is that the Palestinians are in a *less* advan-tageous position than any of the other regimes in the region to resist the Bush Doctrine, if only because, if they lose American support, the state-hood they seek will most surely elude them.

Do the Palestinians really want statehood if it means giving up the dream they have always dreamed of eliminating a Jewish state from the Middle East? Arafat showed that he wanted no part of statehood on such terms when he rejected the offer of it made to him by Barak and Clin-ton. In this, the most crucial respect of all, it remains to be seen just how new the new leaders of the Palestinian Authority truly are.

FRIDAY, FEBRUARY 4 – WEDNESDAY, FEBRUARY 9

All the many experts we meet for the rest of our stay fully share in C.'s skepticism about the Palestinians. Even those who tend to credit the sin-cerity of Abbas's stated opposition to terrorism, and who take his pro-fessions of conversion to a two-state solution more or less at face value, also doubt that he possesses either the personal or the political strength to act upon them. But this is a positively sunny analysis as compared with what we keep hearing about Sharon. One briefer after another pours scorn on every feature of the admiring picture that had been drawn for us by A. when we first arrived.

The exceptions are few, and even they are less positive than mixed. For example, D., who acknowledges that Sharon has his virtues and who supports the disengagement plan as the least bad of the available alternatives, also complains that Sharon is no respecter of democratic norms. In similar fashion, E., while grudgingly admitting that Sharon framed the right strategy for defeating the second *intifada,* goes on to attack him for failing to finish the job by dismantling the entire infrastructure of violence sheltered or operated by the PA.

From there it is all downhill into the swamps of motive-mongering. According to F., the only reason Sharon came up with his disengagement plan was to distract attention from the attorney general's investigations into various accusations of corruption against him and his sons. According to G., Sharon was courting favor with the Left so that he could betray his own supporters without losing power. According to H., Sharon the soldier may have been a hero, but Sharon the politician is only out to save his own skin, even if that means jeopardizing the safety of the country for which he once risked his life.

This kind of stuff puts me off, and I am relieved when I. comes along to present a respectable case against the disengagement plan. Sharon, I. maintains, has everything backward. By this he means that if there is to be a withdrawal from Gaza, it should follow upon, not precede, democratic reform. This is the position most famously associated with Natan Sharansky, whose own way of putting it is that the time for Jews to move out of areas heavily populated by Palestinians, if they should wish to do so, is when they are free to stay without having to fear for their lives.

My heart goes out to this idea, and I would like nothing better than to run with it. But the trouble is that, even in a best-case scenario for democratic reform within the PA, it will take a very long time before the lambs will be able to feel safe in lying down next to the lions of Gaza, Judea, and Samaria.

Why not wait, then? This is what I myself once thought was the best course for Israel to follow: that is, to stall until the arrival of that happy day when the Arab/Muslim world in general, and the Palestinians in particular, convincingly demonstrated that they had, however reluctantly, reconciled themselves to the existence of a sovereign Jewish state in their midst. And it was precisely because it was obvious no such day had arrived when the Oslo accords were signed that I felt sure the agreement would end in another violent assault against an Israel weakened by unilateral concessions.

· · · · ·

Today, the opponents of the disengagement plan who see it as Oslo II, with Sharon cast as Rabin in wolf's clothing and Abbas as Arafat in a suit, seize upon every sign that the requisite change of heart has still not taken place. Yet even though I am inclined to agree with them about the Palestinians, I think they are wrong about Sharon.

Like Sharon in 2003, Rabin had been prompted to act in the early 1990s by a big change in world affairs. In his case, the change was the demise of the Soviet Union. As he saw it, this momentous event had completely altered the old "strategic equation" in the Middle East by depriving the "frontline" Arab states of the armorer they had previously depended upon for engaging Israel militarily. In consequence, there was almost no likelihood that they would start any more conventional wars, as they had done several times in the past. This meant in effect that the Palestinians were now on their own; and while they could, on their own, assuredly make life miserable for Israel through terrorism, they were too weak to pose an "existential threat" to the Jewish state. The only serious threat now came from the missiles of Iran and/or Iraq. To protect itself from that threat, Israel needed the help of the United States in building an effective system of antiballistic-missile defense.

Thus, for Rabin, the overriding strategic objective—merging military with political imperatives—was to ensure continued American support. How to do this? Well, the Americans were convinced that giving the Palestinians a state of their own was the answer to unrest and instability throughout the Middle East. It followed that if Israel were to drop its "intransigent" resistance to this solution, relations with Washington would be more or less permanently shored up. This would in one stroke eliminate any future possibility that Israel might be denied the advanced military technology on which its survival now rested and which it could get only from the Pentagon.

Whatever the other merits of this analysis, Rabin should have known, even if Washington did not know and did not wish to know, that the demise of the Soviet Union had not been accompanied by the end of Arab rejectionism in general or, in particular, by a new Palestinian willingness to accept a two-state solution. And Rabin should also have known, even if, again, Washington did not know and did not wish to know, that a Palestinian state ruled by Arafat was a formula for more and not less unrest and instability throughout the Middle East.

In short—as the outcome of Oslo would so vividly demonstrate—Rabin badly misjudged the significance for Israel of the big change that had taken place in the strategic environment of the early 1990s.

Obviously the count is not yet in on the significance for Israel of the big change wrought by 9/11 and the American response to it in the form of the Bush Doctrine, to both of which Sharon's disengagement plan is itself a response. But it is already safe to say that, as the second *intifada* killed off the Israeli illusions behind Oslo, 9/11 marked the demise of "stability" as the be-all and end-all of American policy in the broader Middle East. "For decades," Bush now declared, "free nations tolerated oppression in the Middle East for the sake of stability. In practice, this approach brought little stability and much oppression." And so the United States under Bush adopted exactly the opposite approach, and has ever since been working to destabilize the old despotisms on which, in the pre-9/11 era, Washington had long relied.

The corollary—to say once more what cannot be said too often— is that George W. Bush will not cooperate (as his predecessors were ready and even eager to do) in the creation of a Palestinian state run by the likes of an Arafat. From this it follows that Arafat's successors—to repeat another thing that cannot be said too often—are being confronted by the Bush Doctrine with the choice between a two-state solution and no state at all. Therefore, even if the Palestinians have not undergone the change of heart on which I myself once thought Israel should wait for as long as it took, the Bush Doctrine will force them to behave (behave, not just talk) as though they have done so: to crack down on terrorism, to set a course toward political and economic freedom, and to forget about the "right of return."*

Surely, then, it is too much to demand—as I., echoing Sharansky, does—the creation of an environment in which Jews can live at ease under Palestinian sovereignty. Surely, waiting indefinitely upon this happy eventuality would entail a failure to seize on the new possibilities created by the same Bush Doctrine of which Sharansky, who in this respect goes far beyond it, is otherwise a great booster (as is its author of him). Surely it is enough for now to demand of a Palestinian state-in-the-making that it convincingly demonstrate its intention to live on peaceful terms with the Jewish state beside it.

. . . . .

---

*Bush made this last condition explicit in writing to Sharon on April 14, 2004: "It seems clear that an agreed, just, fair, and realistic framework for a solution to the Palestinian refugee issue . . . will need to be found through the establishment of a Palestinian state, and the settling of Palestinian refugees there, rather than in Israel."

Other elements of a respectable case against the disengagement plan are presented by J., whose main theme is that, far from making Israel safer through a shortening (whether military or political) of its defensive lines, Sharon's policy will make it more vulnerable, and in at least two ways. First, since the Palestinians are entirely justified in interpreting Israel's withdrawal from Gaza as cutting and running in the face of terrorism, it will inevitably encourage more terrorist attacks. Second, with the redeployment of the army, the Israeli towns within reach of the Kassam rockets will now become even more naked unto their enemies than before.

Reasonable though these arguments may be, I am less moved by them than I am by I.'s Sharanksy-like stand. As to the prediction that terrorism will increase after the withdrawal from Gaza, I have already come to the conclusion that if it turns out to be right, it will bring about the loss (or, at a minimum, the suspension) of American support for a Palestinian state. So, too, if neighboring Israeli towns continue to be shelled. If these things happen, the outcome J. most fears and opposes will be headed off by yet another instance of the notorious Palestinian habit of never failing to miss an opportunity to miss an opportunity.

J., however, also raises an objection to the fence that is harder for me to dismiss. Not that he questions its success as a security measure. How could he when, in areas where it has been completed, not a single suicide bomber has gotten through?* Nevertheless, if it is true that the fence, when finished, will mark the de-facto border between Israel and the nascent Palestinian state, the question arises of how many Jews now living in Judea and Samaria it will be able to encompass. Is J. right in darkly predicting that as few as 50,000 of them will wind up within the new borders of the Jewish state, and that the other 190,000 will be added to the 8,000 of their fellows already slated for eviction from Gaza?

Some months ago, perhaps trying to mollify alarmists like J., Dov Weisglass, Sharon's top adviser, told an interviewer that, in exchange for the withdrawal of 8,000 Jews from Gaza, 190,000 Jews in Judea and Samaria would be able to *stay* in their homes. This statement was then subjected to denials and disavowals. Still, the impression I receive from a long one-on-one meeting with K., a high official of the Sharon government, is that the denials and disavowals were only an attempt to stuff a prematurely sprung cat back into the bag. The de-facto border being

---

*It appears that the one who got through into Tel Aviv a few weeks later was able to make it only because that part of the fence had not been completed.

drawn by the fence, this official assures me, will encompass the big settlement blocs whose combined population does indeed add up to about 190,000 people.

When I ask K. how he thinks this will go down with Washington, he pulls out a copy of Bush's letter to Sharon of April 14, 2004, and—adding his own heavy emphasis—quotes from the relevant passage:

> In light of new realities on the ground, *including already existing major Israeli population centers,* it is unrealistic to expect that the outcome of final-status negotiations will be a full and complete return to the armistice lines of 1949 [i.e., the '67 borders].

Well, I think to myself, 190,000 is better than 50,000. But how on earth will Sharon pull it off without unleashing a mini civil war? Already there is much speculation about the violence that may erupt once the withdrawal starts in Gaza, where there are "only" 8,000 to be relocated. Already there are rabbis decreeing that it is forbidden for a Jew to force another Jew out of the land of Israel. And already people are wondering how many members of the IDF—about a third of whose officer corps is now religious to one degree or another—will pay heed to these rabbis and refuse to carry out what they might well consider illegal orders. And what about secular Israeli soldiers, especially those who sympathize with the settlers? (One such is my own grandson, who makes his mother look like a moderate, and who is now serving in the very unit of the IDF that will be sent to assist in the relocation.) What will happen if, God forbid, they are fired upon or otherwise assaulted and are required to use their guns in order to get the job done?

There is, I now learn from a briefing by L., a theory according to which Sharon is hoping for just such a horrendous outcome in Gaza so that he can persuade Washington that evacuating even as "few" as 50,000 settlers from the West Bank would be impossible. I very much doubt that Sharon has that much Machiavelli in him. I also doubt (wishfully?) that the settlers will go beyond passive resistance or force a bloody confrontation with the IDF. But at this stage, no one—certainly not an outsider like me—has any way of knowing for sure.

As an American, however, I think there is one thing I know better than any of the Israelis who have been briefing us all week, and it again concerns George W. Bush.

·　·　·　·　·

Anti-Semitic conspiracy theorists imagine that a nefarious cabal of neo-conservative advisers—all of whom are Jewish "Likudniks" and are also either paid or unpaid agents of the Israeli government—have seduced this fool of a president into a policy whose stated goal may be to fight terrorism and to spread democracy throughout the broader Middle East, but whose real purpose is to serve Sharon's expansionist designs. Yet in almost comical contrast, what worries most of the *Israeli* Likudniks by whom we have been briefed this week is that Bush, in his eagerness to resolve Israel's conflict with the Palestinians through the establishment of a Palestinian state, will allow them to get away with violating the conditions he himself has attached to American support for such a state. At its most nightmarish, the fear is that Abbas will appease Hamas, Bush will appease Abbas, Sharon will appease both Abbas and Bush, and the lives of tens of thousands of Israelis will be disrupted and even ruined to make room for a terrorist state standing next to an Israel pushed back to the indefensible borders of 1967.

To me, after almost four years of watching Bush in action, this seems wildly off the mark. Indeed, just as I would be flabbergasted if Bush were to break faith with his pledge to help sow the seeds of political and economic freedoms throughout the broader Middle East, so I would be astounded were he to renege on the preconditions he has attached to his support for a Palestinian state. And here a fascinating irony occurs to me concerning my original misgivings about the road map.

I still think that the road map embodied an attempt by the usual suspects to sabotage the June 24 speech, but I now think that the joke may be on them. Yes, the authors of the road map did manage to reintroduce the old framework of "moral equivalence" that Bush had rejected on June 24. Nevertheless, the pretense that they were implementing his "vision" coerced them into including under phase I the demand that the Palestinian leadership "undertake visible efforts on the ground to arrest, disrupt, and restrain individuals and groups conducting and planning violent attacks on Israelis anywhere." Beyond going after these individuals and groups, the Palestinian Authority was also required to mount "effective operations aimed at ... dismantlement of terrorist capabilities and infrastructure."

Now, however, Abbas—who wants to negotiate with the terrorists of Hamas, Islamic Jihad, and those connected with his own party—is asking to be relieved of the demand that he crack down on them immediately and hard. There can be little doubt that the authors of the road map would like to support him on this, but Sharon is in a position to rub their noses in their own words, and that is just what he is doing.

Something similar seems to be shaping up with respect to the borders of the future Palestinian state. Under the road map, as soon as it is agreed that both parties have met all their obligations under phase I, they enter phase II, which is supposed to culminate in "the creation of a Palestinian state with provisional borders." But Abbas would like to skip over this stage as well and go directly into phase III, when the "permanent-status agreement" is to be forged on "borders, Jerusalem, refugees, settlements." Here again, the authors of the road map would like to accommodate him, and here too Sharon is in a good position to see them hoist by their own petard.

The upshot is that unless Abbas amazes everyone by turning out to be willing and able both to undertake a genuine struggle against Palestinian terrorism and to speed up the pace of democratic reform, the process will probably get stalled in phase II. This will—just as Bush clearly envisaged in his June 24 statement—give the Israelis a chance to find out whether the Palestinians have truly decided to call off their war against the Jewish state before the most intractable issues get shoved onto the table.

Perhaps because there is so much talk of Sharansky in the air, this ironic turn in the role played by the road map brings up memories of what happened to the Helsinki accords of 1975. At the time, those of us who opposed the policy of détente with the Soviet Union denounced this agreement because it ratified the Soviet domination of Eastern Europe in exchange for nothing more than a paper promise by Moscow to respect certain basic principles of human rights. Although we were right in thinking that the Soviets had no intention of living up to this promise, neither they nor we understood that it had put a very powerful weapon into the hands of dissidents like Sharanksy in their struggle against the Communist regime. Ultimately, Helsinki, instead of ensuring the permanence of the Soviet empire, contributed to its eventual demise.

The analogy is no more perfect than analogies usually are, but I suspect that the road map, which Sharon had good reason to resist endorsing, will wind up protecting him against the Quartet's unremitting campaign to let Abbas off the hook by diluting the demands that Bush made of the Palestinians on June 24, 2002, and which he keeps on reiterating in the same forceful terms whenever he returns to the subject.

· · · · ·

In the end, then, it all comes back to Bush. So relentlessly have I harped on this that one exasperated briefer accuses me of harboring a veritably religious faith in him. The accusation stings because, if true, it would mean that I am again violating the vow I originally made to myself after the election of my old friend Daniel P. Moynihan to the United States Senate in 1976.

Like so many others who had worked to get him there, I had expected Moynihan to persist in the battle we had all been waging against the steadily leftward drift of the Democratic party. But when he broke our hearts by joining in that drift himself, I resolved that from then on I would abide by the words of the Psalmist: "Put not your trust in princes." I managed to keep that promise even in relation to Ronald Reagan, who in those days seemed to me overly cautious in walking the walk of his thrilling anti-Communist talk. But then another old friend, Benjamin Netanyahu, became prime minister of Israel, and out the window went the exhortation of the Psalmist, only to fly back in when Bibi disappointed my hope that he would slam the brakes on Oslo.

Is it now flying out again in relation to George W. Bush? I cannot in all honesty dismiss the possibility. And yet neither can I dismiss the possibility that this is one prince who, on the basis of repeated demonstration, deserves to be trusted.

When I suggest as much to Ruthie as we part, she shoots back without missing a beat: "What is it with you aliens? Weren't you satisfied with corrupting my father politically? Did you also have to go and turn him into an idolator?" As I did when she greeted me on my arrival, I laugh in appreciation of still another new twist on her antic idea of what has happened to me (this one inspired by my book celebrating the prophets of the Hebrew Bible as generals in a great war against idolatry).

But this time—affected as I have been by a week of exposure to the anxieties pervading the Israeli air—the laugh comes out sounding more than a little uneasy. And fully aware as I now am of the heavy price many thousands of Jews will have to pay for the increased security and the peace that I still believe Bush and Sharon, working together, will bring, it is also a laugh that—in accord with an old Yiddish expression now springing into my mind—carries within it the unmistakable intimation of tears.

—April 2005

Hillel Halkin

Israel After Disengagement

It was necessary, it would seem, for the disengagement from Gaza to take place for the strategy behind it to be revealed as unworkable.

That strategy was based on two assumptions that have guided the Likud government of Ariel Sharon, both clearly held by him yet only partially articulated for reasons of political expediency. The first is that Palestinian and Israeli positions are too far apart, and the Palestinian leadership too weak and untrustworthy, for successful negotiations between the two sides to take place in the foreseeable future. The second is that, in the absence of a negotiated agreement, Israel cannot afford, either politically or demographically, to remain forever in the greater part of the territories now controlled by it.

Sharon's operative conclusion from these assumptions was that Israel would have to act unilaterally, withdrawing its army and settlements from most of the territories to borders determined by itself, with no formal quid pro quo from either the Palestinians or the international community. On the one hand, this would relieve it of the moral and physical burden of millions of Palestinians who, even if technically under the jurisdiction of the Palestinian Authority, were unable to live their lives freely with Israeli settlements and military forces on every side of them. On the other hand, it would enable Israel to retain, behind physical barriers now under construction, many of the Jewish settlements established beyond the 1967 ceasefire lines, including all the major "settlement blocs." Such a course of action, it was deemed, would also greatly reduce Palestinian terror, while the new borders, even if not winning international recognition, might gain tacit acceptance from the United States and other countries.

The disengagement from Gaza in August was the first stage in the implementation of this plan. The next stage, even if Sharon and his advisers refused to speak about it openly, was obviously meant to involve a much larger evacuation of settlements from the West Bank, the mountainous region north and south of Jerusalem that was held by Jordan until the 1967 war.

Gaza, then, was a test case. The preliminary results of the test are now in, and they are negative. They show that what was possible with 8,000 settlers in the Gaza Strip will not be possible with the estimated 60,000 settlers who, out of some 250,000 currently living in the West Bank, will end up on the other side of the security fence once it is completed.

This is not a cause for rejoicing. On the contrary, it leaves one deeply perturbed. As readers of *Commentary* know, I supported the disengagement from Gaza because I thought its logic was correct. I did not believe the Palestinian-Israeli peace negotiations that broke down for the last time in early 2001 could be renewed with any hope of success, and I agreed that the greatest dangers facing Israel in the years to come were neither Palestinian terror nor Arab military might but international delegitimization and the erosion and ultimate disappearance of the country's Jewish majority. Unilateral withdrawal seemed the best—indeed, the only practical—way of dealing with these problems. I take no pleasure in having changed my mind.

· · · · ·

The disengagement from Gaza has been widely praised, both in Israel and around the world, as a resounding success. Why, then, do I perversely insist on viewing it as a failure?

In itself, indeed, it was no failure. Despite its many difficult moments, the evacuation of the Gaza Strip settlements went as well as anyone had hoped it might and far better than many people had feared. There was little violence, no serious injuries, and such sparse physical resistance on the part of the settlers and their supporters that the army, which had originally budgeted nearly a month for removing them, finished the job in a week. Dire predictions of civil anarchy and widespread military insubordination proved false. The country held together and weathered the storm handily.

The failure rather consisted in not having understood that even a "successful" disengagement from Gaza would be inconceivable elsewhere if multiplied by a factor of seven or eight.

One might dwell on a few simple statistics. An estimated 42,000 policemen and soldiers took part in the evacuation of the 8,000 Gaza settlers, with another 13,000 held in reserve—that is, at least a third of Israel's police force and the equivalent of four or five army divisions. If proportionally the same number of men in uniform had to evacuate 60,000 equally uncooperative settlers from the West Bank, close to 400,000 of them would be needed. This would require Israel to mobilize all of its military reserves and to assign every policeman and soldier at its disposal to the task.

What would be the cost of evacuating 60,000 settlers? The total expense of the disengagement from Gaza, from paying compensation to the evacuees to chartering the buses that took them away, may approach $2 billion. Taking a conservative figure of $1.5 billion and multiplying it by seven, we arrive at $10.5 billion—one-sixth of Israel's national budget. Such an expenditure, even if spread, say, over a period of three years, would increase the government's annual deficit from a tolerable 3 percent to a hyper-inflationary 10 percent.

And where would 60,000 West Bank settlers be put, pending the construction of new homes for them? To house Gaza evacuees with nowhere to stay, 2,000 hotel rooms had to be rented on a long-term basis. A sevenfold number of 14,000 rooms would amount to a third of Israel's total hotel capacity.

Needless to say, these are crude projections. Yet they do give an idea of what a Gaza-style disengagement from the West Bank might entail. Moreover, they would have to be continually revised upward, since the Jewish population of the West Bank is currently increasing at a rapid rate.

In addition, and this is crucial, a West Bank disengagement would be far more confrontational than was the case in Gaza. The Gaza settlers were, for the most part, ideological moderates living in a remote area of little strategic or Jewish historical importance that could be physically sealed off without difficulty—in spite of which, thousands of diehard protesters managed to join them and to cause most of the trouble once the evacuation began. The West Bank, the biblical heartland of Judea and Samaria that geographically dominates Israel's central coastal plain, is a short drive from Jerusalem and not much farther from Tel Aviv. Many of the settlements that stand to be evacuated there have ideologically hardcore populations that could not be prevented from being massively reinforced from outside. Nor would the leaders of the settler movement, who acted as a force for restraint in Gaza, be that again. This time, faced with what would be for them a catastrophe of far greater magnitude, they would pull out all the stops. In such a situation, the chaos that failed to materialize in August could very well come to pass.

· · · · ·

"But all this," I will be told, "is based on a misguided premise. You are supposing that a West Bank disengagement would have to be carried out in one fell swoop, as in Gaza. If, however, it were to take place gradually, each phase involving a smaller number of settlers, it might be perfectly manageable."

Logistically, this might be so. Psychologically and politically, though, it would not be. This brings us to the next point.

In the past months, Israel has undergone a severe trauma. One aspect of it, the shock of the disengagement to the settler movement and its principal source of support, the country's half-million-strong modern-Orthodox or "national religious" community, was on public display well in advance of August. Although this community's painful reckoning with its punctured illusions has only just begun, it has come as a surprise to no one.

Less predictable were the reactions in other quarters. Sitting in front of their televisions, which provided nonstop, around-the-clock coverage of the evacuation until the last settler had boarded the last bus, many pro-disengagement Israelis had strong visceral responses. According to the polls, 20 percent found themselves more anti-settler than before. But 30 percent moved in the other direction.

Some among this latter group, it can be assumed, were experiencing no more than ordinary human sympathy. Even if you are convinced of its necessity, it is hard to watch people being evicted from their homes without feeling for them. But for other Israelis, it was more than that. As they watched the settlers marching to the waiting buses with their children and Torah scrolls in their arms, they had a deeply disturbing sense of déjà vu. Although they were aware that what they were viewing was in part a media event, staged for their benefit, they could not help associating it with other scenes from Jewish history.

To be sure, the evacuation of the Gaza settlers was no medieval expulsion. If many of them had been turned into temporarily homeless refugees by a Jewish government, that was principally because they themselves had refused until the last moment to negotiate the terms of their relocation. Still, the fact remained that they were being forced from their homes because they were Jews whom a non-Jewish population, justifiably or not, refused to tolerate in its midst. Otherwise, why could not those who wished to remain have done so under Palestinian rule?

Nor was that all. As the TV images shifted from houses being emptied to houses being demolished, the bulldozers and backhoes pulverizing in minutes what had taken long years to build, there were viewers who felt a shiver of concern for their own future.

Zionism, after all, was always a movement of construction. It was indeed the only great revolutionary movement of modern times that did not set out deliberately to destroy anything—not a foreign occupation, not an *ancien régime*, not an oppressive ruling class. It wanted only to build a home for the Jewish people, and from the outset it built wherever it could. "We will clothe you in cement and concrete, / We will spread a rug of gardens at your feet": many Israelis still know by heart lines like these, addressed to the land of Israel by the poet Natan Alterman, that were once sung as anthems of Zionist pioneering.

One cannot understand the post-1967 settlement movement in the occupied territories without realizing that, long before it became an Israeli policy, it was an Israeli instinct. From the arrival of the first Zionist pioneers in Palestine in 1882, Zionism had one grand obsession: to find available land and put Jews on it. That this land might be arid, or swampy, or surrounded by hostile Arab villages was no deterrent. Zionism took what it could get, often paying absurdly high prices for it, and did what Jewish determination could do with it. Israel arose in 1948 along the lines that it did only because this determination was great.

It was this same instinct that caused the Labor government of Golda Meir to found Gush Katif, the main Jewish settlement bloc in the Gaza Strip, on uninhabited sand dunes in the region's southwest corner in the early 1970s. There was nothing particularly rational or equitable about this. The Gaza Strip was already then an impoverished area, crowded with Palestinian refugees, that needed whatever land reserves it had. A Jewish enclave at one far end of it, separated from Israel proper by the Palestinian city of Rafah, was pointless. It came into existence not, as was once said of the British Empire, in a fit of absent-mindedness, but in a fit of habitual creation.

Nevertheless, it is one thing to say that the Gaza settlements should never have been built and quite another to raze them to the ground. (How much better it might have been had they not been razed, and had some of the Palestinians living in Gaza's hovels been given the benefit of them. But both sides, for reasons of their own, were bent on their demolition.) When a great historical movement begins to destroy what it has built, a frisson may seize the observer. Watching this happen was like watching a river turn around and run backward. It felt instinctively wrong. It caused the political commentator Ari Shavit, comparing the televised evacuation to a movie, to write in the pages of the Hebrew daily *Ha'aretz:*

> What was this movie about? About reversibility. From a bulldozer you came and to a bulldozer you shall return.... What made the disengagement a formative Israeli movie was the fact that even at its conclusion, the type of reversibility it describes remains unclear. Was it that of Gush Katif, of Judea and Samaria, or of all of Israel?

How many Israelis agreed that the events of August were emotionally searing? A very large number. In a post-evacuation survey published by Camille Fuchs of Tel Aviv University, 61 percent chose the phrase "hurting and pained" as best describing their country in disengagement's aftermath.

How many changed their minds about supporting a second-stage disengagement in the West Bank? Perhaps as many as 10 percent. A survey conducted in late August by the veteran pollster Mina Zemach reported 54 percent prepared to evacuate more settlements in Judea and Samaria—down from 63 percent in July.

Of course, 54 percent is still a majority. Yet it is a precarious one. Although no one knows what will have become of this figure a year or two from now, it would be difficult to conceive of any Israeli government undertaking a major evacuation of West Bank settlements with so slim a margin of public support.

Indeed, if Israeli politicians have learned anything from the bitter experience of the 1993 Oslo agreement, it is not to make fateful decisions for an almost evenly split country. Ariel Sharon was able to evacuate Gaza without shattering Israel too deeply because he went into it with two-thirds of the country behind him—enough to convince anti-disengagement Israelis that the popular will was against them. Had he done so with the support of only a skimpy majority, the repercussions would have been far greater.

To this must be added a political corollary: a clear national consensus in favor of the surrender of territory can be forged in Israel only when the mainstream Right, or a large part of it, joins the Left in backing it. This happened in 1979–82, when Menachem Begin kept most of his Likud party in line while negotiating and implementing a withdrawal from Sinai, and it is what happened again now, too, despite a far more serious rebellion in Likud's ranks. But any attempt to evacuate areas of the West Bank without significant support in Likud is a sure prescription for a disastrously ruptured society such as Israel was between the signing of the Oslo agreement and the 1995 assassination of Yitzhak Rabin.

Yet the chances of mobilizing even a part of Likud on behalf of a Gaza-style disengagement in the West Bank are, in the coming years, nil. The party is still smarting from Sharon's rebuff of it when, in May 2004, he ignored its anti-disengagement vote in an internal referendum, and there is a strong likelihood that before the next national elections are held—an event that may come as early as the winter or spring of 2006— it will have replaced him as its leader with Benjamin Netanyahu. Having come out strongly against the withdrawal from Gaza at the last moment while resigning from Sharon's cabinet, Netanyahu is not about to endorse a magnified West Bank version of it. And even if Sharon were to retain control of the Likud and win reelection at the head of it, he would certainly not provoke it into a second insurrection more furious than the first.

That is why it is senseless to think that a unilateral evacuation of most of the West Bank could be made more manageable by breaking it down into phases. Just suppose that Israel had to go through not one more trauma but seven or eight, each considerably worse than last August's and each preceded by long months of savage political warfare. Perhaps the many commentators and the many spokesmen of governments and international organizations who have lauded the disengagement from Gaza as a first step toward more of the same can picture this. I cannot.

· · · · ·

Contrary to the common perception, then, the settlers did not lose in Gaza. Rather, they won by demonstrating that a repeat performance is out of the question. This was indeed their leadership's central goal from the moment it realized that it lacked the votes in the Knesset to block disengagement's first stage. From then on, the real battle was over Judea and Samaria.

This is a battle that began in 1967. From the outset, the settler movement strove to populate the West Bank with enough Jews to make their removal from it impossible. For many years, it seemingly stood no chance of success. Even at the time of the Oslo agreement in the early 1990s, there were barely 100,000 Jewish residents in Judea and Samaria. The astonishing increase that has taken place since then under the most inauspicious circumstances—Israel's handing over of much of the West Bank to the PLO, twelve subsequent years of Palestinian terror, the growing condemnation of the international community—is above all a tribute to the tenacity and resolve of the settlers themselves.

But it would not appear to be a tribute to their ultimate foresight. For where does Israel go from here? In the eyes of nearly all the world, it is still, after the disengagement from Gaza, an illegitimately occupying power in the West Bank. It is also still burdened with millions of Palestinians whose rate of increase far outstrips that of Israeli Jews. True, without the Gaza Strip, the ratio of Jews to Arabs west of the Jordan River has risen from approximately 53–47 to 61–39. But the Palestinian Arab birthrate, which is higher than that of Israel's own Arab citizens, is capable of eliminating that gap—and with it the existence of Israel as a Jewish state—in a generation.

In thinking about where Israel now goes, one might begin with where it cannot and should not go. First on the list is a capitulation to Palestinian demands for a near-total withdrawal to the 1967 ceasefire lines, plus a real or symbolic "right of return" for the Palestinian refugees, in exchange for a formal peace treaty—the Palestinian position when negotiations broke off in 2001. Given the history of PLO and Palestinian Authority mendacity, and the unlikelihood that a state on 22 percent of historical British Mandate Palestine could satisfy minimal Palestinian aspirations, it would be the height of folly for Israel to surrender all of its 1967 gains, with their military and strategic advantages, in return for a piece of paper worth no more than the 1993 Oslo Declaration of Principles. Such a "peace" might last five years or ten; it would almost certainly break down in the end, overridden by Palestine irredentism and the still simmering refugee issue. Meanwhile, the price Israel would have to pay for it would be the evacuation, not of 60,000 West Bank settlers, but of 150,000 or even more—that is, of the Gaza disengagement multiplied by at least twenty.

Additional "mini-disengagements" should also be ruled out. In the absence of productive peace negotiations, there is every reason to expect continued international pressure on Israel to carry out further unilateral withdrawals in order to "keep the peace process going." One temptation might be for an Israeli government to try relieving such pressure by minor pullbacks similar to the one executed from four small settlements in the northern West Bank in tandem with the evacuation of the Gaza Strip. The idea has also been floated of coordinating such pullbacks with the establishment of a "provisional" Palestine state with undefined borders that would expand in the future. Yet even if politically feasible, this would be inadvisable for Israel. It would do nothing but buy time while inviting pressure for more retreats whose limits would not be set in advance.

. . . . .

And time is not in Israel's favor. This is so not just demographically. In recent years, the propaganda push to depict Israel as an apartheid state in which ruling Jews victimize helpless Palestinians has been gaining frightening momentum. Apart from the United States, there is scarcely a Western country in which, despite years of Palestinian terror, anti-Israel sentiment in the media and intellectual life is not dominant and getting stronger.

This is especially the case in Europe, whose large and feared Muslim populations have also helped tip the balance of public opinion against the Jewish state. But even in America, Israel's image has steadily eroded, as evidenced by the recent disinvestment campaigns of large liberal church groups. Although fortunately there is still a long way to go, it is no longer unimaginable that Israel may one day come to be so widely regarded as a latter-day South Africa that public pressure will encourage Western governments, in any case anxious to cozy up to Arab and Muslim nations, to treat it as one.

From the South African analogy, moreover, has flowed an idea that is increasingly voiced even though it is the most absurd of all. If a resemblance to apartheid South Africa is the problem, this line of reasoning goes, then let a resemblance to post-apartheid South Africa be the solution. Turn Israel/Palestine into a single, one-man, one-vote country, and let justice and harmony reign.

How much justice and harmony now reign in South Africa is a debatable question. What is not debatable, however, is that there is no meaningful parallel between apartheid South Africa and present-day Israel/Palestine. On the eve of apartheid's dismantling, South African blacks outnumbered whites by five to one; it was thus a foregone conclusion on both sides that, in agreeing to a single, democratically run state, whites were ceding political control to blacks with no chance of regaining it or of ever again being a dominant force in their country. Their only hope was to continue living there as a legally protected minority with enough economic power to defend their interests. On their ability to retain this power, and the black majority's willingness to let them do so, rests their still far from certain future.

By contrast, a one-man, one-vote Israel/Palestine would be a country in which two more or less numerically equal populations, divided not only by culture, language, religion, history, transnational allegiances, economic and social interests, and territorial disputes, but by a hundred years of bitter enmity, would be required to administer between them a single polity, its institutions, and its military. Can any rational person suppose for a moment that such a country would not soon fly apart at the seams, with far worse bloodshed than it has known in the past? One has to be either naïvely utopian or unscrupulously Machiavellian to promote such a scheme. Yet the longer the status quo continues, the more backing it will win, rendering all the more intolerable a military presence, originally conceived of as temporary, that, almost four decades after the 1967 war, has become ruinous for everyone.

· · · · ·

Still bordering on the seemingly utopian is a solution that, although it has been proposed by different people in different places (including by me in the pages of *Commentary*),* has never gained wide currency. Although it has a great deal of poetic justice on its side, it is doubtful whether it has as much reality.

This solution would be for Israel to offer the Palestinians a confederation of two independent, side-by-side states bound to each other by mutual commitments, among them the agreement of each to allow the other's citizens—perhaps up to an agreed-on population cap—to reside within its borders. These borders, open to the free passage of people and goods in both directions, would run along the 1967 Israel-Jordan ceasefire lines. Jewish settlers could remain in a demilitarized state of Palestine as Israeli citizens; Palestinian citizens could have a similar status in Israel. Israeli troops would be withdrawn from all of the Palestinian state except for the sparsely populated Jordan Valley, where they would be allowed to retain permanent bases.

Such a confederation, which would preserve Israel/Palestine as a single geographical unit while dividing it into two closely linked sovereignties, would have genuine advantages for both sides—as well as offering some bitter pills to swallow and some even greater dangers.

For the Palestinians, it would mean getting the state and the borders they have been insisting on, with the added bonus that the remaining 78 percent of British Mandate Palestine, though under Israeli rule, would be open to them to visit, work in, and live in. Besides giving them

---

*"Why the Settlements Should Stay," June 2002.

all the benefits of participation in the Israeli economy, this would go a long way toward satisfying their demand for the "right of return" of the 1948 refugees. In exchange, however, they would have to accept the permanent presence of settlers and of the Israeli army on land from which they have sworn to eject both.

For Israel, a confederative solution would permit the settlers, or those so choosing, to remain where they are and maintain the Jewish people's historic connection with Judea and Samaria while giving the West Bank's Arabs their freedom. It would also, by retaining the Jordan River as Israel's defense line, provide a high degree of security against any future military threat from the east.

On the other hand, such an arrangement's open borders would provide very little security from Palestinian terror, whose elimination would have to depend on a general state of Palestinian contentment and a strong Palestinian government with the will to suppress violence. Moreover, Israel would be required to surrender sovereignty not only over the "settlement blocs" but over much of Jerusalem, while running the risk of a large influx of poor Palestinians drawn by economic opportunities. Although such migrants would not be eligible for Israeli citizenship, they could, added to the more than one million Israeli Arabs holding such citizenship today, create severe tensions and aggravate nationalist animosities. And who is to say that the Jewish settlers in the state of Palestine might not also end up in bitter disputes with their Arab neighbors, who might be compelled to put up with them but not to like them? Could the Jews count on a Palestinian government to protect them?

In short, the success of a confederative solution would depend on the prior existence of the same good will that it is its goal to achieve, thereby repeating the mistake of Oslo all over again. One lesson of the "peace process" was that such circularity does not work in politics any more than in logic. In situations of conflict, open-ended agreements that do not clearly terminate all major sources of friction tend to exacerbate more than to conciliate. A Palestinian-Israeli confederation, while perhaps not as clearly suicidal as a binational state, would nevertheless be asking for trouble. And of trouble, Israel has had quite enough.

· · · · ·

Is the impasse, then, total? Not necessarily. But the way out of it depends as much on the United States as it does on Israel.

Thus far, the Bush administration's position on disengagement, the West Bank security fence, and Israel's ultimate borders has been consistently ambiguous. U.S. officials, including President Bush and Secretary of State Condoleezza Rice, have spoken repeatedly of the need for further West Bank withdrawals without specifying what areas these should include. They have defended Israel's right to build the fence while also referring to it as "a problem" whose existence should be "temporary," a mere "security barrier" rather than a "political barrier." And although the president has said explicitly that Israel cannot be expected to withdraw to its pre–June 1967 frontier with Jordan, he has declined to state unequivocally that all the major West Bank settlement blocs must remain within Israel.

Thus, in a much-cited letter to Prime Minister Sharon last April, soon after the latter's visit to the Bush ranch in Texas, the president wrote:

> As part of a final peace settlement, Israel must have secure and recognized borders, which should emerge from negotiations between the parties in accordance with United Nations Security Council resolutions 242 and 338. In light of new realities on the ground, including already existing major Israeli population centers, it is unrealistic to expect that the outcome of final-status negotiations will be a full and complete return to the armistice lines of 1949 [which lasted until June 1967], and all previous efforts to negotiate a two-state solution have reached the same conclusion.

The trouble is that, in every one of the "previous efforts to negotiate," the Palestine Authority has categorically refused to agree that all these "existing population centers," which occupy some 10 to 15 percent of the West Bank, should be incorporated into Israel. At most, it has been willing to consider yielding some of them as part of a land swap giving it an equal amount of territory inside Israel—a demand that Israel, which came into possession of the West Bank after being attacked by Jordan in 1967, has quite rightly rejected. This was one of the main issues over which the 2001 talks broke down, and the Palestinian position has if anything hardened since then. For the United States to tell Israel that it should have borders reflecting "new realities on the ground" but also "emerging from negotiations" is thus to deliver a thoroughly contradictory message.

Nor will this contradiction be resolved by changes in Palestinian politics. Even if the much talked-about "democratization" of the Palestinian Authority takes place, the leadership elected will not soften its negotiating positions. On the contrary: the more "democratic" a Palestinian government is, the more uncompromising its leaders will most likely become, since popular sentiment has regularly been even more hardline than that of the Palestinian Authority's top echelons. The strong political influence of Hamas in a democratic Palestinian society would in itself ensure that negotiations with Israel could never get off the ground.

If there is any hope for the two peoples to disentangle themselves in the West Bank before it is tragically too late, therefore, it does not lie in sterile negotiations. It lies in America's resolving the contradiction. This alone would enable the second stage of disengagement to take place.

True, I have argued that a Gaza-style disengagement in the West Bank is impossible. But this style, let us remember, was unilateral. Whatever the balance of its risks and benefits, Israel has received, in return, no concessions, no commitments, and no guarantees from any other government. And indeed, in return for such nothing once again, the Herculean effort that a withdrawal from most of the West Bank would require *is* impossible. There is simply no way in which an Israeli government could marshal sufficient political support for it.

But this need not be the case if the withdrawal were in return for something. If that something were substantial enough, a clear national consensus in favor of a second-stage West Bank disengagement could in all likelihood be mobilized despite the turmoil caused by the first stage. The political struggle would still be titanic, and the evacuation itself, whether single- or multi-phased, of colossal difficulty. But it could be done; most Israelis would be willing to pay the price.

· · · · ·

What would they be paying for? For a presidential declaration from Washington that said something like this:

> Although the government of the United States continues to believe that the Israeli-Palestinian conflict would best be resolved through negotiations as called for in the Road Map, and has every hope that this will one day prove possible, there is no prospect of its happening at the present moment. In the meantime, since Israel is prepared to withdraw all of its settlers and armed forces from close to 90 percent of the West Bank to the security fence it has built, the United States will regard this withdrawal, once completed, as constituting full compliance with United Nations Security Council Resolution 242, and will recognize the new line as Israel's border with the Palestinian Authority.

Such a declaration, of course, could not come out of the blue. It would have to be preceded by private negotiations between Israel and the United

States over just where the still uncompleted parts of the security fence should run. But as long as Israel received all of its settlement blocs and had its interests guaranteed in Jerusalem, it could be expected to take American concerns into consideration.

Were the United States publicly behind such a move, Israelis, knowing they would at last have a recognized eastern frontier along militarily tolerable, demographically viable, morally acceptable lines that are also relatively safe from terror, would, I believe, vote decisively—although many with a heavy heart—for leaving the rest of Judea and Samaria.

Can the United States afford to make such a change in its policy? The Palestinians would initially react with fury; the Arab world would squawk; the Europeans would grumble about a perfidious sellout to the "Jewish lobby"—but all this would pass. Some countries would come around and endorse the American declaration in principle. And once Israel's evacuation of the West Bank actually took place, one can imagine that the real reaction—in Europe, in the Arab countries and elsewhere around the world, and among the Palestinians themselves—would be of relief. Finally, the Israeli occupation would be over.

Such a step, moreover, would be in true compliance with Security Council Resolution 242, over whose exact wording the United States led so hard a fight at the time. That resolution, adopted soon after the 1967 war, speaks of "the withdrawal of Israel's armed forces from territories occupied in the recent conflict," not of withdrawal from "the territories"; that is to say, the withdrawal it calls for is not total. At the end of the 1967 war, Israel held nearly 30,000 square miles of militarily occupied territory in the Sinai Peninsula, the Gaza Strip, the West Bank, and the Golan Heights. After pulling back to the West Bank security fence, it will have evacuated 97 percent of this area. How much closer to both the spirit and the letter of 242 can it get?

It is true that the Palestinians may find it difficult to build a viable state in the tiny territory of Gaza plus nine-tenths of the West Bank. But they would have found it difficult to build a viable state in Gaza plus ten-tenths of the West Bank, too. In all likelihood, sooner or later, state or no state, they will do the obvious thing and join up once again with Jordan, between which and the West Bank there will no longer be a barrier once the Israeli withdrawal takes place. Jordan's land area is fifteen times the West Bank's; it is more than three times Israel's. But this is a matter that can be left to the Palestinians and the Jordanians.

As for Palestinian irredentism, it will continue to exist. Perhaps organizations like Hamas will occasionally lob rounds of rockets or mortar shells over the security fence, to which Israel will have to respond, just as it does to Hezbollah attacks from Lebanon. Nor will an Israeli withdrawal to the fence put a total end to terrorism, either, although it should be able to contain it effectively. Much will depend on the degree of civil unity or strife within Palestinian society itself, and on how long this society takes to normalize and prosper economically. A long time will pass before a Palestinian or Palestinian-Jordanian government will recognize Israel's new frontier. All this, however, will be infinitely preferable to the present state of affairs—and to any of the other alternatives on offer.

For years, the United States has urged Israel to make bold and courageous decisions in order to help solve its conflict with the Palestinians. Here is a chance for America to make such a decision itself.

—October 2005

Contributors

David Bar-Illan, a frequent commentator on Israeli affairs who died in 2003, was the editorial-page editor and chief editor of the *Jerusalem Post*, and served as director of communications in the government of Benjamin Netanyahu.

Yigal Carmon, a former colonel in Israeli intelligence, served Prime Ministers Yitzhak Shamir and Yitzhak Rabin as adviser on countering terrorism (1998–1993). He is the founder and president of MEMRI, the Middle East Media Research Institute.

Douglas J. Feith, an attorney in Washington, D.C., served in the Defense Department and in the National Security Council during the Reagan administration, and as undersecretary of defense for policy in the George W. Bush administration.

Dore Gold, the president of the Jerusalem Center for Public Affairs and the author of *U.S. Strategy in the Middle East,* among other books, was Israel's ambassador to the United Nations in 1997–1999.

Nadav Haetzni, an attorney, writes about Palestinian affairs and other military and political matters for a number of Israeli publications.

Hillel Halkin, who lives in Israel, is a columnist for the *Jerusalem Post* and the *New York Sun* and the author most recently of *A Strange Death: A Story Originating in Espionage, Betrayal, and Vengeance in a Village in Old Palestine.*

Efraim Karsh, head of Mediterranean studies at King's College, University of London, is the author of *Fabricating Israeli History; Arafat's War;* and *Islamic Imperialism,* among other books.

Neal Kozodoy is the editor of *Commentary.*

Joshua Muravchik is a resident scholar at the American Enterprise Institute and the author of *Exporting Democracy; Heaven on Earth: The Rise and Fall of Socialism;* and, most recently, *The Future of the United Nations.*

Fiamma Nirenstein, an Italian journalist who writes from Israel for the daily *La Stampa* and the weekly *Panorama,* is the author of *Israel: Peace in War* and *Terror: The New Anti-Semitism and the War Against the West.*

Daniel Pipes is director of the Middle East Forum and the author of, among other books, *Conspiracy: How the Paranoid Style Flourishes and Where It Comes From* and *Militant Islam Reaches America.*

Norman Podhoretz is editor-at-large of *Commentary* and a veteran observer of the Middle East peace process. His most recent books are *My Love Affair with America; The Prophets: Who They Were, What They Are,* and *The Norman Podhoretz Reader.*

Ruth R. Wisse is the Martin Peretz Professor of Yiddish Literature and professor of comparative literature at Harvard. Her books include *If I Am Not for Myself . . . : The Liberal Betrayal of the Jews* and *The Modern Jewish Canon.*

Index